Jamie's storytelling blends poetry, journalism, and autobiography into a beautiful oral history of Cedar-Riverside. She captures the personalities and culture of the neighborhood with a warmth and love that flow out of each page.

—JD Duggan, The Uptake

In _Butterflies and Tall Bikes_, author Jamie Schumacher takes readers on a journey to an urban island on the West Bank of the Mississippi River in Minneapolis, Minnesota. This "island" is not surrounded by water as you would think, but flanked by interstates and transit ways creating a tight-knit community, divided by ideas, but united in serving each other.

The book amplifies stories of the unique businesses, people, and institutions on the West Bank while weaving in Schumacher's transformative experiences in helping businesses navigate big changes with vision, advocacy, and creativity. Reading between the lines, Schumacher discusses why accessibility matters in all forms. It is clear that the Covid-19 pandemic has forced us to look at community differently. However, as a transit professional, I was challenged to re-think how community engagement can bring even better resources directly to families, businesses, and organizations.

—Queen Tea | Theresa Nix

Cities need neighborhoods like the West Bank, and storytellers like Jamie. In her practical, observant style, _Butterflies and Tall Bikes_ captures the people, peculiarities, and policies that have shaped the neighborhood and the community bonds that have made the West Bank vital and vibrant through it all. Reading _Butterflies and Tall Bikes_ is like taking a stroll with a good friend—invigorating and enlightening, and it makes you love a place even more.

—Carl Atiya Swanson, CAST Consulting and Springboard for the Arts

Jamie's warm and down-to-earth reflections shift easily between memoir, thoughtful oral history, and insights gleaned from years eking out small but important wins as the leader of a scrappy neighborhood non-profit. *Butterflies and Tall Bikes* is a thoughtful document that faithfully captures a period in the West Bank's raucous and ever-changing momentum. It's a welcome read for anyone longing for their next half-drunk beer and conversation on the patio at Palmer's.

—*Aleah Vinick, former tour guide*

I've worked in and around the West Bank in the political and live music worlds. I've seen four of my all time top ten bands within blocks of each other here and watched a dear friend buy a bar here. Jamie captures the energy of the community while shining a light on the right places that showcase why my friends fly into Minneapolis and have me pick them up at Palmer's instead of the airport.

—*Andy Holmaas, former political staffer, local musician, and Minneapolis enthusiast*

Crafted in a time of isolation, this book brings healing nostalgia, warmth, community, and hope. What a gift to have someone write so deeply about this neighborhood unlike anywhere else in the world.

—*Hailey Colwell, Minnesota Playlist, Spektrix*

I LOVED the book. It felt like the walking tour Jamie gave me in my first months at Our Streets—feeling her deep love for the neighborhood and the people we met on the way, but ultimately getting to know her better, too. The painful and slow work it takes to make change resonated with me.

In *Butterflies and Tall Bikes*, Jamie Schumacher paints a thrilling portrait of Minneapolis's West Bank neighborhood and its extraordinary inhabitants. Part biography and part travel guide, Jamie's love for one of our city's most interesting and diverse communities shines through. While grounding us in the West Bank's history this book fills us with a soaring optimism about the future of our city.

—*Ashwat Narayanan, executive director, Our Streets Minneapolis*

From Koerner, Ray & Glover to Bonnie Raitt to Semisonic, from Bedlam to the Southern Theater, from the Triangle Bar to Palmer's to the Triple Rock, the West Bank has historically been a center for one of the most creative and diverse music, arts, and culture scenes in Minneapolis, possibly the universe.

Jamie Schumacher's book weaves threads of history, memories, and hopes for the future into a rich tapestry of her personal stories intertwined with those of fellow West Bankers who love this neighborhood as much as we do. *Butterflies and Tall Bikes* is a beacon, an inspiration to we who have loved the West Bank for decades and to those who want to know more.

—*Cyn Collins, host of KFAI's* Spin with Cyn, *author of* West Bank Boogie: Forty Years of Music, Mayhem and Memories *and* Complicated Fun: The Birth of Minneapolis Punk and Indie Rock 1974–1984—An Oral History

Margaret Mead said, "What happens on the growing edges of life is seldom written down at the time. It is lived from day to day in talk, in scraps of comment on the margin of someone else's manuscript, in words spoken on a street corner . . ." Happily, the West Bank and its community has Jamie Schumacher to honor and preserve those precious "scraps of comment," weaving them beautifully into this love song to a neighborhood and a city.

—*John Capecci, coauthor,* Living Proof: Telling Your Story to Make a Difference

Jamie Schumacher tells these West Bank stories much like she paints: by refracting thousands of tiny details into a vibrant portrait of the multifaceted neighborhood.

—*Sage Dahlen*

Such a niche story in the hands of an artist like Jamie gives it such mass appeal, weaving together the stories of non-profit life with the unique world of the West Bank and adding the color to make *Butterflies and Tall Bikes* a beautiful piece of work.

—*Sarah Salisbury, Freelance Stage and Production Manager*

Butterflies and Tall Bikes

Butterflies and Tall Bikes

West Bank Stories of Community, Creativity, and Change

JAMIE SCHUMACHER

Illustrations by **CORINA SAGUN** and **KEVIN CANNON**

ISBN 13: 978-1-7326350-29
Library of Congress Catalog Number: 2021904116

Printed in the United States of America
First Printing: 2021

25 24 23 22 21   5 4 3 2 1

Cover art and interior map by Kevin Cannon
Illustrations by Corina Sagun
Book design by Ryan Scheife, Mayfly Design

Wise Ink Creative Publishing
807 Broadway St NE
Suite 46
Minneapolis, MN, 55413

wiseink.com

To order, visit www.itascabooks.com or call 1-800-901-3480, or contact the author at www.jamie-schumacher.com.
Reseller discounts available.

for anybody who
has ever longed for a place
where you can be your weird little self

CONTENTS

FOREWORD

BY ANDREA SWENSSON

While most of us were screaming into our pillows and eating our weight in quarantine snacks, my friend Jamie researched and wrote an entire book, and I will never stop being a little mad at her about it. (I'm kidding, Jamie . . . mostly.)

The audacity! And I mean that sincerely: the amount of tenacity that it requires to produce not just any work but an entire book in the midst of 2020's gale-force winds—an upending pandemic, a global uprising around racial justice that sprang from our very city, and the darkest and most harrowing political election of our lifetime—can't be measured in mere chapters. But that's how I've always known Jamie to operate. She confronts problems with the same scrappy ingenuity and artistic fury that has kept her beloved West Bank neighborhood of Minneapolis whirring and weird for longer than we've both been alive.

I've been thinking a lot about the importance of a place. Absence makes the heart grow fonder, and with access cut off I've become positively infatuated with the music venues, theaters, coffee shops, restaurants, bookstores, record stores, and boutiques that keep my internal dials calibrated to remind me that I'm here in Minneapolis. These are the places where the small, happenstance encounters have kept me tethered to the community that surrounds me, and without them, it's hard not to feel unmoored. The body aches to return to the bustling chaos of humanity, IRL.

But does a building itself have a soul? If you've ever helped a band load into a venue before sound check or tiptoed into a darkened theater late at night, you may be familiar with the cold spots, spirits, and whispered stories that haunt these spaces while everyone else is away. But as Jamie knows so well, and as the stories on these pages will outline in vivid detail, it's the people that make these places come alive. And on the West Bank—that dense, dizzying, churning little town within the big city—so many of these people have become interwoven with the places they love.

One of the musicians most closely associated with West Bank history, the dearly departed harmonica player and writer Tony Glover, had his archives put up for auction recently, and as I scanned through the collection, I stopped on a pay stub for some work he did on the production of *Purple Rain*. The address listed on the check caught my eye: instead of his home, it was sent to his attention at the 400 Bar, the longtime watering hole and music club. It reminded me of how once, when I asked West Bank music scholar Cyn Collins whether she had advice on how to reach Glover's longtime bandmate "Spider" John Koerner, she told me to just call him up at Palmer's. And if I ever needed to mail anything to Spider, she added, I could also send it to Palmer's and he'd receive it within the day.

There's something old-school and romantic to me about the idea of a bar being so significant to a person that it literally becomes a second home. I know I've had my fair share of spots around town, including up and down Cedar-Riverside, that I frequented so often they began to feel like extensions of myself—the Nomad, the Triple Rock, Hard Times, the Cedar, that beautiful back patio at Palmer's. In fact, Jamie and I first bonded by hopping around to some of these spots, talking late into the night about music, writing, and life (and communing with an especially memorable ghost at the Southern Theater). My memories of these spaces have little to do with architecture, barstool arrangement, or the beat-up wooden stages scuffed by hundreds of amps and stomping boots. It's the bartenders who become trusted confidants; the writers and artists who work beside one another in coffee shops like soldiers-in-arms; the security guy who *finally* cracks a smile at you the hundredth time he checks your ID; the unexpected booth full of friends who scream when you walk in the door and scoot over to make room for one more. These are the moments we will soon have again, when the city's arteries reopen to make way for new life, and these are the stories—so small, but actually everything—that we hold dear now and forever.

I am so grateful for people like Jamie who collect these stories. This book is a time capsule, a living history, and a love letter. And it makes my heart go a-flutter.

—*Andrea Swensson, November 2020*

INTRODUCTION AND WRITING THROUGH THE PANDEMIC REVOLUTION

People make a place.

A neighborhood is so much more than a built landscape. It is also the people that bring the space to life.

This isn't my story alone. My Twin Cities friends and colleagues continue to shape and inspire me—and the West Bank, too. I wanted to make sure some of their stories were interwoven with this text because they give a glimpse into the tapestry of amazing humans that breathe life into the West Bank.

While editing this book, I had the opportunity to hear Jana Shortal, a Minnesota KARE 11 news reporter and a tremendous storyteller, give a keynote speech at the Minnesota Council of Nonprofits' Advancement, Communications, and Technology convention. In it, she said, "Too often we talk about people experiencing things, but we do not talk to them." Her news style aims to shift a norm of interviewing around an issue in media to a more direct approach, giving more agency to each interviewee. I hope the interviews in these pages help do the same, and uplift voices in the community and the voices of friends I hold dear.

I wrote this book in the fog of exhaustion that we have all been struggling through since the start of the pandemic. It has been like therapy in a time of social distancing—every interaction I could remember with any detail was not unlike a gem to be mined for the touch, smell, and feel. Every interview was a gift, a connection.

People make a place.

Many of my friends, family, and colleagues are evaluating their roles right now. Millions of artists find themselves out of work, wondering what to do next. Most of us do not want to leave the arts; with creative expression, there is no better way to operate other than to be our truest selves. In that vein, between distance learning, parenting, and pandemic, thrusting myself headfirst into another writing project seemed the natural way to manage my own inner chaos.

The first etches of this book began with my friend Andrea before the global disruption. We'd get together in the early mornings to have coffee, chat for a little while, then turn our pensive minds to writing, hammering out chapters and passages. When visiting coffee shops and bars in other cities, I often seek out spaces where famous authors used to hang out together. I would envision them with fancy hats and smart conversation, dazzling a small audience with their wit and revelry. Now I imagine they were probably just nerds like us, sitting together with a notebook and a pencil or a fountain pen, quietly scrawling out the contents of their minds in creative, comfortable company. The West Bank buzzes with this same type of energy, a neighborhood that nurtures creatives in all their iterations.

Time right now feels simultaneously paused and in fast-forward. Many online are referring to this as a great global pause. But perhaps this is not the right image. Perhaps instead it is a great molting, an opportunity to shed an uncomfortable skin.

What doesn't belong in the world we return to? We will return in jolts and pauses to a world in a global recession. Stunning inequity beyond what we already know to be true. In part we are choosing not only what to go back to but what to rebuild, recover, and preserve. We should keep people centered in this process.

After the initial shock of pandemic wore off, things for me settled into what so many have been calling the "new normal." Fueled in part by angsty energy, during naptimes and after bedtimes I threw myself into writing and interviewing for this book.

But my writing took a big pause on May 26, 2020. The murder of George Floyd took place twenty minutes from our home. Video of this act spread quickly around the world, and an uprising soon followed. Protests turned dire, with a mix of righteous anger and outside instigation. The protests and subsequent riots and fires left great loss in their wake: in the end, more than 1,500 businesses in Minnesota were damaged or ruined. Minnesota's grief, stitched inextricably with our country's complicated history of racism, raised the Black Lives Matter movement to a global level.

The days that followed were a blur of urgency and emotion, and I'm certain lengthy books and studies of this pivotal time in history are to come. What I can say from here is that watching the Minnesota community come together to show solidarity and support has been remarkable. Organizers around the Twin Cities activated immediately, initially for protest as well as taking care of immediate needs and resource deployment. Indeed, many of these systems were already in place—the Twin Cities' constituents are engaged community members.

I am ever impressed with creative folks' ability to rally and have a positive impact. Stage technicians collaborated with generous local theaters and used plywood from set supplies to board up businesses for safety. When that plywood ran out, they went to lumber shops to get more. Text trees, email chains, and other networks kept people connected during the overnight turmoil. When shops and pharmacies burned and neighborhoods were without resources, residents tapped those networks to keep resources flowing to neighbors in need.

The West Bank rallied, the little island proving a safeguard of sorts. Residents and business owners formed overnight watches in partnership with the businesses while neighborhood kids rode around the district on bikes, checking incoming cars. Mothers, safely masked, went from watch to watch, handing out Somali tea to the volunteers. While damage on the West Bank was significant for our small businesses, it paled in comparison to neighboring districts.

And then, another remarkable phenomenon, though one not all that surprising if you know our community. All along those plywood windows, artwork popped up. Muralists volunteered their time and supplies to contribute, businesses hired local artists to decorate their temporarily boarded windows, nonprofits commissioned works of larger scale. The Twin Cities, rather than being solely a display of desolation after the riots, also became a citywide exhibit on protest, despair, hope, and action. Do we have some work to do? Yes. But there are things to honor in this moment as well.

Anybody who knows me well already knows my take on this, but it bears repeating: art is a language of the people. Somewhere along the line it became a commodity for rich merchants and wealthy churches; artifacts from colonized communities were stolen, melted down for gold, destroyed, or placed behind museum walls. I am grateful to be in my line of work at this particular time, and a part of the movement to upend these systems.

In a dream world, foundations would be loosening their purse strings in a bigger and broader way. What better time to invest in the infrastructure of our buildings than when they are not being fully utilized and we don't have to interrupt shows to make upgrades. What if we came out of this era with our historic spaces renovated, fully accessible, with safe, good jobs for artists and construction workers funded along the way? Supporting arts organizations through the economic downturn with not just bare-minimum maintenance, but inside-out renovations that would allow them to emerge from the pandemic fully functional and able to serve the community as a whole? In addition to being the change we want to see in the world, perhaps we could build the change, too.

And even more important than those built environments we hold dear are the people who breathe life into them.

This book is a just snapshot, a glimpse of a particular place through the lens of individual experiences and memories. Our stories are important, and the seeds we plant are, too. I continue my own personal journey of learning, and hope it is never-ending.

This book had a title before I wrote it. I remember the first time I saw someone riding a tall bike while visiting Minneapolis; I was sitting outside the original Purple Onion, the prospect of a move from California to Minnesota still off on the horizon. I watched as a single tall-biker rode by. They stopped at a stoplight nonchalantly, arm outstretched to a post at the corner, before the light changed and they rode on.

Tall bikes are emblematic of what drew me to Minneapolis: a creative culture so deep it permeated everything from galleries to transportation. Not being a tall-biker myself, there's still something that feels almost magical about them. Seeing one is a reminder of why I fell in love with, and am still in love with, this imperfectly perfect city. Tall bikes represent an environment where creativity can thrive.

To put it another way: on the spectrum of cycling culture, tall bikes are everything the pedal pub is not.

Or, to put it yet another way: it's always awesome to see a butterfly go by.

One of my favorite prints from my artist friend Amy Rice is her work *Butterfly on a Tall Bike*, which was inspired by a photo taken at Minneapolis's annual MayDay Parade. The phrase and visual have stuck with me as symbolic of the West Bank spirit. Perhaps it is because butterflies are to nature as tall bikes are to Minneapolis. And now more than ever, we need to support the kind of systems that let creativity flourish.

There have been many times in systems change work that I have felt alone. Experimenting with new ways of working, new systems, new visions of collaborative leadership. Art and activism as part of a broader network of change. But this time feels different. I am not a lonely splash anymore; I am part of a body of water, in a sea surrounded by people I love, part of a forceful wave that's headed in the right direction. Whatever happens next, we'll get through this together.

As things reopen, I hope our values hold steady, including the importance of in-person contact. Prioritize it, make time for it, fight against efforts to reduce those in-person connections within our work for more "efficient" methods of communication.

I write this intro amid another striking Midwest summer storm—the kind that rolls in with a dense heat, as the colors in the sky shift from gray to black to yellow within a dazzlingly short time. The rain pounding sideways at the windows, the lights flickering menacingly as thunder rumbles through. I shut them off and sit in darkness to watch the storm outside. There's something comforting about being at home during the storm, about *having* a home during the storm. I sit with gratitude.

We are at the precipice of something larger than us, a historical point that the world should never forget. We hear often the saying "This moment is bigger than us." I wonder whether it would be truer to say that, rather than a moment bigger than us, we're in a movement made of us. A movement propelling us forward along the arc of justice,[1] powered

---

1. As Dr. Martin Luther King Jr. said, "We shall overcome because the arc of the moral universe is long, but it bends toward justice."

collectively by the force of our rage, grief, fear, creativity, activation, and hope.

What seeds will we plant now, in the wake of this burning?

What kind of new world do we want to grow?

Will a phoenix rise from the ashes, or something else?

The answer to those questions will be up to us.

WELCOME

Welcome to the West Bank, new friend!

Every week I find something more to love about this
neighborhood. While you're here in our international
community, I hope you'll pause in a moment of
appreciation for everything that surrounds you.
Vibrant murals, theaters, music venues, cultural
centers—in a thriving district where local businesses
still wildly outnumber chains. With so many
bustling shops and spaces, there's always something
interesting happening, always something incredible to
eat, and always a great show to see.

And West Bankers also have no shortage of opinions,
so don't hesitate to reach out for recommendations!
Whether you're here for school, work, or play, I hope
this directory serves as a good resource for you. Try
something or someplace different!

You may find a new favorite as you explore the world
on the West Bank.

———————————————

—*From the West Bank Area Directory*

    —*The author*

It Began in Manchester

This story doesn't start in Minneapolis. It begins in Manchester, United Kingdom.

Well, *my* story actually starts in Tor-rance, California, where I was born. My journey brought me to the Midwest in 2003. With California becoming in-creasingly expensive, moving was an attempt to find my path and my call-ing in a beautiful and more affordable place to live. In Minnesota I found my path and so much more!

In 2011, I was living in Minne-apolis, in a little Craftsman house in the Northeast Minneapolis Arts District.

Manchester, UK

I worked at a web development company as the nonprofit communica-tions specialist, helping foundations and community organizations de-sign websites and work on their SEO (search engine optimization, for any non-nerds in the audience). Our office was in the historic Northrup King Building, an amazing, sprawling warehouse full of artists and cre-ative businesses—one of the cornerstones of the arts district. About two miles from my home, it certainly wasn't a bad commute. The artist in me loved being surrounded by creativity on the daily.

My husband, Nick, and I had recently married, sharing our vows with friends and family in the parking-lot courtyard of the nonprofit I founded, Altered Esthetics. On a chilly fall night we danced, a bonfire roaring in the background. We were now on our honeymoon, a dream trip to the home of some of our favorite and most formative music: Manchester.

Manchester felt like being home in all the best ways. No city has ever reminded me so much of Minneapolis in terms of music and social architecture—and I loved it for all those reasons and more. For readers who were not impressionable youths in the '80s, Manchester was the source of some incredible bands of music history. For a good peek into this era, I highly recommend the movie *24 Hour Party People*, which does a great job of capturing this formative time.

We arrived in the city via train early in the morning, dropped off our bags, and stopped by the local visitors center. We then headed out for a music history walking tour, following gray streets lined with tall, tidy brick buildings all the way to the city's center. Our trip very fatefully overlapped with two historical walking tours of Manchester—the first a "Manchester Music" tour and the second "The Smiths' Manchester," departing the following day.

Of all the guided tours we did while traveling, these two were the best. Our guide was clearly a fan of the area's music and creative forces, and he was also well versed in the historical and social context surrounding the development of both the music and the area. The tour groups were small, and many of the participants were from Manchester themselves. You know you're in for something good when even the locals are interested!

Focused on the music history and path of the Buzzcocks, Joy Division, and New Order, it ended with a trip to the Haçienda. We collectively sighed at that point as, quite sadly, what was once a vibrant club is now apartments. Behind them, along the water, is a commemorative sign highlighting the Haçienda's historical and musical significance.

As the tour wrapped up, our guide asked how long we were in town . . . and excitedly told us that we were very, very fortunate. There was a club where, once a month, they spin Smiths and Morrissey songs all night, and tonight was the night. Did we go? We sure did.

That night we headed to the Star and Garter. *The Star and Garter*. A punk venue, club, and community staple, the Star and Garter is a beautiful historic building right in the heart of Manchester. The lower lounge, with its album-lined walls and velvety red curtains, was straight out of a David Lynch movie, and I loved it.

Just after ten, the upstairs rooms came to life. We danced for hours, and it was magical—the Smiths were a huge part of my formative teenage years. To be in Manchester dancing with Nick and so many Mancunians in such a warm, welcoming environment was incredible. Music can bring people together.

We woke up early the next morning, had some breakfast, and headed out to see more of lovely Manchester. The Smiths tour was every bit as good as the Manchester Music one. The weather was drizzly and gray—in other words, absolutely perfect weather for truly experiencing the Smiths' Manchester. Geese honked noisily along the water's edge as we wound our way around the city.

The tours also had very little overlap as far as information went, so they didn't seem repetitive. We did, however, repeat our walk past the Haçienda tribute sign ourselves before leaving.

When we left Manchester in the late afternoon, I wished we could have stayed even longer. On our way out, we stopped through the visitors gift shop downtown. Coasters, shirts, and other goods proudly marketed the city's style and culture—one inexorably shaped by music and the Mancunian spirit. I couldn't help but wonder: why wasn't Minneapolis marketing itself in this way?

Minneapolis, and Minnesota broadly, has a remarkable music history. In addition to being the chosen home of Prince himself, Minneapolis has been home to a flurry of other musicians—Bob Dylan, Judy Garland, and Semisonic, to name but a few. We have incredible music venues throughout our city, small enough to be intimate and special, each one of them unique. In my opinion, we weren't doing enough to celebrate and preserve that part of what makes the Twin Cities so special.

"This has to change," I thought to myself. "And when we get back, I need a new job."

You're Hired!

Nick and I returned from our honeymoon with the glow of the trip still fresh. As I somewhat reluctantly headed back into work, I kept my finger on the pulse of the job market, hoping to transition back into a more community-focused job like the roles I'd had before joining the web development company.

An opportunity came along sooner than I anticipated, in one of Northeast Minneapolis's neighboring districts: the West Bank. A colleague was leaving her position as executive director of the West Bank Business Association, and she encouraged me to apply for her role.

Not really being a suit-wearing gal, I wore a pumpkin-colored skirt and black sweater to the interview, clutching a black folder and notebook with copies of my résumé and references. Two men met me in a small conference room in the Bailey Building on Riverside Avenue, home to the association as well as KFAI Radio and Mapps Coffee. The smell of roasted coffee permeated the building.

I leaned in to the advice a friend had given me years prior: "Don't try to pretend you're something you're not for a job interview. You're a terrible liar anyway. Just be your nerd self. Is a job that doesn't want you for who you are the kind of job you want, anyway?" As the interviewers went through their list of questions, I talked excitedly about the work I had done in Northeast, founding a gallery and helping the small businesses along Central Avenue through my work with the Northeast Community Development Corporation. When asked about my comfort level working with folks of different cultural backgrounds, I was able to share the story of my own immigrant family and my parents' paths to this country.

I got the job.

My role would be to help build the capacity of the organization, market the area, and support the needs of its businesses. The West Bank being a transit-friendly district full of music venues, cultural organizations, and tons of personality, I was thrilled to be able to move my energy in this direction. After giving a respectable few weeks' notice at my development gig, I moved on to the next new thing. I was excited to begin, to learn, to grow. Adrienne, the former director, gracefully helped me transition in as she transitioned out. The board helped me as well, with two board members taking me from business to business throughout the district and introducing me to the various owners and managers. I had frequented the neighborhood often, first as a guest of many of the coffee shops and music venues and later as my main hang during grad school times, but now I was here in an official capacity.

As we toured the district, my fellow board members pointed out weird property anomalies, shared gossip and rumors about the area's history, and told their own stories of how they found their way to the neighborhood. As so often happens with any good night on the West Bank, it ended at Palmer's Bar, a West Bank institution (but more on that later).

After we were done, I returned to my new office in the Bailey Building—a closet of a room barely able to fit the desk and file cabinet that were its only furnishings. While I waited for the buzz to wear off, I pored over the archives, finding news articles for the West Bank Music Festival, grant contracts, and a *Playboy* magazine shoved in the middle of a folder of board meeting minutes. "Welcome to the West Bank?" I thought with a laugh.

Initiation complete and successful, I lay down on the floor of the office and fell contentedly asleep.

Painting a Picture

Every urban landscape is its own unique fingerprint, patterned in soothing swirls of streets and sidewalks, each neighborhood and each city wholly distinct from any other. I love the fingerprint of the West Bank; though it is connected to other parts of the city and state via freeways and public transportation, the area exists as almost an island within Minneapolis. The sambusa-shaped wedge is bordered on its three sides by the I-94 and I-35 freeways and the Mississippi River. The estimated population for our 1.5-square-mile area is more than eight thousand people, making it one of the most densely populated areas in the state.

The active commercial community of the West Bank neighborhood, also known as Cedar-Riverside, comprises over two hundred small businesses, but there is also an institutional presence: Augsburg University,

the University of Minnesota, and Fairview Health. The universities do their best to connect their students and faculty to the surrounding neighborhoods, with staff working diligently to improve the Universities occasionally problematic history of expansion within the neighborhood.

In addition to the hospital and universities, the neighborhood has been fortunate to have its own clinic, too. Created in the 1970s by grassroots organizers, People's Center was one of Minnesota's first free medical clinics. It is still active to this day, serving the residents and students of the West Bank and others in need of quality affordable healthcare. Its staff members are community minded, many of them neighborhood residents themselves. When COVID-19 broke out, People's Center was one of the places folks could go for drive-up testing—one of the many assets making this a great place to be.

In the middle of the neighborhood is its busy namesake intersection of Cedar and Riverside Avenues. Shops and restaurants stretch up and down Cedar and continue along the Riverside Avenue node that connects to parks and additional housing. The backdrop for the neighborhood and probably our most iconic feature is the Riverside Plaza towers, high-rises that house a majority of the neighborhood's residents. A cultural district as well as an arts and entertainment district, the West Bank boasts a large number of music venues and theaters, one of the best known being the Cedar Cultural Center.

While very much an urban setting, the neighborhood does not lack entirely for green space. Currie Park lines the eastern border, providing soccer fields, playgrounds, and pedestrian pathways to downtown Minneapolis. Adjacent to the Augsburg campus is Murphy Square, the city's first officially designated public park. The West Bank also has several popular urban gardens, the plots highly sought after. And, of course, there is the mighty Mississippi.

The West Bank landscape is a series of seemingly contradictory features. An island-like neighborhood, yet one interconnected by two light rail lines, rapid buses, and two major freeways. Car-centric yet pedestrian, with only about half of residents owning cars. Full of hippie liberals, some Green Party advocates, and some staunch libertarians. While political banter and heated debates are not uncommon in coffee shops and restaurants, everybody coexists and is proud of the neighborhood's diversity.

West Bank dudes on a summery day

Such is the neighborhood as it sits now. But how did it get to be this way? When I joined the West Bank Business Association, I benefited from the work of students and researchers who have explored the neighborhood's fascinating history. One session I attended early in my tenure was "Cedar-Riverside: From Snoose Boulevard to Little Somalia." Curated by Anduin (Andy) Wilhide, the presentation and the fascinating compilation of the neighborhood that went along with it are currently housed among Augsburg's Digi-Tours, a collection of virtual tours created by students, faculty, and staff.

Minneapolis, and the West Bank specifically, has been a major entry point for newcomers to Minnesota for over 160 years. The neighborhood has an incredible history—stories enough to fill a series of books. But to help paint the picture for our journey, here is a very brief introduction.

The West Bank occupies land that is part of Mni Sóta Makoce, the historic homeland of the Dakota people who moved through to hunt, fish, and tap the maple trees that once grew along the Mississippi River. When I joined the WBBA, most of the "neighborhood history" summaries on the organization's website and elsewhere began with immigrant arrivals—but this, like most American history, creates a false picture. Cedar-Riverside has always been a densely populated and active neighborhood, starting well before Europeans arrived here. Before colonization, it was a hub for trading and connection, the banks of the Mississippi River a perfect backdrop to a vibrant community.

Waves of Immigration

In the nineteenth century, the Dakota land was occupied by immigrants and colonizers. In the 1850s, many new waves of European immigrants came to Minneapolis in search of home and work. They lived in houses that stretched from the river to Ninth and Tenth Streets, forming the Minneapolis we know now. Tragically, the Indigenous presence on the West Bank remains conspicuously low.[2]

Bohemian Flats

The river flats have been a distinct area since the 1870s, a flat, low-lying area along the banks of the Mississippi. For the better part of a century, immigrant families lived here in a village community. While the flats were home to many communities over their history, the nickname that endured was Bohemian Flats, a reference to the Slovak and Czech residents who lived here.

Snoose Boulevard

In 1910, the population of the neighborhood peaked near twenty thousand, including students of the Augsburg seminary school. Residents and guests would pack dance halls, saloons, and bars—so many bars! Cedar Avenue eventually earned the nickname "Snoose Boulevard" (or *Snusgatan* in Swedish) for the Scandinavian *snus* tobacco that locals spit on the street after nights of revelry.

---

2. As of the last census, the Indigenous population of West Bank constituted 0.5 percent of residents—even lower than Hennepin County as a whole, which hovers at around 1 percent.

An Increasingly Global West Bank

In the late nineteenth and early twentieth centuries, African Americans, Russian and Romanian Jews, and small numbers of Italian, Chinese, and Japanese immigrants joined the Scandinavians and Eastern Europeans living in Cedar-Riverside. Taking up residence, opening businesses, and starting families, wave after wave of newcomers shaped the West Bank's landscape.

The Haight-Ashbury of the Midwest

By the 1960s, many first-generation immigrants and their descendants had moved to other parts of Minneapolis. Those who stayed on the West Bank were joined by hippies, college students, and radical activists from around the US. It's not hard to draw comparisons to the Haight-Ashbury district of San Francisco, which was widely known as a hippie hotspot in the '50s and '60s, home to a very diverse population, and the site of many civil rights protests. Like its California counterpart, the West Bank landscape was thick with music and mayhem—Minneapolis's radical problem child.

Every neighborhood has a history and drama, but the West Bank is special. It would not be accurate to talk about the West Bank without talking about its political history and lengthy reputation for rowdiness. A hotbed of political activism is still alive, drawing energy from the remnants of an antiestablishment spirit embedded firmly into our neighborhood tapestry.

Farewell, Dania Hall

Dania Hall was a cultural and entertainment center of the neighborhood for almost a hundred years. It was also plagued by a series of fires that damaged the building, the last one, in 2000, destroying it completely. This is still mourned as a great loss for the community—and we'll talk more about Dania Hall later.

A Tapestry of Faiths

Opening originally in 1998, the Riverside Islamic Center was Minnesota's very first mosque. By that time, Cedar-Riverside had become home to one of the state's largest concentrations of Somalis, many of whom were Muslim and continued their cultural and religious practices after immigration. The name of the Riverside Islamic Center changed in 2013 to the Islamic Civic Society of America, which includes Dar Al-Hijrah Mosque. The presence of Augsburg University, Trinity Lutheran Congregation, and their students and parishioners add to the religious diversity of the neighborhood.

"Little Mogadishu"

Beginning in the 1990s, the West Bank was the locus for a huge influx of East African immigrants. Current residents proudly claim Cedar-Riverside has the world's densest concentration of Somalis outside of Mogadishu. While neighborhood-specific numbers have not been confirmed, Minnesota as a whole does indeed have the greatest population of Somalis in the United States. To commemorate these communities, Fourth Street, Sixth Street, and Sixteenth Avenue South west of Cedar Avenue were renamed Oromo Street, Somali Street, and Taleex Avenue.

The West Bank Vision

While the neighborhood continues to change, its vision remains the same. A tightly knit and diverse community, Cedar-Riverside is a hub where the world connects to Minneapolis and the greater Midwest. Residents and businesses, a majority of which are still small and locally owned, work hand in hand to make the neighborhood a beautiful place to live, learn, work, and play.

Perhaps this is what makes the West Bank so special. They say the soul of a people never leaves a place. Since the West Bank has been an international hub for centuries, it has long been a soul of the world.

First Things First

The West Bank Business Association was founded as the Cedar Riverside Business Association in 1983. For several decades, it remained largely a volunteer organization, its board of delegates from the business community using it as an arm to advocate for their needs. Over time, with city support, the organization grew to have part-time staff—administrative at first, then programmatic. District support in the form of banners and festivals was added to its work, and things continued to grow from there.

When I arrived in 2011, the West Bank Business Association was working off a few grant contracts with the city for business associations and commercial districts. A large annual event, the West Bank Music Festival, soaked up much of the organization's capacity. With no long-term plan in place but a fair amount of ambition, I worked with the board to create a short-term plan around our goals for the next year as a starting point.

But like many small nonprofits, the organization was very underresourced to do its work of serving over two hundred businesses with wildly varying needs. Those businesses with representatives active on the board would naturally steer the organization's limited resources to focus on what they deemed pressing, which gave the WBBA a reputation for being primarily a bar-owners association for a time. Cash flow for the organization came from two sources. The biggest portion was through grant funding, mostly via resources from the city of Minneapolis to support business districts and business associations. The other, smaller revenue stream was membership dollars.

Our goals for my first year centered around getting things in order: updating our 501(c)(3) status, our bookkeeping and accounting, our goals for the neighborhood, and continuation of our district marketing. After conversations with businesses in the community, we landed on a set of priorities that everyone agreed on. We were off!

Alongside this work, it became clear we needed to address the pattern of the West Bank when it came to policy and planning. The area was a bit of a problem child when it came to city planning. Tending to be a more . . . reactive neighborhood than most, the West Bank was left out of many planning decisions, even those that directly affected us. As we carved out the path for our organization, we also aimed to shift this dynamic, moving toward being more proactive than reactive. Members of the WBBA board stepped up to join additional regional boards and commissions. Helping to guide the map of planning is a good strategy to employ, especially if you like to know what direction you're going and have some semblance of control.

With a short-term plan in hand, an engaged board, and a new and exciting job to do, I hit the road.

My Place, My Role, My Timing

Though I was far away from the city where I was born, I felt so at home on the West Bank. Why? About ten years ago, I began the journey of unpacking my own roots, and as part of that I examined what my family's history meant to me in the context of today's world. My family's story is not unlike those of so many of my friends and colleagues on the West Bank, and others who somehow found their way to this unexpectedly remarkable place.

Both of my parents are immigrants, my mother from Poland and my father from Sri Lanka. My mother came with her parents and brother. My father's family came bit by bit, and members are all over the world now—some still in Sri Lanka, some in England, some expatriating elsewhere after first coming to the States.

I grew up in a hectic environment full of aunties, uncles, and cousins. We connected over the years with others, especially other immigrant families, who became like extended family for all of us. More aunties, uncles, and cousins from all around the world.

My parents immigrated during an era when assimilation to American culture was the norm. On the best days, our household felt like an international celebration. On the quiet days, I felt awkward and undeniably different from my peers. Was it my bookishness, skinny legs, and lack of fashion sense? My background? The smell of curry that made our house smell "funny" to friends who would come and play or "ethnic" to a college boyfriend (who, for the record, didn't last)? What seemed odd to others was my norm.

After high school I took a dive into historical exploration. Reading books like *Lies My Teacher Told Me* and *A People's History of the United States*, I began a reeducation of sorts, seeking out all those bits of history a more child-friendly historical retelling tends to leave out. I stepped from American history to global history, intertwining what I learned of my parents' cultures with my own creative exploration.

This exploration became part of my creative practice as an artist. I listened to audiobooks and podcasts, learning as I painted, processing with every brushstroke. Gradually my teenage confusion gave way to understanding as I learned more about my background. I reclaimed the bits and pieces with pride and belonging. I found like-minded artists who were processing similar dynamics in their creative work, like Sun Yung Shin. Born in Seoul, South Korea, she now lives in Minneapolis. Her poetry is both a salve and a support for me and others like me who have had to fight for access to our own history.

As that personal work unfolded for me, so did the realization that I had been looking at my place in time haphazardly. As a mixed-race person in America, I often felt at home everywhere and nowhere all at once. Our family carried some generational weight and trauma connected to the war, violence, and other history of our former countries. However, as a newly American family, I know we had a lot of privileges, which I tried not to take for granted. I had the right to vote and the ability to go to college; I was the first person in my family to obtain a four-year degree and then a master's. My parents encouraged me to focus on my education and growth. And the more I knew and understood about my own self and history, including my many shortcomings, the better both my creative work and my vocational work became.

My learning continues, but I feel like a greater understanding of myself has allowed me to navigate the choppy waters of tricky work with a little less wreckage. I move forward and, as my colleague Shauen Pearce eloquently put it, "carry our history but not our baggage."

I think the coastal cities tend to underestimate the international population of Minnesota. Having grown up in Los Angeles, I know there are myths about the Midwest that persist, but it is a remarkable blend of rural, urban, and international—and it is full of creative talent. Not only is it a place for refuge, it's also a place for reflection. Minnesota prides itself on literacy and education, a center of writing, poetry, and spoken word. Our cultural assets speak to that resource in organizations like the Loft Literary Center, Open Book, the Minnesota Spoken Word Association, and countless collaboratives and centers that revolve around creativity in word.

Who writes our stories? Who speaks for the neighborhood?

As I moved through my role on the West Bank, I aimed to amplify other voices so they could share their own stories in their own words.

In addition to the overall welcoming nature of the West Bank, a big part of why I felt so comfortable was that I could just be me. Tragically unhip but enamored with music. Distanced from aunties and uncles of blood, but near to new aunties and uncles of choice.

I wonder whether others are so pensive about their place of employment, or if that's why some people in particular find themselves flocking to the nonprofit sector. So many of us are trying to find the ever-elusive balance between vocation and avocation. A friend of mine works with a marketing agency and doesn't find the need to align that passion with her work; she is able to maintain more of a separation, instead finding passion through her music and creative expression. "My job gives me the freedom and the income to be able to create those opportunities elsewhere, without the same financial struggle I had when I worked at a nonprofit," she tells me.

While the struggle of work-life balance in the nonprofit and community sector may be a challenging one, it's hard to imagine myself in any other line of work. I'm grateful that it allows me to pursue creative endeavors like writing and painting alongside the work, and as I continued in this career path, I was lucky to meet other like-minded nonprofit creatives.

Comedy and Community

› RANA MAY

Known locally for her stand-up comedy, Rana May is also a program manager at a local nonprofit, the Link, whose

> " The first place I hung out on the West Bank? Hard Times Cafe... "

mission is working with youth and families to overcome the impacts of poverty and social injustice. She is a sharp AF activist working within the system to help countless[3] youth navigate a complicated system of barriers that seems hell-bent on keeping kids in a cycle of poverty.

Rana is also a force in local comedy, helping organize events and other curated efforts to highlight women in a male-dominated industry rife with sexism and abuse. One such event, PSSY CTRL, is a monthly stand-up comedy showcase held at the Corner Bar's Comedy Corner Underground that features lineups of female, nonbinary, LGBTQIA+, and BIPOC comics.

One afternoon, Rana and I find the Corner Bar to ourselves for conversation. The bar is in the part of the West Bank known as Seven Corners—an area of the city that at one point had, as its name suggests, seven corners as the streets from two city grids collided. That was until additional development reduced the number of unwieldy corners to the intersection, leaving it at a more usual number. The bar is hopping when there's a sportsball

---

3. Countless except in the context of grant reporting, in which case I'm sure there's a tidy measure of outcomes and deliverables tracked neatly within a customer relationship management system to ensure accountability to the funders that be.

Rana at the Comedy Corner Underground

game downtown, and its happy-hour specials are also a big draw for down-towners and university faculty getting off work.

We cozy into a booth, sharing an order of mozzarella sticks and mar-inara sauce while B-sides and '90s hits blare in the background. We share memories of our mutual friends and remember when we first met.

"Was it Hard Times?" she asks, referring to the worker-owned coop-erative coffee shop on Riverside. It serves incredible vegetarian fare and baked goods—including vegan goods so delicious they have me convinced their baker is some sort of magic maker. The vibe is about as anti-Starbucks as it comes, from the décor to the ownership structure. It's one of the last remaining cooperatively owned businesses in the neighborhood.

"No, I don't think so," I respond. "I think it may have been Palmer's, on the patio."

"That sounds right," she laughs, and we begin.

› On her connection to the West Bank...

"I think the first time that I was here I was a freshman. I had made two friends who lived in different dorms, and we popped over the Tenth Avenue Bridge and I got a quesadilla at Hard Times. I was like, 'What the fuck is this place?!' I immediately associated the West Bank with artsy, gritty stuff—that was my introduction. I hung out with a lot of punk rockers in show spaces, seeing shows at the Bedlam, too." Rana is referring here to the original Bedlam Theatre, a beloved venue originally located on Cedar Avenue. "I helped run a studio and had punk shows there. It was the precursor to the Medusa. Right after we closed, that's when Medusa opened up—about a year later."

The Medusa was an off-the-radar West Bank club; the House of Balls, an artist-owned art gallery and studio, occupies the space where it used to be. Rana hasn't been there yet, but we're both grateful that the space evolved into an artist space rather than condos.

› On food...

"The Wienery was my favorite spot for lunch. I slept during the day and was working at night—so I'd often hit up the Wienery or the deli right across from Palmer's. The Med Deli when it was in the really little spot. I'd get chicken and a giant pile of cheese curds."

› On changes in the neighborhood...

"So much has changed since I first started hanging out here. The fire in the building where Bedlam was and near the mosque. And Grandma's Saloon getting torn down. But those kinds of changes . . . that's every part of town. The University of Minnesota buildings took up space in the time I was here. I loved the Triple Rock before there was a show space. There used to be a beautiful patio outside, and it became a great show space, but that patio was awesome.

"But there are good changes, too. It's been great to see the East African community claim space and become more obvious. They have more storefronts now. Before, it was less obvious that they owned businesses—they were in malls but didn't have storefronts.

"Oh, also, the Taco Bell got a facelift!"

"Hey, that's not the West Bank. That's Seward," I counter, and she laughs.

› On her "West Bank story"...

"When I first started going to Palmer's, they used to sell chalices. Afterwards, I went to Med Deli for dinner. I remember one time it was the winter and I realized too late that I wasn't wearing a bag and I didn't have any pockets, but I had to ride my bike home. So, I put it in my belt in my pants. It was so warm, and it was so cold outside! I got it home safely, but I nearly peed myself doing it."

We laugh, then go downstairs to take a photo set in the club's green-room—the break area for talent. We chat a bit more about what's coming up at the club before heading our separate ways.

Rana last saw somebody on a tall bike a few months ago, somewhere in Minneapolis.

Clean Up, Clean Up, Everybody Everywhere

As I began my new role, I added a few activities to our programs. Out of everything, neighborhood cleanups were the thing everybody agreed most wholeheartedly on: they were universally positive for businesses, residents, and guests. So we set out to organize these events regularly—neighborhood cleanups being the original #TrashTags, before the internet phenomenon took root. Every spring, the melting snow would reveal soggy bags, boxes, and remnants from too-full public trash cans. We'd kick off around Earth Day, regrouping regularly for another round of neighborhood cleanups staffed by the WBBA team, board members, residents, and staff from the other local nonprofits and restaurants.

Every year, volunteers would fill hundreds of bags with trash from the neighborhood. Plastic bags and cigarette butts were some of the worst culprits, and Minneapolis eventually proposed a plastic bag ban. While a full ban was prevented from going into effect, the city did require stores to start charging customers for them in 2019. Soon after, as part of a pop-up art installation, youth from Cedar Riverside Community School participated in one of our cleanups. They put up a temporary installation of bunches of plastic bags hung from the trees in an effort to educate residents about the fee and recurring litter issues.

The Cedar Riverside Neighborhood Revitalization Program (now Cedar-Riverside Community Council), our neighborhood residents organization, also helped clean during regular safety walks. Residents of the West Bank—mostly Somali elders—would don safety vests and inspect the streets, picking up trash with little grabbers and tidying sidewalks as they walked. They helped with cleanup while also providing "eyes on the street."

The city would do its part to help, providing trash cans and ash receptacles to any businesses interested in "adopting." The more adopted trash cans we had on the street, the less likely they would fill to overflowing and spill out onto the sidewalk. My goal was for us to reach the "Disneyland" effect: I had noticed that at Disneyland, there seems to be a trash can accessible no matter where you look, and staff check and empty them regularly. A neighborhood that's well cared for brings this vibe, too. We encouraged businesses to adopt cans and receptacles for cigarette butts. Especially with all the bars in our district, having ash receptacles throughout helped cut down on smokers tossing their butts onto the sidewalk.

The universities, particularly Augsburg, were also a big part of this effort. Every fall, Augsburg students would participate in a city service day and help with cleanups, neighborhood landscape projects, and more. Faculty would join us each spring for a staff effort—leading by example.

On these days, teams of ten to twenty Augsburg students and faculty (or Auggies, as they call themselves) would head out to support the neighborhood, walking over from the campus, undeterred by even the rainiest day.

The cleanups themselves were greatly helpful. They had an added benefit of outreach to businesses, which allowed us to introduce them to larger programs like the Façade Improvement program. Several new façade grant projects were instigated as a result of the outreach we did during cleanup—an added, unintentional benefit that triggered greater neighborhood improvement.

One year we coupled our cleanups with a dedicated outreach campaign, hoping some awareness would help reduce the tendency for patrons of restaurants and bars to toss their trash on the sidewalk. We supplied businesses with trash bags and graffiti wipes (graffiti removed quickly after it appears is less likely to reoccur). Businesses were on board, joining us for cleanups in record numbers and helping to sweep up spaces in front of their storefronts. While pitching in to clean up was not a universally accepted practice, things did get better little by little. Businesses also placed signs in their storefronts: "We live here, we work here, we learn here. Please help keep our neighborhood clean."

A Got-Dang National Treasure

› TONY ZACCARDI

Palmer's Bar is quite possibly the perfect dive bar—with awards to prove it. A cornerstone institution of the West Bank, it's the entry point for many guests to the neighborhood. And for many regulars, Palmer's feels like home.

As you enter on the west side of Cedar Avenue, a painting of a dapper man in a suit and top hat guides your way. Inside, you are immediately surrounded by a comfortable smell unique to dive bars with *real* history in them: aged wood, the deep smell of sunlight baked into the walls, and classic Grain Belt tile aged with whiskey, time, and the beat of countless souls.

Keith and Lisa at the West Bank Ride

I'd been to Palmer's countless times before taking my job at the WBBA—half the time for music, half for simply hanging out. There are few better spaces for camaraderie and communion in the spring than the bar's back patio. When I started my new gig, Lisa Hammer and Keith Berg were the owners and, as such, de facto hosts of the West Bank community. Both welcomed me warmly into the fold and supported me and the association throughout their tenure. Chatting with Keith on quiet mornings became one of the highlights of my regular outreach. When he passed away unexpectedly in 2015, I mourned the loss together with my Palmer's family.

After a few years of running the bar solo, Lisa made a difficult decision with wisdom and care: selling the institution to the right owner, at the right time. Not willing to let just anyone come in and turn Palmer's into something it's not, she waited until the perfect person came along.

> **The West Bank is the Brooklyn of the Twin Cities. It's *every* kind of thing.**

Palmer's Bar

Tony Zaccardi, to quote our friend Andy Holmaas, "is a got-dang national treasure." He is indeed something of a local legend, not unlike Palmer's itself. He's an accomplished musician in the acclaimed band Eleganza! Many of us got to know Tony on the other side of the bar—not on the West Bank but at Grumpy's Northeast. I was lucky to know him this way, and I was absolutely thrilled when the news broke that he would be taking the dive into dive-bar ownership.

After the dust settled from the rapid closing of spaces during the pandemic, I sit down with Tony and Zach Swenson via Zoom for a catch-up and interview. Zach is a West Bank regular who has worked as staff at a variety of West Bank spots. Today, he is helping Tony.

"How are you doing, friend?" I ask.

"Honestly," Tony says, "my mind is racing. I'm stressed out, but so is everyone else right now. A day or two behind the reality, but ... cautiously optimistic."

› On his connection to the West Bank ...

"I started out on the West Bank at twenty-one playing at 400 Bar. My music brought me here, but I worked in Northeast. And since being here I've gotten to love the history. Lisa left me a lot of archives. I love hearing the stories, I love digging and researching. There's still more to learn and more to do.

"When I bought the bar, people were excited to come down here. It's smaller than the Triple Rock, so it's also a little more intimate. Zach, who also works at the Wienery, works here. I'm excited to see it still thriving, in my little corner. Talking to people like Matty O'Reilly [owner of Republic] and Erik Funk [former owner of the Triple Rock—more about him later], they are all excited that I'm here, wishing me good luck. I love that people have an appreciation for the West Bank. That's a great sign for what's to come."

› On changes in the neighborhood ...

"Well," Tony says, rolling his eyes, "that Tony guy bought Palmer's!" We laugh, and he adjusts his glasses, wiping his eyes. "Honestly, though, this bar transition is big. I feel the weight of it. You can see it's a bar that's got such great history.

Tony and Zach at Palmer's Bar

"That guy, though," he says again, laughing, as he pours himself another drink and invites Zach to sit next to him.

› On what remains the same . . .

"The neighborhood, in my time playing shows here, is still incredibly diverse. It's still an immigrant culture that goes back over a hundred years. The Towers, the diversity—I tell my family members that it's kind of the Brooklyn of the Twin Cities. It's every kind of thing.

"The West Bank is like New York in that there are all kinds of people. Old hippies, old bike club people.[4] And somehow we all get along and coexist.

"There are people curious about old-school actual bars, not just distilleries. People feel like they can just come down here, and they can. People can come in and it's a cultural tour, just being in the neighborhood. There's all sorts of things that don't happen in Northeast, or Eden Prairie. And I say that as a Northeasterner!

"The thing I've learned, too, is there's a misconception about the crime that's maddening. That's been a big thing that I'm fighting. Oh, and on that

---

4. The Black Label Bike Club (originally the Hard Times Bike Club) has a historic presence on the West Bank, as do its members. They are known internationally for Victorian-inspired tall bikes and a DIY/punk ethos.

note, actually, you can find a place to park. Every day at happy hour, I've got nine spots literally right out front. Get the fuck over here!"

He laughs again.

› On his "West Bank story" . . .

"Oh, I have a good one!" Tony says, his face lighting up. "A former employee told me this one, so I have no idea if it's actually true."

"That's the making of a great West Bank story," I laugh. "A little bit of fact mixed with a little bit of fiction."

Tony dives in excitedly. It all starts with "Spider" John Koerner and Willie Murphy, two legendary musicians local to the West Bank.

Spider John at Palmer's Bar

"Okay, so, before they built the Towers, there were all these houses. Spider John and Willie Murphy made a record. On that album *Running, Jumping, Standing Still* there's a song, 'Red Palace,' for which they made a video. This is years before videos were common, and [musician and activist] Wavy Gravy made an appearance. He showed up with a hippie bus full of hippie girls unannounced on the farm in New Jersey where Willie Murphy was filming the video.

"The real Red Palace was an after-hours spot here on the West Bank. It had notoriously wild late-night parties. One night at Red Palace, Red [James 'Red' Nelson] was doing his thing on a West Bank afternoon. Grilling food, eating steaks, cooking lobsters, what you do. Then, as he was cooking, he started shooting steak bones through a potato cannon. Just, like, going wild, shooting steak bones. Then, eventually, they start running out of steaks.

"So, he sends one of his guys to go get more steaks from the grocery store downtown. Except the dude doesn't have any money, so he shoves them in his pants and steals them. Well, he ends up getting frostbitten somehow, so he has to go to the hospital because of the frostbite from the stolen food.

"While he's in there, a prostitute comes in with a steak bone stuck in her leg. She's like, 'Help! This steak bone—it came out of nowhere!'"

Tony laughs and lights a cigarette.

› On what he imagines for the future . . .

"It's hard because, you know, I can imagine a lot of things . . . I think a little more honor towards the historical aspect. There are some amazing photos of historic Cedar Avenue. I hope it remains a fierce little independent quadrant of Minneapolis, with respect from city leaders. Let's honor that this is still here. The North Loop—that's like the shining emerald right now of Minneapolis. Meanwhile we've got bus stop signs that have been missing for over four months. . . .

"I'd like a little more respect, attention, and acknowledgment from the leaders and those in power. You know, what little respect we do have, what seat at the table we do have, is thanks to folks like you demanding one."

Aw, shucks. I guess I can be stubborn when I need to be.

Tony last saw somebody on a tall bike about three days ago, in Dinkytown, Minneapolis.

Hugs

eeting with businesses one-on-one was a regular feature of my daily work with the West Bank Business Association, and spring outreach became one of my favorite activities of the year. I would make the rounds, updating our spreadsheet with any businesses that had closed or opened and saying hello. I'd let owners know about any grants or other opportunities coming up, and policy decisions happening at the city that would affect their businesses. The streets becoming active again as the weather warmed up always felt hopeful and cheery—springtime in Minnesota is a welcome balm after the roughness of winter.

This mass exodus from indoors to outdoors is a common feature of the season here. Residents spend months cooped up during the state's long, snowy winters, and the slightest hint of spring will draw out even the most introverted of introverts. I'd gear myself up for a full day of social contact, which was exciting but a little exhausting. I would prepare myself mentally for these exchanges—it felt like I was fighting a mix of imposter syndrome and introversion. Why did I have my job? What if all the businesspeople secretly hated me? Our quirks pop up at the most inconvenient times, don't they? But once I was out and about, the worry fizzled away. Hugs abounded, and the personal connections were great reminders of not just why I took this job, but why I loved this job.

I would ask folks how they were doing, and they would share or vent with me. More often than not, I'd get a heavy dose of the latest West Bank gossip. Minneapolis being a small community, there was a lot of social crossover, so as we talked business, we'd also catch up about friends, family, and kids.

In-person outreach became a critical, regular activity for our team. We'd send email blasts from the organization to get the word out electronically as well, but by far the best way to get things done was in person. Touching base about a major event? In person. Grant? In person. Big city news that required us to show up at a council meeting? In person. The board and our various committees would help when we had particularly pressing issues at hand, swinging by to chat with businesses. While programs and events were the things we talked about in grant reports and annual newsletters, the effectiveness of those programs was undergirded by the relationships, the people.

As the years continued, our stated goals shifted to reflect this regular outreach. "Every business, every quarter" became an internal motto—making sure to carve out time for those conversations with regularity. I look back on that time with gratitude. A precious gift we often don't allocate enough time for: time with each other. The human connection is every bit as important as the work.

Dancing through the Numbers

› KATE BARR

> **The West Bank always felt like a little island. It's such a small, easily walkable place.**

Kate Barr is an icon in the local nonprofit community. Known for her clarity, wit, and responsiveness, she's the director of Propel Nonprofits. I first met Kate ages ago, when I took the reins at the Northeast Community Development Corporation. Spiraling in the economic downturn during the Great Recession at the time, the organization was in dire stakes. Though she barely knew me, Kate took the time to give me guidance as I worked to lead it through a darkly turbulent transition.

She has played this role for countless others in the nonprofit community. Kate brings a calm and steady presence to her work, and her penchant for mentoring others radiates through Propel and its programs, which support the financial literacy of nonprofit leaders and the stability of nonprofit organizations. We have stayed in touch over the years, connecting here and there for coffee to chat about nonprofits, transition, and spreadsheet nerdery.

› On her connection to the West Bank . . .

"I first moved to Minneapolis in 1978—and the reason I moved was because of the Nancy Hauser Dance Company. . . . I danced there and I worked there. And then, after a few years, I went to work for Riverside Bank. I was there for a long time but spent about three years at the West Bank location. Riverside Bank is where Associated Bank is now, at the corner of Cedar and Riverside."

So many businesses have come and gone over the decades—both before I started working on the West Bank and in the years since.

Kate Barr

› On food . . .

When I ask about Kate's favorite lunch spot, she responds excitedly: "Edna's!"

"What?!" I exclaim. "Wait, you knew Edna?!"

"Yes! Edna and her son Willie, who was the cook. I ate there a lot, and Annie's Parlour sometimes, too. But my lunch spot was Edna's, along the stretch near the post office, by Global Village. In fact, the guy who was the manager of that Annie's I think lives in our area of St. Paul."

Edna's Diner occupied the space that is now the Wienery, kicking off a long tradition of affordable, tasty meals in the location on Cedar Avenue.

› On changes in the neighborhood...

"You know, the biggest change I see has been who lives there. I was there in the late '70s, and that was the place where hippies lived. It was the center of counterculture in Minneapolis. Everything from Riverside Cafe to the co-ops . . . it just was the vibe of the neighborhood. Now, because of the changing demographics, and the Somali presence, that's shifted some. Also, the University of Minnesota is a *lot* bigger now than it used to be. There's just so much more university to the district.

"There also used to be so much independent retail there; that's fading out now. Midwest Mountaineering has been there forever, and they were there then, too. They were smaller, though—they had one storefront. Now they have that block!

"When I worked at 504 Cedar, Palmer's is where we hung out. Palmer's has been there a long time, too . . . 400 Bar was there for a long time, and Riverside Bank was a part of it all.

"I don't want to give the bank too much credit for some miraculous thing. But the bank really started as this . . . experimental bank to be in that neighborhood. Shares to Riverside Bank were sold individually—like, walking up and down. Individual people owned one and two shares of the bank. Where else do you see that? So on the one hand, Riverside was truly a community bank. But I also don't want to sugarcoat the fact that it was still a banking system even though it had an egalitarian feel to it, especially for the '70s and '80s. It was the first bank in the Twin Cities to bank co-ops, which was huge. Being there at the dance company and then at the bank, you just felt really a part of the neighborhood. . . .

"I think part of what's changed is that it's a completely different demographic than it was before. This is not a bad thing; it's just different. And the more that it is about the East African community or serves the primary residents, the better."

› On what remains the same . . .

"There are some institutions like Mixed Blood Theatre that have been there for a long time. The fact that Palmer's is there I find comforting. And I think the other thing about the West Bank that still feels the same . . . it's still a small, little, easily walkable place."

› On the nightlife . . .

"There was the 400, the Viking Bar, Triangle Bar. And then, when you went up the hill to Seven Corners you could go to Sgt. Preston's, or the Haberdashery. Dudley Riggs's original theater, which is now Town Hall Brewery. There was lots of music. And Dania Hall was still there. The fire was when I was there."

"Oh, wow," I gasp. "Do you remember what happened?"

"I remember when the fire happened, but I don't remember the fire itself. I just remember how shocking it was. There was a performance space in there, and every now and then a performer would need a particular size, and they would go to Dania. Once I went there to see a dance performance that had aerial works—it was beautiful. Such a loss for the community."

› On her "West Bank story" . . .

"This is one of my favorite stories. In the early '80s, the hippie crowd was ready to stand up for things; there was a rent strike. And part of doing a rent strike is you do have to actually pay your rent, but you have to escrow it—the bank will hold those funds for you without passing it through to the owner tenants are trying to negotiate with. This way, tenants cannot be evicted for nonpayment of rent.

"Well, Riverside ended up accidentally being the escrow. One by one, people started coming in, saying, 'Can you hold this for us?' After the third or fourth person, we realized we had to hold the escrow. I don't remember it being particularly organized on our end at first!

"I remember there were signs on the window at Riverside Cafe, and our bank became a part of this whole protest, because we were the community bank. It was exciting to have this rent strike. Everybody was taking action, and people were marching for what was right."

Rent strikes were a common feature of the West Bank, especially in the 1970s and continuing into the '80s. Strikes in this era were significant in making strides in rental rights, resulting in more formal lease agreements and minimized rent increases. Locally, they even led to the bankrupting of a development company, with its parcels eventually sold off.

› On what she imagines for the future . . .

"The West Bank always felt like this little island," Kate says as we close our conversation. "There's something great and wonderful about an island, but the separation feels vaster than it needs to be. I would like to see more capital investments made in the West Bank so that people there can determine what they want it to be and what they want it to have."

The future is uncertain for so many small businesses and nonprofits in this era. So much of our work today centers around retaining options for them and helping them see the next phase of whatever this future will be.

The last time Kate saw somebody on a tall bike, it was somewhere in St. Paul.

It's All in the Wrist

my parents discouraged me from getting a job in high school. "School is your job," they said, and went on about grades and college. But at sixteen, in want of gas and CD money, I walked down Candlewood Street to the local mall, and one by one I filled out paper applications. Availability: after theater rehearsal on weekday evenings, plus weekends.

The cashier at the Wherehouse, a local record store, had worked there for upwards of a decade. A Tom Petty lookalike with shoulder-length blond hair and black cowboy boots, he smiled at me as I slipped my neatly filled application onto the counter. "You want a job here, bright eyes?" he said, and I nodded. "Well, I'll see what I can do." He smiled again and winked at me as he placed my application on a not-small stack of what I assumed must have been a hundred other apps under the cash register.

Not surprisingly, with my stunning display of availability, it took some time before I was hired anywhere. (I did fulfill my dream of working at a record store a little later in life.) Most people know Marie Callender's for its frozen meals, pot pies, and various comfort foods, but I came to know Marie's in a slightly different way: as my first real, regular employer. I was hired as a hostess at one of the chain's restaurants for a whopping $4.15 an hour (gather round, kids). I dutifully wiped menus, sat customers, and helped bus tables. If it was slow, I'd wipe the windows between the booths, tracing each little diamond pane until it was clear and free of countless kid fingerprints. Pro tip: Did you know coffee filters are excellent for cleaning glass? No fuzz, no residue.

Every restaurant staff has its own slew of horror stories, and my experience was no different. In that, I found Debra Ginsberg's *Waiting* to be quite a relatable read.

> "In my experience," she says, "I've noticed that waiting on tables is one of two things that almost everyone thinks they can do. The other is writing. Perhaps it's no accident that there is only one letter of difference between waiter and writer."

There was the time a customer trashed our women's room, turning it into a quite literal bloody mess—my boss offered to buy me lunch if I cleaned it up. "Please," she begged me. "I'll give you gloves!" Cleaning the blood off the toilet, trash can, and door was a nightmare. How had they even managed to do it? Not surprisingly, I was not hungry for lunch. I got my food to go and ate it after I took the world's hottest shower.

My time at the restaurant was good practice for the introvert in me, though I was probably a shy and terrible hostess compared to my more extroverted counterparts. But apparently not so terrible—I made the promotion to waitress after only a few months on the job. I was promoted in advance of another hostess who had been there longer than I, much to her frustration. A surly teenager about my age, she took out her frustration by giving me the cold shoulder and gossiping about me with some of the other servers, who in a satisfying turn took great pride in sharing everything she told them with me. "Watch out for her," they advised me. "She wants to get you fired." While I felt bad about management's decision, I'm 95 percent certain cleaning up that bathroom triage scene helped inform it.

One time, a family of ten were on their way to the airport—all going to Florida's Epcot Center. They made it clear their flight was departing in short order and they were in a great hurry for their meals. (Apparently Southern California's Disneyland was not fancy enough?) I brought out crayons and toys and met the whims of six very needy kids I was sure would be super fun to travel with on a packed airplane. I time-checked for them to ensure they didn't miss their flight and packaged their leftovers in a hurry. I cleaned mushy cornbread off two high chairs and swept peas and french fries and crayons off the floor. No tip.

A lot of my friends who worked for other big chains have horror stories about the quality of food and management. I had no major issues, and I'm grateful. But the way it infected my subconscious was a fascinating phenomenon—oh, the nightmares! Servers have the most ridiculous nightmares. In my most common dream, I made the rounds over and over, watching helplessly as the hostess brought me table after table. Try as I might, I kept forgetting table eight's lemonade. My station was filled to the brim, I hadn't taken a single order, and I kept running around in circles carrying a tray with endless waters but no lemonade. Even the smell of whipped cream that soaked deep into the fibers of my clothes after a long shift permeated into my dreams.

I continued to work for the Marie Callender's chain through college, hopping from location to location depending on where I lived at the time.

I had to reapply and interview each time, but fortunately there always seemed to be a need. Each spot had its own personality and quirks. One was next to a retirement community in Seal Beach, California, quirky enough to warrant its own sitcom. On Tuesdays and Thursdays, a big bus would drop off elders at the strip mall to do their shopping and get their hair done, and they'd pop in to Marie's for the slice of the day. Groups of freshly coiffed little old ladies would ask for split checks, paying in change and tipping in nickels. Even in the late '90s, this situation felt like an adorable time warp. The Huntington Beach Marie's, where I worked later in college, had an incredible brunch, and the after-church rush on an Easter Sunday could take the edge off that month's rent payment.

I must have worked for over twenty managers among the various locations—so many I learned to predict who would be good or bad based on their path to leadership. The best managers by far were those who had risen up through the ranks. They managed with the dexterity and wisdom that can only come from years in the trenches (and by trenches, I mean server stations laden with cornbread and potato cheese soup). When things were slow, they would help the cooks in the back with prep. When things were busy, those managers were like superglue up front: stocking, prepping, making runs out to tables so the food stayed hot. Cooks, the best judges of character, loved the seasoned managers the best. They would give them a hard time and serve up samples of test recipes only for them. On the other hand, you could always find the book-taught managers in the office behind closed doors during a rush, some paperwork in need of "urgent" addressing. They cared less about what you needed during a rush than about how you filled out your time sheet and whether you were following the "ten points of exceptional service" on which we were quizzed and graded by secret shoppers.

Relationships were the best part of the job. Lalo, my favorite chef, taught me how to crack an egg with one hand. He laughed as I made mistake after mistake—mistakes he scrambled into a breakfast for us to share. Nick, a fellow server, once brought in a bunch of plastic farm animals. Hiding them in his apron, he dropped them into the potato cheese soup one by one as he passed the soup and salad bar. When a customer asked to see the manager because "there was a cow in his soup," it was all she could do to not laugh. (Nick, by the way, was disciplined but not fired.) Mona, a server about four years my senior, became a close confidante. She'd pepper me with questions about school and relationships, giving me sage advice on work, dating, and sex.

I learned to carry a tray of food that weighed probably half as much as I did, thanks to the thick ceramic dishes and bowls we used. "It's all in the wrist," Mona said as she taught me how to hoist the tray onto my left shoulder and balance it with my left hand before walking it out to the table, flicking open a tray stand with my right hand, rotating the tray off my shoulder, and setting it on top of the stand.

There was the time I threw a hot-sauce bottle in my apron during a speedy cleanup only for it to leak everywhere, through the apron and through my pants. By the end of my shift my thighs were raw and red from the pepper and vinegar chafing them all night.

That wasn't the only way the job wreaked havoc on my body—I still have pains in my thumb joint from the repetitive weight of the heavy ceramic dishes—but I loved the work. I lived for the peaceful moments at the end of a shift. Larry, one of my favorite managers, was a quiet person like me. One time after a particularly loud night for the restaurant, we sat in an empty station after the shop closed up. We ate soft-serve ice cream smothered in chocolate sauce, compared family notes, and laughed. Neither of us were doing exactly what our parents had expected us to do.

Experience. Customer service. Camaraderie. You don't always learn these things in college, but you'll always get them in a service job.

As my part-time office-job hours gradually consumed my waitress-job hours, I kept those lessons close with me. I found the ones about teamwork and humor critical. Not surprisingly, I also found those I hired who had a restaurant background to be incredibly reliable and resilient, even in an office setting, unafraid of digging into the work. Maybe it was a bias for my own experience, or maybe it was because a restaurant is a fantastic place to learn about customer service and quick thinking.

These lessons were grounding for me and my work on the West Bank, especially with our restaurants. At the WBBA I got to work with a whole community of bars and restaurants—only unlike the ones I'd worked in, they were locally owned. We even had our own bakery, Keefer Court Bakery and Cafe.

The international food selection is a staple of our district, and during

the time I worked there we had over two dozen
restaurants and cafés. While we did some traditional marketing, we tried to be unique
in our implementation. We shared interviews with the owners, many of them
immigrants, and stories about the importance of food and culture. We hosted
a sambusa-making class with Abdirahman Kahin, owner of the expanding Afro
Deli. We encouraged the relationship be-

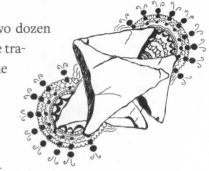

A plate of delicious sambusa

tween the restaurants and the theater venues, given that an overwhelming majority of theater and music venue audiences reported in surveys
they would often go to eat before a show, for drinks after, or even both.

We also crafted an area directory, district website, and social media
pages. We used unique events highlighting the culinary culture of the
restaurants, like storytelling sessions with the owners and cooking classes
with the chefs. We made videos featuring the restaurants, food, and seasonal offerings, like one on how to make mooncakes for the Chinese Mid-
Autumn Festival.

Possibly the most impactful addition was providing assistance
like designing logos, websites, and menus—particularly for small,
immigrant-owned businesses that otherwise would not be able to afford
them. We helped coordinate discounts and incentives for theater audiences in the district. We gave out loyalty and coupon cards to encourage
cross-traffic and return visits. We curated pop-up galleries in restaurants
featuring the work of local artists. And I, personally, spent a good chunk
of my wages on eating out. (I wouldn't say that one was a specific marketing strategy—just too many tasty temptations!)

All throughout, my foundation of experience in the food industry
helped as I worked to support the needs of our local businesses and brainstorm ways we, as the association, could support their bottom lines, as
well as their staff.

Seeing Double at the Triple Rock

I love that awkward, exciting, butterfly-filled stage when you're first dating a new person. Everything is a little brighter, more intense, full of momentum. When I first started dating my husband, Nick, it was a lot of that. One morning at his house I noticed a guitar, and at my request he let me hear him play. I remember that feeling of anticipation, that wonder, the unanswered question: What do I say if he kinda sucks?

Fortunately, I was pleasantly surprised.

So, Nick had talent. But what about his band? I vividly remember seeing the group play for the first time—even what I wore to the show itself.

The Triple Rock Social Club was a bar, venue, and restaurant on the West Bank, co-owned by Gretchen Funk and Erik Funk (the latter of the punk band Dillinger Four). It was a part of my early experience with Minneapolis and already one of my favorite venues, so when Nick said he had a show there, I knew exactly where I was going. I drove my clunky Volvo down Cedar Avenue, scoring one of the last remaining parking spots in the lot behind the Triple Rock. I walked round the big brick building to a little entrance on the corner, sharing my ID with the bouncer before heading inside.

The restaurant side of the Triple Rock was a long, skinny hallway of a space with booths along the outside wall and a bar along the inside. Bathrooms at the far end, separated from the booths by a pinball machine and an exit door between. To the left of the bathrooms, the corner kitchen and performance venue: a rectangular room with a sunken area for the audience, stage at the far end. There was almost always a spot to see from, an asset for a short person like me. A second bar ensured the concertgoer would never run out of tallboys (or whatever their drink of choice may have been).

So there I was, all dolled up for a rock show, and the question returned: What do I say if they kinda suck?

Of course, they didn't! Not only were they a great band, they were tremendously fun to see live. As Nick's and my relationship continued, I had more and more opportunities to hear him play, and there was rarely a dull moment. One thing that always gave me peace was knowing no matter what, our lives would be full of art and music.

The Triple Rock continued to be a big part of my Minneapolis music life. One night we danced to King Khan and the Shrines, the fragments of dropped beer bottles crushed and crunching under the feet of excited fans. On another memorable evening we headed to First Avenue to see Mastodon, and after the show we hit the restaurant side of the Triple Rock for late-night snacks. Lo

The Anchor Windlass outside of Triple Rock (a different band, a few years later)

and behold, members of the band joined us in the booths that lined the walls. I sat opposite singer/guitarist Brent Hinds and talked about tattoos, art, and Minneapolis (a slow and fuzzy conversation as, admittedly, most folks had had one or two beers by that point). It's the stuff of fan dreams—but it was also normal for the venue. The names of Triple Rock guests were carved into tables and bathroom doors, and I think close encounters like this are part of how the club scratched its name into the heart of the Minneapolis music community. The Triple Rock continued to be one of my favorite places to see live music until it closed in 2017: big enough to have good acoustics, but small enough that shows still felt intimate and up-close and personal—literally.

Acts of Service

› RUSSOM SOLOMON

Russom Solomon, owner of the Red Sea restaurant and bar and a longtime WBBA board member and community leader, was my first West Bank Business Association contact. He and Mark Dudek Johnson from the Cedar were the two-person team that brought me in to interview for the executive director position. Russom was always ready with an honest opinion, bringing his insight and wisdom to the board.

> " I don't go to meetings thinking 'What is there for me?' I go there thinking 'What's there for all of us?' And that has served me well. "

In addition to great food, the Red Sea also has a music side, with a show section juxtaposed in between the bar and the restaurant. While the entertainment part of the Red Sea has become known more recently for hip-hop, it played a prominent role in the reggae scene of the '90s.

Russom is somebody who leads by example, though he may be too humble to use the term "leader" to describe himself. A soft-spoken parent of two great kids, he is deeply committed to the community beyond the walls of his bar. He has long been an advocate for safety in the neighborhood, and it's his work and persistence that helped create the Cedar-Riverside/West Bank Safety Center. He has been connected to the area for over twenty-five years.

Russom Solomon

› On his connection to the West Bank . . .

"Before the Red Sea, I went to school at the University of Minnesota, in the early '90s," he tells me. "I focused on civil engineering and environmental engineering. But my main connection was through the restaurant."

"Around what time was that?" I ask.

"That was . . . around '94. I bought the restaurant as the Red Sea. The Red Sea started in 1990 with a different Eritrean guy. It was called Asmara at one point—the capital city of Eritrea. The guy who sold it to us bought it in 1990 and renamed it to the Red Sea from Asmara. He expanded from the restaurant side to the two little rooms, which used to be different things— one was a clothing shop. He eventually sold the business to us in 2002. A year after that, we were able to buy the building, too."

› On changes in the neighborhood . . .

Russom echoes others' comments about the area's changing demographics.

"The West Bank is an immigrant hub. Over the years, different immigrants have come here—Koreans, Ethiopians, different people at different times of history. When I came in . . . the demographic used to be more of a hippie place, but still very diverse. Things are changing a little bit now. And then there is the reduction of businesses—significant reduction, like 400 Bar, Depth of Field. Those things have changed a lot.

"Predominantly, the folks that reside in the neighborhood now are from the Somali community. The West Bank is vibrant with the different groups. That has an impact. The culture—it is still diverse, but diverse in a different sense than it used to be. I was part of the business association from 2002 on, and then I was a part of the [West Bank Community] Coalition in early 2005. At that time I was one of two East Africans there. On the business association board, it was the same. We are missing some people from the institutions that used to be more involved, but there are new faces, too."

› On what remains the same . . .

"The theaters are still here. The Cedar, Mixed Blood Theatre, Theatre in the Round. But you can feel the change. It's especially noticeable for those that come into the area from other areas."

› On his favorite "West Bank story" . . .

"When we did the successful West Bank Music Festival, it was great for us. Unfortunately, that can never happen again. It took a lot of logistical resources. But having some major artists outside our bar, like Brother Ali, that was amazing. That's the peak, from my perspective.

"Zombie Pub Crawl was a busy time for us, too. But the West Bank Music Festival, the energy it brought—it was unbelievable. It's a good thing that there were pictures you can see. Reminds you the amount of work that went into it. We had a lot of great people helping out."

› On what he imagines for the future . . .

"To be honest with you, I don't know. The way things are changing, it might be a little tougher. One has to really be up front about this because you are as relevant as your neighborhood is. You have to be able to cater to that neighborhood.

"If the population in the neighborhood is changing, you have to adapt. You can't be an island. That's why it's important for my kind of businesses to have places like Palmer's, Acadia. We're all in this together. We're music venues, but the entertainment industry is changing.

"The people who support events like live music are changing, that's also another problem. One has to adapt to those changes and be creative. But no matter what you do, that industry is slowly but surely slowing down. And this, COVID, is not going to help.

"The people on the West Bank help support each other. By taking part in these meetings, like the association, we made a lot of friends who other-wise we would not have met. I don't go to meetings thinking 'What is there for me?' I go there thinking 'What's there for all of us?' And that has served me well. The overall goal is that you do work for everybody and try to sup-port and give your input for everybody's sake, and then you will benefit in the long run. I've made close friends, and people have supported us when we've needed the help.

"Had I not taken part, I think it would have affected my businesses, and our connection to this community."

The last time Russom saw somebody on a tall bike was a few weeks ago, biking past the Red Sea.

Barriers to Participation

The WBBA board had all the blessings and curses that can come with a nonprofit board in an engaged community. The organization had a member structure with a hierarchy to the board and executive committee. For those unfamiliar with nonprofit management, the board is the body tasked with oversight and responsibility for the organization. Traditionally, boards set the vision, hire executive staff, and oversee the financials and governance of a nonprofit. While every nonprofit is different, most federally recognized models operate with a hierarchy of responsibility that ends with the board of directors. Board meetings were open to the public and well attended, usually focusing on a topic of interest in addition to the board governance, which took a back seat to neighborhood issues. Our board was composed of members from the community—bar and restaurant owners, nonprofit staff, and residents.

I came to the organization shortly after it had instituted paid membership benefits for businesses. While our program services were available to all businesses, paying members received discounts on things like technical assistance and shared marketing opportunities like ads in our brochure. They were also eligible to serve on the board of directors, creating a hierarchy from members to the board. The paid aspect of membership felt like walking a tightrope: Would we be a truly representative organization when there was a monetary requirement for board participation? Staff worked to make sure all businesses knew they could participate in programs such as events, committees, and façade grants regardless of paid membership status. And as awareness about our programs grew in the district, so did participation.

With a subgroup of engaged businesses and executive committee members, we set out to update our bylaws, last revised in the '80s. There are 1.6 million 501(c) tax-exempt nonprofits in the United States, all of which are required to operate with a board of directors. While we were an engaged board, we were heavy on the bar and restaurant side. Wondering how well our composition reflected the community, we conducted a survey of the neighborhood businesses.

We began to see how we could open our organization up to greater participation from the business community. Were our board meetings accessible? Was our organization accessible? Staff put together a series of recommendations.

We improved where we could, and where the board was willing. At the request of the membership committee, the board also instated a pro bono membership level for new businesses and those under financial constraints. We moved meetings to a more accessible central location.

We picked up snacks before meetings and provided free training to board members. Training proved to be a big positive, and our board members went on to serve other organizations, helping rectify a systemic issue in the sector: not enough board members of color and not enough board members trained in nonprofit management and accounting. This continued skill building and education was a priority—not just for us, but for other boards as well. We folded continued learning into our board membership and considered it part of our programming. The more barriers to participation we removed, the more we saw businesses getting involved.

Recognition was important, too, and I and our membership committee did our best to recognize the contributions of board members who kept our organization going (especially those on the executive committee, who gave additional time). The membership committee began an annual party that gave West Bank businesses and staff a chance to celebrate one another and commemorate the year's accomplishments.

A healthy nonprofit board can be a powerful tool, and boards can be a path to learning, experience, and leadership. Boards guide organizations and steer resources. Boards shape visions and help staff as they cultivate the organization's culture. They are great access points—we just need to make sure the path is navigable and there are as few barriers to access it as possible.

We tried to grow the West Bank Business Association and maintain a healthy board with good practices. But in the end, it was good to keep in mind that a board is composed of people. And not just any people—people who generously give their time to help shepherd a vision for a community they love. I think we in the nonprofit community need to talk more about paying people to do this work. Quite often, having a seat at the table is not enough; many serve on boards even while their own businesses are on the brink. They and their time are gifts. We should try to make sure the nonprofit board model, especially for smaller organizations, helps right-side inequities rather than exacerbate them.

The West Bank Music Festival

When I started at the WBBA, the West Bank Music Festival was its biggest event of the year. Each August, people flocked to Cedar-Riverside for music, food, art, and more. But before we talk about the West Bank Music Festival, we have to talk about Cedarfest.

What was Cedarfest? Only the festival of Minneapolis lore and yore, a giant exhibition of community, togetherness, debauchery, and, of course, music.

In the 1990s, the heyday of Cedarfest, piles of mostly twenty-somethings would spill onto Cedar Avenue, filling parking lots that had been taken over, packing themselves like sardines around the outdoor stages. Businesses would set out booths and tables with their wares, and thousands would stroll up and down the street with beers in hand. It was a musical hippie free-for-all full of love and sound. Or so I'm told. I was never there—I was a teenager making mixtapes in Los Angeles, wondering why my father wouldn't let me listen to the devil's music and wondering how on earth he kept finding my CDs in all the places I'd hidden them.

Cedarfest, which was entirely free for guests, offered an eclectic mix of music with something for everyone. The event, however, proved unsustainable, and it ended in the late '90s.

On the walls in the alley behind Midwest Mountaineering, you can see a door on the second story that opens out into nothing. An office

The West Bank Music Festival

The Delilahs at Cedarfest, 1994

somewhere in that building had a back door, where there must have been a rear entryway from a staircase that no longer exists. The door, partly covered by overgrown ivy stringing its tendrils haphazardly across the wall, is marked by big block letters: CEDARFEST.

The West Bank Music Festival was, for all intents and purposes, an attempt to recreate Cedarfest. The brainchild of the West Bank bar owners, its goal was to highlight the district, draw traffic to the neighborhood, serve as a fundraiser for the WBBA, and boost the income of the local bars. As the years went by, the event did . . . some of those things successfully.

It was in its third year by the time I came on board. Fortunately, I had the support of a great committee and my predecessor, Adrienne Peirce, to help me along. My decade of experience running events at Altered Esthetics gallery and throughout the Northeast Arts District didn't hurt. A short but helpful guide from the prior year's festival helped pinpoint profitability, key contact people, and suggestions for the upcoming year.

We started planning early on, a variety of folks from the district helping. The Cedar Cultural Center staff helped with booking talent, and the bar owners helped with logistics. We invited businesses to set up tables and restaurants to create easy grab-and-go foods for festival guests. The event itself was a festive occasion, with guests and neighbors coming out to dance in the streets and celebrate life, music, and, of course, the West Bank.

Growing a little bit each year, the summer festival involved shutting down Cedar Avenue and placing a stage at the far end. Vendors would line the streets, and food trucks would be invited (but not so many as to eclipse the neighborhood restaurants). The bars closest to the stage, obviously, did best, but the event was a good night in general for the restaurants and venues. The retailers that were not involved, on the other hand, would fight the street closure, their days inevitably dampened by the flood of concerts. The hope was that the event still created an overall awareness of the neighborhood and served as a tool for district marketing.

The day of my first West Bank Music Festival came—not my first rodeo, but my first large-scale music event. I had a clipboard in hand, the awesome kind with the compartment underneath to hold my three-ring festival binder. Volunteer info, contact sheet, festival manual, safety plan, cell phone, spare cell phone battery, checks for vendors, deposit bag, spare wristbands. Check, checkity check on my preparedness checklist. I arrived on-site at 6:00 a.m., early enough for the porta potty drop-offs and other vendor arrivals. Walking down Cedar Avenue in the early morning, the smell of Keefer Court's fresh buns baking filled the air.

Growing up in Southern California gave me an education in preparedness thanks to its regular earthquakes. We had gallons of water in the garage, each with a drop of bleach—water reserves for "just in case." On the first day of school each year, I'd bring one full change of clothes along with my pencils, books, and school supplies in case of an earthquake or other situation in which my parents would be unable to pick me up. Most families I knew kept an earthquake kit of some kind. And though we never lost water during an earthquake, we did boil water before we used it, all the time. Plan well, worry less.

I was told later by my board chair, one of the bar owners, that the beer vendor asked how I was doing, remarking, "She seems so . . . calm." Apparently they'd worked enough festivals to be acquainted with the organized-but-frazzled type. I put that compliment up on my festival planner's wall of achievement because (pro tip) if you've done your job right, the day of your event is one of the easier days of event planning. It's the day when everything you've orchestrated is in full swing and—except in the case of emergency—you get to ride the wave. Engaged but no longer in control, you get to see how all that planning went and whether the event is or is not truly going to go off without a hitch.

The afternoon was full of art and energy. *City Pages* hosted a booth with art projects for little kids and grown-up kids to paint a large-scale canvas, which, I believe, later hung in their offices. The Infiammati Fire-Circus opened the evening portion of the festival with fire and dance before the night gave way to music.

While I made the rounds, checking in on volunteers and staff, the warmth of the summer day broke into a much cooler evening. As Astronautalis took the stage, I felt the weather shift. The crowd enjoyed a full set and encore before a light drizzle began to fall, gently ushering festival patrons into bars as though the clouds were helping volunteers scoot, scoot, scoot—so we could take down tents and stages to reopen the closed avenue.

The rain continued to fall on Cedar Avenue. Wrapping up the last of our packing as quickly as we could, we cleared the street to head home—but not before a quick celebratory beer at Palmer's for a festival well done.

Something I discovered in this process is that even people who don't like big crowds, like me, can make decent festival planners. Perhaps because we'll do our best to make it a comfortable experience for extroverts and introverts alike.

That year we had the blessing of being supported by the city of Minneapolis via a Great Streets event grant, which helped cover a big portion of the stage, safety, and contractor fees. We were also able to procure a few local sponsorships. Combined with beer sales from our organization's tent, this helped the event break even.

(A side note: If you, dear reader, happen to be any sort of event organizer and watched either of the documentaries on the infamous Fyre Festival while holding a pillow to fight back panic attacks, let's be new besties and consider this an invitation to discuss. Organized event planners are a particular ilk, and we need to commiserate over that travesty together in solidarity.)

The festival drew mainly nonresidents, though many residents were among the staff and volunteers. That made me wonder: Was this a community festival or a festival to serve the community in this neighborhood specifically? And while liquor licensing required us to section off areas for alcohol consumption, in a densely populated neighborhood with a high percentage of nondrinkers, I wondered whether it was problematic to shut off the streets to vehicles, then block off access and fill the road with drunk festivalgoers.

While we broke even from a hard costs standpoint, that didn't reflect my time spent planning and organizing—or the broader community impact. With a load of year-round needs, was a festival the best use of my time and energy for the district as a whole? I brought these questions to the board, and we agreed to do the festival another year and continue to evaluate things.

"Next year," they said, "things will be even better."

💬 The Merry Merries: Mary Laurel True & Merrie Benasutti

I came to know Mary Laurel True through Augsburg College. A warm, personable, and colorful ambassador for the neighborhood, she helped welcome me to the West Bank and encouraged me in my work, step by step.

I met Merrie Benasutti early on in my time at the West Bank as well. Working with the Cedar-Humphrey Action for Neighborhood Collaborative Engagement (CHANCE) program at the University of Minnesota gave us the opportunity to work together on student-led engagement projects. CHANCE is a collaborative program between the University of Minnesota and Augsburg to nurture student engagement with the district.

Merrie and Mary Laurel worked closely together, and one of my board chairs at one point referred to them as "the Merry Merries," insisting I meet with them ASAP. And they were merry! Always so warm and helpful. The silly nickname stuck with me for years.

› MARY LAUREL TRUE

› On her connection to the West Bank . . .

"I have been officially working at Augsburg as director of community engagement since 1990! That's thirty years of work life and connection with the community.

"But before that I went to St. Catherine's. I found Augsburg in 1978 through the Center for Global Education and Experience—I was on the program Cuernavaca Mexico, with Augsburg students. I learned a lot about Augsburg through them and came to love what I heard about them. I loved St. Kate's, but the experiential education was interesting to me.

> **I think it's miraculous that people with such great differences live together with so much mutual respect.**

"Then I found the West Bank—this was in the spring/summer of '78. After that, I pretty much moved over to the West Bank and had friends that were living on the West Bank. I lived between West Bank and Seward from 1978 to 1983. I'm from Massachusetts originally.

"As a young woman, I was going to bars and just loving all the music. I was gone from '83 to '89, when I went back to Massachusetts and went to graduate school. I thought my life was going to be there until my first husband decided he wanted to come back to Minnesota. I was fine with coming back; I loved the Twin Cities so much. I was the oldest of twenty-seven

Mary Laurel

cousins, and pretty much all of them were here. When I came back, I had a two-and-a-half-month-old baby, and that's also part of why we moved back to the Twin Cities.

"My connection is not only through thirty years of work, but also my college years of hanging out on the West Bank and becoming a West Banker. I was involved with the vegetarian movement, the cooperative movement, the antiwar and antinuclear movement on the West Bank.

"When I came back, I spent a lot of my work life and private time on the West Bank because I loved the Cedar. I have been on the board there for about six years. I love Palmer's and Acadia café and was on the board of the Bedlam for years. I was on the Sisterhood [Boutique] board also and helped to create that program. My connection is deeper to the West Bank than to any other place.

"Also, when the East African community came, that changed my life in significant ways. My connection to the Somali and Oromo communities grew. I grew up in a pretty liberal, radical Catholic family, learning about Islam and Africa. Aside from Mexico I hadn't done a lot of traveling. But the friendships and the connections and the deep love of the East African community—the colleagues I've had, it's not just work, it's real life . . .

53

"The West Bank totally fits who I am."

› On food . . .

"My ultimate favorite forever is St. Martin's Table!"

St. Martin's was an organic café in the garden-level basement of Trinity Lutheran Congregation. Staffed entirely by volunteers, it was a charity-based operation that worked to end hunger in the Twin Cities. Money from customers' bills would go toward a different hunger-focused charity every month. Just hearing the name evokes fond memories of thick, hearty slices of bread covered in veggie spread and sprouts, conversations with colleagues, and a cozy, welcoming environment.

"Ohhhhh" I say. "I miss St. Martin's so much!"

"I know!" Mary Laurel says. "I was there at least a few times a week. I'm sad to have lost that. I'm sad to have lost the Afro Deli in the neighborhood, too. But I loved St. Martin's, their whole mission and what they were up to. Sisters' Camelot is open, by the way—in Bethany Lutheran Church. Hundreds of people come. They're even staying up during COVID time." (Sisters' Camelot is an organic food shelf for folks in the Twin Cities.)

› On changes in the neighborhood . . .

"I guess I would say what's changed for me in the past years—and it's scary for me—I see one of the quintessential features of the West Bank evaporating. The musical elements of the 400 Bar, Bedlam, the Viking, the Triangle Bar, Blondie's, the Triple Rock. Some of these changes, especially the buildings, they can't be redone—they are destroyed. They are not coming back, and the nature of them is not coming back. You know, they had music for old people and young people, and now they are gone. It's the saddest thing I've seen.

"I remember even about ten years ago being able to go from a show at the Cedar over to Viking, then over to Palmer's. Then something would be happening at the Nomad, and then you could go to Bedlam and see a show or sit on the rooftop and get some food. It was just an era where there was really good music in the bars.

"Before that, in the late '70s and early '80s, it was similar . . . when Willie Murphy was still playing around, and Spider John was around. You knew these folks were famous and important, but we had no idea how important they were to people like Bob Dylan and other musicians. And we were just sitting with them at Palmer's.

"That annex with Cabooze, Whiskey Junction—there was a rollicking good nightlife there. The density of good music within three blocks was unheard of. Some blues, R&B, Americana. And the casualness of the places, too. People knew each other and people were very accepting of everybody's strange behavior. You know? Like—this is a scene. This is *love*."

The Cabooze is a large venue just on the edge of the West Bank, in a little strip of venues that include the Whiskey Junction and the Joint, a take-out bar. Also in that strip is Scooterville, a motor scooter dealer. The little node was known for music, summer festivals, and motorcycles.

› On what remains the same . . .

"I still think the West Bank has got its funky nature; it's got an alternative-to-the-mainstream kind of feel. I love seeing the East African community. The West Bank is a mixture of all different kinds of people.

"I love the resilience of the place. I don't know where in the country you would find so much resilience and acceptance of different kinds of people living side by side. I think it's miraculous that people with such great differences live together with so much mutual respect. Being right in the mix and people kind of saying, 'Yeah, well . . . that's what they do, and that's okay. This is what I do, and that's okay.'

"And when people go to Palmer's, there's a mutual acceptance and appreciation. That's what I've always loved about the West Bank. There's a lot of counterculture, and with KFAI there still—there's a lot of interesting and continuing-to-be-alternative ways of seeing the world. I don't think you realize that as much until you leave the Twin Cities and see how different that is. When you leave, you realize how that isn't the way many places in America are."

› On her "West Bank story"...

"One thing I remember is the first fire benefit we planned as a fundraiser. Just being there with a lot of local musicians who loved the West Bank—being at the Cedar and having a band with Somali musicians that were recently reunited.

"It was just an amazing world, to have all these people that care so much about a place and have so much talent that can raise money. What could you ask for more in a community? That was when the Cedar had gotten more involved. An old venue taking on a new venture that was apropos to what they were and what they were trying to do in their neighborhood. World music. You now had what was one of the best music venues in the world bringing their neighborhood in.

"And after a late night, being able to bike from the West Bank back home, on the Greenway. The joy—so much joy. Where else would you find that much joy?!"

Mary Laurel says music is the heart of her life, and I believe her.

› On what she imagines for the future...

"I think my dream and my hope is that more Minnesotan/Twin Cities folks who have influence realize that a big part of what the West Bank is could be lost if we don't do something and save what we have now. We can do that while we celebrate our East African neighbors that are making it a more interesting and rich place. I think it's a combination of saving what it is and celebrating the new part of it. They bring a lot of strength to the neighborhood. They make it a livable, safe place to be. This place is unique in what it is, and many people who live here are from another part of the world. They are entrepreneurial, they are self-reliant. And Fairview has been so helpful by hosting Sisterhood's location, and that's one of the best storefronts in the whole neighborhood!"

Jennifer, Merrie, and Ben at the West Bank Music Festival

Sisterhood Boutique, a secondhand shop located just off Cedar on Riverside Avenue, is a great example of entrepreneurship within the West Bank immigrant community. It was developed by young East African women in the neighborhood as part of Brian Coyle Center's youth entrepreneurship program to help develop hands-on job skills and real-life retail and managerial experience.

"Everyone talks about transitioning all these organizations to East African leadership. Well, Zikki and Amal run [Sisterhood Boutique] right now, and they aren't even twenty-five years old!" says Mary Laurel. "That Coyle has encouraged young women to run that is amazing. Not many white-led organizations intentionally turn over leadership to the East African community."

Run by the nonprofit Pillsbury United Communities out of a building overlooking Currie Park, Brian Coyle Center is a cornerstone of the West Bank. In addition to a large gym used by the neighborhood for everything from voting to late-night basketball, it provides a variety of services. Teachers offer English-as-a-second-language classes, there are tutors for after-school homework help for kids, and both kids and parents can take classes to increase their computer literacy. A big kitchen is used for events as well as entrepreneurial businesses that need a space, and Coyle offers the area's only non-geography-based food shelf—meaning it is open to anyone in need of staples, no matter where they live.

"I didn't say much about the importance of certain organizations in the neighborhood," Mary Laurel adds. "I'm honestly so proud of Augsburg— that's the reason why I stay here. I saw Augsburg's reputation in the '70s was very contentious, perhaps because of the homes they purchased. But in the last ten or more years, it keeps getting better. Folks like Coach Jennifer Weber that have come out of the institution and stayed. And Jane Buckley-Farlee's commitment and how she interacts as a faith leader. It's not like we're perfect, but the love that we have, it's deep and it's real and it's committed. I'm proud of that, and I'm proud of the ways we've been engaged with the neighborhood."

The last time Mary Laurel saw somebody on a tall bike was about a week before our chat.

› MERRIE BENASUTTI

› On her connection to the West Bank . . .

"When I was pregnant with my daughter, I was working at Metro State University. It was a federal grant-funded position; I helped connect Metro State to the Dayton's Bluff neighborhood. When Congress reappropriated the funding elsewhere, I was out of a job. But I also was pregnant! So, I stayed home with my daughter for her first year, then accepted a new part-time job with Mary Laurel. I was there for ten years, and that was my first introduction to Cedar-Riverside. This was around 1995."

› On food . . .

"You know, Mary and I went to lunch a *lot* at St. Martin's Table—and we recruited students to help staff the kitchen. I would also go to North Country Co-op.[5] Seward Co-op was over on Franklin up the street, and we'd go there occasionally, too. Those are the places that stick out the most to me."

> ❝ Our walking tours . . . end with people saying, 'Oh wow, I didn't realize so much was here.' ❞

› On changes in the neighborhood . . .

What has Merrie seen change over the years?

"That's a big question! It feels like at different times there has been more engagement. I feel like things are pretty good right now in spite of all of our challenges. But also, you see these different waves of people engaging and disengaging—and different waves of new immigrants, too. The Somali community has stuck around longer than previous groups.

"One of the things I've often talked about regarding the neighborhood is the disconnectedness. Basically, when the interstates went through . . . even though we're in the middle of Minneapolis, the neighborhood got cut off. Even the three parts of our neighborhood are disconnected from one another by the roads: Cedar-Riverside, Seven Corners, and the Riverside Park area.

"When the light rail came in, I thought it would be an opportunity to knit us back together a bit, but I'm not seeing that as much as I thought I would. I'm not seeing as much inclusion from all parts of the neighborhood as I would like to. The new Cedar-Riverside Community Council board seems like it has great promise, but the group is going to take a while to get on their feet and figure out their path.

---

5. North Country Co-op, Minneapolis's first co-op, closed in 2007 after thirty-seven years of operation on the West Bank.

"I'm cautiously optimistic, but I do think with COVID especially, we're going to see major shifts with a lot of structures."

› On what remains the same . . .

"In spite of the physical disconnectedness of the built environment, I think there's a connectedness, too. That connectedness is a big positive part of the neighborhood. It's relationships. And another consistency is there's always been waves of new immigrants, there's always been the arts. Structurally, there are things that are still there."

› On her "West Bank story" . . .

"I tend to do a lot of neighborhood tours for students, faculty, and different visiting groups. I have a loop through the central neighborhood. There's the spot on Cedar Avenue where Dar Al-Hijrah shares a wall with Palmer's. I feel like that epitomizes the Cedar-Riverside neighborhood—that we have Muslims and a dive bar sharing space. We coexist happily together."

› On what she imagines for the future . . .

"I think we have most of the right ingredients for [the neighborhood] to really thrive. And it doesn't really get credit for how great it is. A lot of where I've centered my work is how to change the perception of it. For instance, with CHANCE, one of the first assignments was a crime trend analysis. We'd have students pick another neighborhood in Minneapolis and compare it. Students would quickly realize that a high crime rate here, well, that's not the reality, especially compared to other areas. These misperceptions make people hesitate to really engage in the neighborhood.

"Even as I would do our walking tours, many would start out [with someone] saying something negative yet would end with people saying, 'Oh wow, I didn't realize so much was here.'"

The last time Merrie saw somebody on a tall bike was only a few days ago. "It's a West Bank thing," she says with a smile.

Mentorship Models

Ben Marcy was one of my first West Bank co-conspirators. An adjunct faculty member at the University of Minnesota, Ben worked with students in the undergraduate leadership minor program on community-engaged projects. Situated so close to campus, the West Bank Business Association was a perfect partner in this effort.

Given our proximity to both the U of M and Augsburg, there could be an overwhelming amount of intern interest at any given time. While some businesses exploit that for free labor, the tide seems to be changing as more businesses institute paid internships as a clear step toward more equitable labor practices. Since I viewed internships as much about training as about help for the association, I would only work with a small number of students each term. The leadership minor was a great fit for this approach.

During my first year with the association, Ben met with me at the office so we could discuss the upcoming semester and what our approach could be. In years past, students had come up with some fun projects—some research based, some practical or product based. But the continual flow of students in and out puts a strain on business partners, who already have too few resources and too little time.

How could we take that awesome student energy and authentic desire to connect with the neighborhood and make it less of a roller coaster? We carved out a new plan: projects that connected students with programs already underway or that would build on the efforts of past student groups. This would allow interns to come up with ideas for student-led initiatives but build on work that had already been done. They could also get hands-on experience with programs already underway.

Since our programs varied from marketing to event planning to business support, there were opportunities that catered to a variety of interests. The students always came from different backgrounds, so making each semester customizable was huge. I appreciated the opportunity to dive back into learning and stay connected with my alma mater.

Among students, as among the public in general, there were some misperceptions about the community. For example, as more than one West Banker featured in this book mentions, the idea that the neighborhood is unsafe. Some of these misperceptions have roots in the crime that was more prevalent in the '80s and '90s; some have roots in racism toward a community with a traditionally large population of immigrants. Time after time, we watched students who more commonly frequented other neighboring districts fall in love with the West Bank and everything it had to offer.

Throughout my time with the association, I worked with students each semester and even during the occasional summer. This continued at its typical seasonal pace until things took a bit of a turn.

One day, Ben and I met at Hard Times—a co-writing session over the winter break. Ben was working on assignments for his PhD, and I was feverishly working on grants for some upcoming deadlines.

"I have some bad news," he said. "Enrollment for the semester is low. I'm not sure what that means for your group, but I'm no longer going to be working as adjunct." He looked understandably crushed.

"What are you going to do?" I asked, my heart sad for my friend and colleague.

"Lots to do for my PhD—I'm going to focus in on that. But I'll miss getting to work with the students."

"You'll be able to do that again," I said, a perhaps-not-great attempt at reassurance. "This is just a pause, that's all."

During my time with the association, I worked with a number of faculty and student groups at the U. There were few people as invested in ensuring students had a thoughtful and meaningful experience as Ben Marcy.

Slowing Things Down

Cedar Avenue is the West Bank's main commercial corridor, but it's more than that. As mentioned, the I-94 freeway and the I-35W freeway don't fully interconnect, so if you'd like to head northbound on 35, you must exit on Cedar Avenue, cut through the neighborhood, and hop back on the next freeway. This is as frustrating to nonlocals as it is to locals, and it's one of the reasons Cedar Avenue is known for high instances of speeding—a tragic combination in an area with heavy pedestrian traffic and plenty of jaywalking. Those simply cutting through the district tend to travel at higher speeds and with less regard for the neighborhood surrounding them than those whose destination is in Cedar-Riverside.

Cedar's sidewalks, not unlike our freeway disconnect, had become a bit of a mess. Several decades overdue for repair, they were only accessible on one side of the street. Disabled guests and residents were unable to use them due to their narrowness, their too-steep slope, and the trees planted awkwardly down the center instead of along the edge, which didn't leave enough room for people in wheelchairs to pass around.

A repaving project gave us the window we needed to make a series of improvements. Minneapolis city planner Joe Bernard met with the business association and community members to discuss a street renovation and sidewalk project for which the city had received some federal funding. While it took several years to implement from start to finish, the end product was a big improvement.

Sidewalks were widened and became accessible to many residents for the first time. Driving lanes were reduced from four to three. Parking was replaced on one side of the street, benefiting businesses and adding a buffer for pedestrian safety. Traffic slowed as a result of fewer lanes. Folks still got from point A to point B, but with fewer accidents and pedestrian injuries. The slowdown is a benefit to business as well, increasing the visibility of restaurants and retail. It increased the walkability of the neighborhood as a result of altering the flow of traffic. My only regret is that we didn't fight harder for a bike lane right on the avenue.

Among the things we did to help with walkability, livability, and pedestrian-friendliness of the West Bank:

> Slowing down traffic
> Benches for pedestrians
> Pop-up outdoor art galleries, murals, and gardens
> Bike racks
> Permanent Murals
> Widening sidewalks and fixing the grade
> Cleanups and trash removal
> Painting and decorating trash cans
> Adding lighting for aesthetics and safety
> Banners and "way finding" (signs)
> Directional maps
> An artist-made Little Free Library
> Bump-outs on curbs at busy intersections
> Pedestrian crossings in areas where there was lots of jaywalking
> Moving a bus stop to improve pedestrian visibility
> Paint-the-pavement projects on the sidewalk leading to local businesses

As city planner Jeff Speck has said, "All the fancy economic development strategies, such as developing a biomedical cluster, an aerospace cluster, or whatever the current economic development 'flavor of the month' might be, do not hold a candle to the power of a great walkable urban place."

West Bank Ladies

When I started in my position, I was the only full-time staff person at the still-growing WBBA, which can be a lonely experience. Fortunately, I made friends along the way. Enter the West Bank ladies! One by one, I met the various business owners and property owners on the West Bank, who welcomed me with open arms and open taps. Our relationships transitioned quickly from festival committee planning to bar hopping and social activities. Lisa Hammer of Palmer's fame was our chief catalyst—full of advice and never short on wit.

"I had your job before, you know," Lisa said as we chatted the first time we met.

"Wait, what?" This was news to me.

"Yeah—I was the director years ago. But not for long. I'm too much of a pain in the ass," she laughed. She shared with me tidbits of advice and information about the work she did while she was with the association. She and other prior directors had also left an electronic paper trail of emails and documents that made stepping into the role as seamless as possible.

The West Bank ladies and I had one of our first evenings out together planned, and I was looking forward to it. On that cold October morning, I went to my doctor's office for a checkup on my prescription only to find—much to my surprise—that I was one month into an unexpected pregnancy! Married for just over a year at that point, Nick and I had talked about kids, but we hadn't decided anything yet. My day was packed with meetings to be followed by a night with the ladies; I wouldn't even see Nick until the end of the day. How, exactly, was I supposed to spend the evening with a bunch of bar owners—all of them parents themselves—and not let my secret slip? I concocted a plan: I would arrive at the venue early and order a nonalcoholic drink that looked like a boozy one. I would sip on my ginger-something-with-a-lime for the evening, nursing it for much longer than any normal person would (but not unusual for me, if we're being honest).

I got to Icehouse early, ordered my fancy not-drink, and journaled a bit while I waited for the ladies to arrive. Once they did, I politely declined additional drinks and shots as we chatted West Bank news and

Secretly pregnant

goings-on. "They don't suspect a thing!" I thought, pleased with myself for keeping up appearances and hiding my little secret. (Reader, the four seasoned moms around the table knew exactly what was going on.)

At home, I told Nick the news. After the shock wore off for both of us, we began making plans, signing up for a variety of classes and appointments. I began to set aside my mild terror around the pregnancy and labor process and replace it with joy. The bud of excitement growing inside me was, according to my new pregnancy app, the size of a poppy seed.

Our next ladies' gathering was at Acme Comedy near downtown Minneapolis, a few months later. We tended to hang out in neighborhoods other than the West Bank so nobody would get sucked into work while we had social time. Sitting around a table for dinner before the show began, I announced the big news to excited screams.

"I fucking knew it!" Lisa said, laughing.

"Sorry I couldn't tell you last time. I only just found out that morning and figured I should probably let Nick know first," I explained. "But that's why I wasn't drinking much last time. I didn't know if anybody noticed."

"Oh, we noticed," Jill said. "We thought maybe you were trying to be extra professional or something at first, but . . ."

"Yeah, no." I laughed. "Not teetotaling. Just pregnant."

"Well, congratulations!" Lisa said. "The West Bank loves babies!"

"I hope so! Do me a favor and don't tell anyone else yet. I still have to let the board know."

They promised. But news on the West Bank travels faster than the speed of light. I knew I had to let folks know quickly.

We headed into the club for a night of comedy, the other ladies ordering additional drinks while I ordered myself a hot cocoa. Grateful for a night out, we sat in our corner laughing hysterically—until a man with a flashlight walked over to us and shined it in our eyes, whispering, "Girls, I'm going to have to ask you to keep it down."

"What do you mean, 'Keep it down'?" Lisa responded. "It's a comedy club. We're laughing."

"You're disturbing the other patrons," he said. "Please try to keep it to a reasonable volume."

"What the hell?" I whispered after he walked away. "It's not like we were heckling."

Lisa shrugged, and we continued to watch the show, all of us still laughing and hooting—perhaps a little louder than before. Perhaps intentionally. Mr. Flashlight stormed back over to Lisa and Juliana, who were sitting in front.

"Ladies, I'm going to have to ask you to leave." His flashlight was like a wagging finger of shame.

"*Fine by me!*" Lisa said as we walked out to the lobby.

We had been kicked out of a comedy club—for laughing?

We opted to head back to Palmer's, where we could continue to be West Bank loud without a bother.

New Developments

A few days after my night with the ladies, I called up Mark, one of my board members.

"Hey. Do you have time for a quick meeting?"

"Sure," he responded. "Come on over."

I ducked out of my office, heading to the Cedar Cultural Center across the street. A revamped movie theater turned music venue, the Cedar's historic building overlooks Cedar Avenue, its bright and iconic marquee welcoming guests to the West Bank. I rang the bell at the front, and Mark came down to let me in, wearing one of his signature brightly colored Hawaiian shirts and cowboy boots. That usually meant there was a show that night.

We meandered up the narrow staircase to the Cedar staff offices, a series of tiny spaces carved into what used to be storage and projection rooms in the building's days as a theater. Mark rolled a chair over from an empty desk toward his workspace and motioned for me to sit down.

"So how's everything going?" he said.

"Pretty good," I responded. I caught him up on some of my activities from the week, and some of the West Bank drama. "So . . ." I hesitated. "I was hoping to chat with you before next week's executive committee meeting about something important."

"What's up?" He looked concerned.

"Well . . . I have some news!" I said, trying to sound positive. "I'm pregnant." I waited at the edge of my chair for a response.

"Are . . ." he said slowly. "Are you quitting?"

"Wait. What? No!" I responded, a little surprised. "That's not why I wanted to meet." I launched into my next steps, outlining my plan for the upcoming months, including how this would work with the West Bank Music Festival. I planned to take some time off after the baby was born, easing back in gradually for meetings and check-ins. By my due date, the logistics would all be in order, and it would be time for marketing to take the reins with promotions. After the festival was over, I would take what would have been the remainder of my maternity leave spread out instead. The timing would actually work out pretty well, all things considered.

We proceeded to talk about the details and planned to bring this up at the executive committee meeting. We talked about the festival, my due date, and our plan for the event and for staffing. I felt a little bit more at ease.

We wrapped up the meeting and I gathered my things, stuffing my journal into my backpack.

Mark gave me a hug. "Well, thanks for letting me know. I'll see you next week. Oh . . . and congrats!"

"Thanks," I said. "This will be fine, I promise." An effort to reassure myself as much as him, I'm sure.

Cadence and Rhythm

› DAVID HAMILTON

> **The neighborhood was always able to welcome and bring together diverse communities, and it's still doing it.**

I checked in with my colleague David Hamilton a few months into the pandemic to see how he was doing. As the summer wore on, so did our pause—and as time stretched, so did my longing for live music and gathering in communion of sound. Although David is no longer a resident of the West Bank, his deep roots in the neighborhood extend through various jobs over the years, living in the district, and, most of all, music.

David is the executive director of the Cedar Cultural Center, which is known for bringing in international music and talent. It is home to Drone Not Drones, a twenty-eight-hour community festival that serves as a fundraiser for Doctors Without Borders, and hosts the Midnimo program, which features Somali artists and has helped bring artists like Aar Maanta to the Twin Cities.

David is a quiet guy, and we often compared notes on leading with introverted tendencies. But his work has been so important to the West Bank community— far more than a lot of people know. It was great to have the opportunity to talk with him more about it.

The Cedar Cultural Center

› On his connection to the West Bank...

"I originally came on the West Bank when I was in grad school in the early '90s. I lived in the Holtzermann; that was when the Cedar first opened. At the time, I had tons of friends from the U of M. This is the time when everybody hung out on the West Bank. There was a thriving bar scene and music scene—I would see Inertia and Willie Murphy at the Viking. I had many African friends at the time.

David Hamilton

Palmer's was there then, of course. Hanging out with all these different kinds of people, hippies and the East African connection, it's exactly what I needed at the time.

"I used to volunteer at Mayday bookstore—that's where my political radicalization started. Tatters was still on the West Bank at that time, too. And back then there were still Korean grocery stores and restaurants, an Indian restaurant, and Global Village was there as well. I had a roommate one time that worked there.

"I was a recently started musician, and it was funny for me to go and see the Maroons at 400 Bar only to play with some of those folks ten years ago.

"So, I lived at the Holtz, then I lived in Blue Goose Co-op, behind Five Corners bar. Then, later, I bought a house on Twentieth Avenue. I was around the West Bank for almost twenty years, and we saw a lot of changes. It was also funny when Pat came and bought the Wienery because I had gone to grade school with Pat!

"I also lived in Seward for a short time. I worked at an org called Access Works. KJ was an intern for us at one point, actually. Minneapolis is a small world."

Access Works is the first harm-reduction syringe exchange in Minnesota. KJ Starr was my colleague at the West Bank Business Association and owns the Wienery with her husband, Pat.

"My older sister, who is about ten years older, was a dancer in an African dance group. They played at the Renaissance Festival. They'd come in a big van and pick her up, and all this weed smoke would come out the back. And Tony Paul was in that band! I've been around Tony Paul forever. I still see people I knew from way back in the day, but it seems like most of the people I knew around the West Bank have left or moved on. It's so weird to be back here working at the West Bank.

"After that I worked at Augsburg for about ten years. I did a couple different jobs there, but when I left I was operations director for [the] Center for Global Education."

› On food . . .

"Of course, there's still Ethiopian restaurants, but the whole Cedar Avenue was completely different. When I first came, Ethiopian food was the big new thing. I never had Korean food before, either, until I came to the West Bank. The Korean restaurant has been gone for ten years or more."

› On changes in the neighborhood . . .

"I think the changes are many forces. Live music, smaller music venues in particular, has been hit hard in the Twin Cities. That, coupled with a demographic shift. You know, the people who did come to the West Bank, they became older, and they didn't go out as much anymore. There are more factors than that, but that's the challenge the Cedar has been grappling with.

"I was there before the larger Somali migration to the West Bank occurred, so I saw the West Bank in the old days. I'd say the Somali community made a mark on the West Bank as many communities had before them. When I was at the U, I had friends that lived in the Towers and went to the U of M. I would go to the Towers and play chess with some friends. But I would say recently, the Somali community has had the biggest influence on the neighborhood.

"What's also interesting is when I worked at Augsburg, I would do Somali immersions with Mary Laurel True. We would bring groups in the Twin Cities—aiming to bridge cultural understanding. We'd come in and visit with mosques, and Abdirizak Bihi would speak to the groups. We would walk around the West Bank, and we would learn about the history of Somali culture, food, language, and religion.

"One more connector: I also worked at Minneapolis Urban League for a year. I had a Somali coworker I worked with—we did outreach and education around sexual health."

It feels like everyone on the West Bank is connected to everyone else and complements one another's work. Abdurrahman Mahmud, another one of my colleagues at the WBBA, worked with the Aliveness Project, which serves people living with HIV.

"A change of many forces happened. And what's interesting is for a while the Somali community did not have its own live music venues or access until the Cedar started bringing the artists to the West Bank and to the United States. So that was helpful in the revival in Somali nightlife, music, culture. It wasn't any one thing but a confluence of things. All these forces.

"It's everywhere, that change. Even over by Cabooze and Viking—a lot of people used to come from outside for shows, and that's been less and less the case."

"I'm hoping our music venues pull out of this," I say.

"Me too." David nods. "I think we'll be okay, we have reserves, but this is going to change the face of music for a long time."

› On what remains the same . . .

"I think what's still there is represented in Palmer's. A very, very diverse neighborhood. The old crowd still goes in there, and there's a new crowd, too. It still has that connection.

"I remember being over on the West Bank before Hard Times started . . . how that brought in a different, younger, what then was kind of a 'punk' crowd into the neighborhood, and they ended up hanging out at Palmer's and the Holtzermann and everything.

"The neighborhood was always able to welcome and bring together diverse communities, and it's still doing it. That has stayed the same. It's funny how communities change by interaction with others.

"It's still a very diverse neighborhood. Keefer Court is still here. Hard Times has survived. Seven Corners morphed. Who knows what will happen after the pandemic?"

› On the neighborhood culture . . .

"What has changed is the university connection. It's still alive a little—like at the Campus Cafe [a Turkish lunch spot] and Hard Times. You don't have all the people from the U of M coming to the bars like they used to and hearing live music to the same degrees.

"It used to be that different groups from the U, counterculture artistic people, would come over to the West Bank. But the draw for that demographic, if they are still at the U, is not necessarily there anymore. And the music tastes have changed too. Reggae lost its big draw."

"When I first moved here," I offer, "there were a lot of festivals—camping festivals, etc. That vibe seems to have changed."

"Yeah," says David. "The music is shifting. I used to play at Blue Nile, in a spoken-word hip-hop group. But things are changing."

The Blue Nile was an Ethiopian restaurant on Franklin Avenue, a few blocks from the West Bank. It was the first place I had Ethiopian food with a group of my new Minneapolis friends—we crowded around a round table in one of their big rooms, all sharing big family-style plates of curries heaped in little piles on spongy injera bread. The Blue Nile also became well known locally for a good tap list in addition to its food. It closed a few years ago.

"I'm not the expert on this, but I think the Somali community in the Twin Cities has changed as well," says David. "I've heard Somali speakers talk about that, with music, dress, and going to school. How traditions start to change and the generational challenges that occur with that."

› On the nightlife . . .

"There was still the old folk influence in the neighborhood. Cafe Extemporé was in the neighborhood, and I remember the New Riverside Café had a huge presence. Reggae was popular with the U and students. I'd see Inertia weekly at the Viking Bar. Then there was reggae Monday nights at Five Corners. Maroons had a night at 400 Bar. Cabooze would often bring in reggae bands also. I saw the Wailers there."

› On his "West Bank story" . . .

"One of the things I loved about living here is that I didn't need a car, or need to go anywhere. West Bank had record stores, clothing, all the restaurants, bars, everything that serves to the subcultures I was hanging out with. At one time I was going to school at the U, volunteering at

Mayday, and living at the Holtzermann—I didn't leave the West Bank for a while. I didn't need to.

"The people I would hang out with, that it would bring together, the people I know, the East African community I knew, it was all-containing.

"I remember when Dania Hall burned down. People would talk about the history of it, and the importance of it. An important historical piece came out of that. I know there were some accusations of malfeasance, there was a lot of speculation at the time. I think the final determination was a cigarette, arson. It's still so much legend. It was a lot of speculation at that time of what happened."

› On what he imagines for the future . . .

"What we have been hoping was to revitalize it as an arts community. How can the arts, all the important arts institutions in the neighborhood, work together? How can we work with the neighborhood, and the youth? I've been saying with the Cedar—our future is working with the youth moving forward. That's a concern for the neighborhood. We want to help and be a part of the community as a whole.

"There's an image problem right now with the West Bank and Cedar and crime, and concerns around that. And that's a concern for the Cedar and it's a concern for the neighborhood and the Somali community. There's also a perception problem.

"So—that's what we were starting to think about and hope for. And we knew we couldn't think about this individualistic vision of the West Bank, nor could we live in the glory days of the West Bank. And the Cedar has been dealing with that mindset, 'Well, so-and-so-doesn't come anymore.'

"The neighborhood can't be based on what it was ten or fifteen years ago. People want us to hold on to the hippie past. That is an important part . . . but we also want to do the new, and we have to change and connect with the youth. There's always all these challenges we have to think about—we have to be relevant and move forward."

› On art and culture . . .

I ask David whether the Cedar is involved with the new cultural districts policy the city of Minneapolis is exploring.

"I have some concerns about the title of cultural districts and the labeling of cultural districts as though other neighborhoods don't have any culture. It's like when people call me diverse. I myself am not diverse. Sometimes it seems like 'cultural districts' is code for 'don't give bank loans.'"

"Exactly," I agree. "And we need to make sure we're not using the same districting tools that have been used to harm communities in the past to now be extractive. We need to make sure we've got good policies and protections in place."

"You know, if the Cedar goes out of business, it will hurt the businesses in the neighborhood," David says. "Acadia schedules their staff based on our schedule. Whenever we have a show, they increase their staffing. They know their waves based on the rhythm of our show schedule."

"It's critical," I agree. "I don't think a lot of people realize how closely things are interwoven."

David continues:

"I've been trying to say this in different ways. Now the Cedar needs to, and wants to, center around issues of racial injustice. This is work I've been wanting to do all along. Well—now there's community support about doing so, which makes it easier.

"We have a lot of different ways we are moving. We are thinking about, What's the future of concert venues? Our big concerts are going to be gone for a while, if not forever to a certain degree. How do we operate and move forward? So there's just so much going on. We're in a period of great transition.

"It is what it is. We have to be open to change and things becoming different."

Cedar Cultural staff on the West Bank Music History Walking Tour

David's been going to the Cedar weekly to get mail, and it's been a few months since he saw anyone riding a tall bike.

Classic Albums

I got to know my childhood neighborhood intimately. In the freedom of summers, I would bike along the sidewalks from block to block in ever-expanding circles before winding my way back home. As I traced the route, it felt like a familiar song on a record. Groove by groove, I rolled my way around the album of Lakewood, California. Each house played a beat. A sidewalk lifted by the pressure of a tree trunk welling up underneath was like a scratch—enough to create a soft fuzz in the tune, but not enough to stop the song.

It's rare as adults that we get to know a neighborhood with that level of intimacy, but community organizers receive this gift. Every quarter,

I would retrace the commercial spaces of the West Bank during that precious in-person outreach. One path on my way in, another path on my way out. Countless meetings in different spots of the neighborhood tucked into commercial spaces, basements, second-floor offices, apartments, and more. As I got to know the neighborhood, I walked a new path each time until there were no new paths to be had and the songs on the album were all familiar.

The West Bank is a great record to play, not least because music is an integral part of its history. When I began to piece together elements for our first public walking history tour, I dusted off my copy of *West Bank Boogie* by Cyn Collins and read it again. I met with my friend Aleah from the Minnesota Historical Society. I interviewed musicians from the neighborhood, including Cadillac Kolstad, an international piano player and West Bank regular—a rock and blues piano player the likes of a lost era. I spoke with Andrea Swensson, my music-writing friend, and others who grew up attending shows on the West Bank. If Minneapolis is indeed a music city, the West Bank is one of its focal points.

Over time, inspired by my Manchester music experiences, we stitched these stories and histories together into our own unique West Bank Music History Walking Tour. I got myself a rolling speaker, created a playlist, and led groups on a musical journey through the West Bank.

Vintage History

Minnesota music is interwoven with the West Bank bars and venues that have come and gone. The world-famous Andrews Sisters of Mound, Minnesota, were playing four to five times a week in the Twin Cities in the '30s and '50s—including spots in this neighborhood.

Counterculture

In the '60s and '70s, the West Bank became known for counterculture. Along with an active art and music scene and war protests, Minnesota was one of the birthplaces of the local worker-owned cooperative movement. Our own Purple Yoda is a part of this history—Prince's *Purple Rain* was filmed in Minneapolis and Los Angeles, and you can see scenes of Cedar-Riverside in the movie.

Everybody's In on It

The music scene was not limited to bars and venues—theaters got into the mix, too. The Southern Theater, one of our historic venues, opened its doors on March 1, 1910. The original theater went out of business eventually, the building repurposed for other things until the Guthrie Theater renovated the space for use as a second stage. The Southern Theater Foundation emerged in its present nonprofit corporate structure in 1983. The building is now a home for, in addition to theater, a wide variety of music performances. The band Cloud Cult filmed *Unplug: The Film—Live at the Southern Theater* in 2015.

Classic Icons

Koerner, Ray & Glover are cornerstones of the West Bank music community. The trio's surviving members, "Spider" John Koerner and Tony Glover, still occasionally perform together in the neighborhood. Bob Dylan and Bonnie Raitt are both said to have been inspired by those prominent West Bank blues acts.

Oblivion Record Store

Oblivion Record Store opened in 1969, in what is now the parking lot for Theatre in the Round. Initially a small venture in front of the Scholar, it was followed by a string of restaurants before succumbing to a fire.

Triangle Bar

Triangle Bar is another one of our older historic bars. As Cyn Collins writes in *West Bank Boogie*, "Many veteran West Bank music fans fondly recall the Bees doing choreographed high kicks and swinging their horns, all while walking along the top of the bar."

By 1969, the Triangle's music slowed down—live music was heard on Friday and Saturday nights only. By 1987, the bar was falling on hard times, and eventually it moved away from music altogether. Steve Parliament, one of the owners, remained active in the community by serving on the board of the Cedar Cultural Center. Rumor has it the bar of the original Triangle Bar is still in the basement of a West Bank building somewhere. West Bank music history museum, anyone?

Viking Bar

Another prominent venue of music for decades was the Viking Bar, which hosted the Liquor Pigs, Willie Murphy, and, of course, Spider John. When it had its fateful last show, Mary Laurel True called community friends: "Come down, come down, the Viking Bar is closing!" (Another story recounted in *West Bank Boogie*.) The night ended with patrons packing the bar space, dancing on the bar and tables. The Viking went dark in August of 2006. The owners put up the message "Gone Fishing" on the marquee before departing. It reopened again for a time in 2015 with a full kitchen renovation and live local music before closing its doors once more.

KFAI—Fresh Air Radio

The West Bank even has its own radio station. Established in 1978, KFAI community radio broadcasts a mix of community talk radio and folk and avant-garde music from around the world. Its locally focused shows include "Spin with Cyn," hosted by Cyn Collins herself.

Coffee and Community

Coffee shops and cafés have been an active part of the music scene here, too. During the twenty-seven-year history of the New Riverside Café, more than three hundred collective members worked there, 1,040 musicians performed there, and approximately ten thousand customers were served. The Coffeehouse Extemporé existed in five different locations on the West Bank over the years, hosting music and artists alike.

Dania Hall

Dania Hall was a beautiful historic building located on Cedar Avenue across from the Cedar Cultural Center. It hosted live music and other performing arts for over one hundred years in a spacious hall on the main floor. Scandinavian American artists from the Olson Sisters to Olle i Skratthult graced the venue, and it continued to serve the community until it fell into disrepair.

Part Wolf

The building that is now Part Wolf—previously Nomad World Pub, among other iterations—was built in 1903 and is considered one of the remaining legends of the West Bank bar scene. Before it housed Part Wolf and the Nomad, the building was part of the Snoose Boulevard Festival from the '50s to the '70s, and acts that have played there include West Bank faves Spider John, Cadillac Kolstad, and even Bob Dylan.

1968 and "the Fetus"

The year 1968 was a critical one for America—and for counterculture movements worldwide. It also happens to be the year the Electric Fetus began its existence, founded by four friends right on the West Bank (or, as they called it, "the center of the city's hippie scene" and "the Haight-Ashbury of the Midwest"). The store sold records, highlighting local music. Of course, everybody's favorite story is the Streakers' Sale, when customers were allowed to take all that they could carry for free . . . as long as they shopped totally naked.

West Bank School of Music

The West Bank School of Music worked with students of all ages and ability levels starting in 1970. Bill Hinkley, who taught himself how to play mandolin, fiddle, guitar, and banjo, taught for decades here. The nonprofit owned the building, practically gifted from the city to support its programs. The language of the contract stated, "Terms of sale have been negotiated that will meet the needs of the Purchaser and the objectives of the City to retain a cultural institution in the Cedar Riverside neighborhood." After decades of operation, however, the West Bank School of Music sold the building, seemingly overnight. It moved to St. Paul, where the school operated briefly using dollars from the sale—until it closed.

The T-Rock

The Triple Rock Social Club opened in 1998. The building had been a variety of things before being a club, including a general store and a restaurant. Owners Gretchen and Erik Funk expanded the club to include a venue portion in 2003. LFTR PLLR reunited for the occasion—the locally adored former band of the Hold Steady's Craig Finn. The inspiration for the name was the Blues Brothers movie: the Triple Rock Baptist Church is where John Belushi and Dan Aykroyd receive their mission from god from James Brown, the church's pastor. NOFX penned an ode to the club, "Seeing Double at the Triple Rock," and the song's music video was shot inside the venue.

The Bedlam

For a history of this West Bank institution, I turn to its former artistic director, John Francis Bueche:

Bedlam was a performing arts and activist group from 1993 to 2016 whose signature show style was high-energy, sardonic comedy with music. Its process was largely collaborative and community engaged. In addition to its parties, plays, music, dance, performances, it was also a part of an alternative lifestyle/ alternative economy thread in Twin Cities history: environmental and social justice activism, bike culture, queer or bi identity, collective organizing.

Along the way, Bedlam found it useful to inhabit several physical spaces, which, among other things, expanded the way they engaged with and were shaped by communities and causes. Though mostly white led and attended throughout its existence, Bedlam was an active ally of Native American organizers in the '90s and Minnesota's growing East African residents from 2004 to 2011, especially Somali and Oromo.

Programming and the Bedlam team became more reflective of the full diversity of the Twin Cities as its Bedlam Social Club ('06–'10) and Bedlam Design Center ('10–'15) increased activity and access. Equity, diversity, and inclusion goals factored heavily in Bedlam's decision to pursue Bedlam Lowertown ('12–'16) in downtown St. Paul as a next club location. The last two spaces, Design Center and Lowertown, were part of an emerging strategy to establish a broader network of multiple Bedlam spaces and mobile operations. It had been intended for a second South Minneapolis club to be opened before or in sync with Lowertown.

In 2004, Bedlam hosted *West Bank Story*, a musical that thoughtfully explored the neighborhood's long history and told the stories of past and present residents of the neighborhood. The *Minnesota Daily* wrote in 2008, "Shows like 'West Bank Story' may be particularly emblematic of Bedlam Theatre's co-artistic director Maren Ward's vision that theater can be and is a means to define and improve a community."

"*West Bank Story* was a creative way to see what role we played in the neighborhood," says John. "In our time, we tried to more consciously be a crucible for the transformation of society." Much to the community's heartbreak, it closed a few years after relocating to Lowertown.

Medusa

Tucked away behind the Blue Line light rail, Medusa operated from 2007 to 2013. It was an underground club and venue for punk music—and community. Even in the age of social media, it remained an off-the-radar venue. Medusa is one of several DIY creative spaces created by West Bankers that peppered the West Bank, including the West Bank School of Art, the MALA studio, and Babylon.

Hootenanny at Palmer's

Palmer's Bar

Palmer's opened for business in 1906 as Carl's Bar. It has survived Prohibition, the Great Depression, two world wars, Vietnam, and the civil unrest of the '60s. It hosts an annual summer music festival called Palmfest.

Cedar Cultural Center

The Cedar Cultural Center, originally a movie theatre and now a music venue, is a cornerstone. In 2015, its outdoor plaza opened as a public-private partnership space for music and community.

The Red Sea Bar and Restaurant

The West Bank is most known for amazing reggae, rock, and boogie, but it's a very important neighborhood for the hip-hop community as well. The Red Sea, located right on Cedar Avenue, is part of that history. As Brother Ali said during an interview for the West Bank blog, "The Red Sea holds a lot of important memories for me and the original Rhymesayers crew because we used to host a weekly Wednesday night."

Mixed Blood Theatre

Peek down Cedar Avenue just off Fourth Street: welcome to the Firehouse! Mixed Blood Theatre has been hosting unpredictable theater, music, and spoken word since 1976. It has also served as a home to community gatherings.

The 400 Bar

The 400 Bar was one of the oldest bars in Minneapolis. It started out as a drugstore, but by 1890, the building's lower level had become a saloon. It remained that way until 1920—Prohibition. The pub opened again in 1935. Willie Murphy, as one of the regular musicians, helped build it as a music venue. Its last ownership transition was in 1996, when it was purchased by Bill Sullivan, who was known locally for his time spent on the road with the Replacements. He ran it jointly with his brother Tom, who has since passed away.

The 400 Bar, in addition to being a stopping point for many touring bands, served as an incubator for up-and-coming talent. The Sullivans would focus their attention on only one or two local acts at a time, pairing them with touring acts to maximize their exposure. But for many, this was a shift from neighborhood community bar, especially as bands like the Jayhawks began to play here. To fit in with what was locally played on the West Bank at the time, they evolved a more "country-esque" sound, but it was still rock. As a result, the 400 Bar served as a welcoming home to artists in the emerging genre of alt-country. This is also where Semisonic first debuted its big hit "Closing Time" and is appropriately where our tour comes to a close.

"I remember the first time we did 'Closing Time' was at the 400, and I forgot all the words and we had to start over," Semisonic's Dan Wilson told me. "But it was very appropriate because I had first heard that phrase, 'You don't have to go home, but you can't stay here,' bellowed by a bouncer at the 400.

And when I was writing 'Closing Time,' I was definitely in my mind picturing—you know when it says 'Open all the doors and let you out into the world'? I was definitely imagining leaving the 400 Bar, you know, to that intersection, to those streets late at night. So it was appropriate that we debuted that song here."[6]

Over the years, the journey we would take on the West Bank Music History Tour became a little bittersweet. Every two years or so, it seemed, another music venue would close. The tour, once a fair split between history and current music, gradually became more historical over time.

Zombies among Us

So, we had the West Bank Music Festival. We had Palmfest, the annual event at Palmer's Bar featuring music and patio festivities. And we had the Zombie Pub Crawl.

Though I've heard there are others elsewhere, as the saying often goes: we were the first. Drinking while dressed up like zombies—in Minnesota! The first iterations of the event were so wild the cops didn't even know what to do about it.[7] The Zombie Pub Crawl started in Northeast Minneapolis and grew rapidly each year until the mob of drunken zombies became too large to be contained in any normal-sized venue, spilling out into the streets. Eventually the organizers had to procure a stadium to contain the brain-obsessed masses, and that's where I came in.

"You gotta meet with these guys," Todd said. Todd was the owner of

---

6. "The 400 Bar may be gone, but its stories live on." —Andrea Swensson
7. In 2006, several zombie protesters were arrested by the Minneapolis Police Department and jailed, though they were never charged. They sued the city and won.

the Nomad Pub and my board chair at the time. "It's a good night for us, and the city's giving them a hard time about permits. You've done this before."

No problem . . . right? I was seasoned from the music festival but second-guessed my ability to help with an event that was a gazillion times that size and scale. But I repped the businesses in the district, and with that I had some voice to offer.

Zombies in love

Over the next few months, I dipped in here and there to help the organizers of the Zombie Pub Crawl advocate for their event, sitting in on city planning meetings and connecting them to businesses. Although it was a boon for the bars, it was a bit of a headache for retail locations—dealing with street closures and the vexing aftermath of drunk zombies.

The following year, the organizers tapped me to help out with photography during the event. In addition to the West Bank, the Zombie Pub Crawl was to be held at Midway Stadium in St. Paul—with rapper DMX headlining.

To join me, I invited Adrienne Peirce, my predecessor at the WBBA, who had grown to be a good friend, and Ben Marcy, my partner from the U who also happened to be a resident of the West Bank neighborhood. We arrived to the St. Paul Saints stadium late in the evening, complete with access passes labeled VIZ (Very Important Zombie).

Did you ever go to the St. Paul Saints stadium, reader? Not the fancy new one. The old one—the good one. The B-movie best of stadiums. If you like Bruce Campbell cult movies, you'd appreciate the vibe of this epic place. It's the sportsball equivalent to what it must have been like to film on the *Army of Darkness* set. Technically, it had all the elements needed for a full production, but there was something wooden, frail, and paint-worn about it all that made it imperfectly perfect.

On game days, the parking lot was an overfilling, pothole-quilted mess filled with tailgaters and smoky grills. The lines were short and the beer was cheap. In the far outfield, past the third-base line, was a decrepit hot tub box-seat section you could rent with a small group of your closest and most scantily clothed friends to enjoy the game in your bathing-suited leisure.

But we weren't in the hot tub on Zombie Pub Crawl night. No, we were in the outfield, surrounding a stage, waiting for DMX to come out so we could Party Up. Adrienne and I wandered around the field and perimeter while a stadium full of zombies grew progressively more drunk and restless. This was a lot of zombies. A dizzying, Guinness World Record–setting number of zombies: 15,458 zombies, to be exact. All . . . waiting. Maybe DMX was scared of zombies?

"Is he going on?" I asked. "'Party Up' is going to feel pretty anticlimactic, *up in here, up in here.*"

"I don't know," Adrienne said, laughing. "But the zombies are getting antsy."

I was supposed to be taking photos—that's why I got VIZ status, after all. I felt bad just standing around. Adrienne wondered aloud how things were going back on the West Bank.

We waited another half hour or so with no luck before meandering our way over to the buses the organizers had commissioned to shuttle zombies back and forth between Midway Stadium and Minneapolis.

The upholstery on the bus was lined with plastic (to protect it from the certainty of fake blood and the possibility of real vomit). As we crowded in with the zombies, I snapped a few photos. The windows were foggy from hot beer breath, giving the world outside an ominously clouded appearance. *Click.*

We arrived on the West Bank to a fabricated apocalyptic scenario. Cedar Avenue had been closed to car traffic, and zombies shambled from bar to bar, playing up the role as they slurred "Braaaaaiiiins" to the bartenders instead of "Beer, please." I wondered: Do zombies tip well?

Click, click.

After checking in on all the bars and snapping photos of the zombie masses, we made our way over to my office in the Bailey Building, which I had prestocked with snacks, pillows, and refreshments enough for us to outlast the chaos. A three-story brick building, it was a perfect place for us to withstand even a real invasion, with four locking doors in between us and the outdoors. As we slipped through the back door and locked it from the inside, several blood-soaked zombies played up the part, clamoring against the glass in their attempt to get at us and our delicious brains. Adrienne and I ran upstairs, giggling, making our way to the closet office and the pizza rolls within.

We watched from the window as the zombies continued from bar to bar. After an hour or so, my phone rang—Ben had arrived!

"Help!" he exclaimed. "I'm outdoors, and"—fake gasp—"I think they see me."

I raced downstairs, laughing as I opened the back door and pulled him inside. By that point, the zombies were drunk enough to be fully absorbed in the live music at Acadia's outdoor tent—perhaps they'd had their fill of brains for the evening. I locked the door behind us, but not before taking a few more photos.

We talked about the West Bank, ate pizza rolls and ice cream, and watched amusedly as the zombies continued their shenanigans around the building. It was a bloody but mostly respectful crowd, though the organizers still planned for a massive cleanup crew once the festival was over to wipe blood off windows, clean trash from the sidewalks, and sweep the streets.

I learned later that DMX did eventually hit the stage but only played for about twenty minutes because of the neighborhood's curfew on live music. As for our crew, we headed home sometime before the sun came up the next morning. I'd biked in to the district to avoid worrying about parking. At home, I showered the blood and sweat off my person—a surprising amount, considering I hadn't worn a costume to the event. After I was fully decontaminated, I crawled into bed, exhausted.

"How was it?" Nick asked, half-asleep.

"You've got red on you," I said sleepily, and conked out.

Neighborhood Connections

› CLAUDIA HOLT

> **"It's a punk rock neighborhood—and I include the refugee populations . . . They are punk rock, too!"**

I first met my friend Claudia during a planning session for the Zombie Pub Crawl. She's a witty and charming fellow community organizer, a creative force, and so much more! Besides being one of the founders of the Zombie Pub Crawl, she is a singer and musician who contributes her vocal chops to Minnesota's Prairie Fire Lady Choir and the Como Avenue Jug Band. By day, she works as a financial capability manager for Prepare + Prosper, a nonprofit that works to build financial health and provide access to quality tax and financial services.

While she may not think of herself as a curator, she is—and an excellent one at that. Curating community space and togetherness is an art, and a hallmark of a good event is this idea of community. Every year during Northeast's Art-A-Whirl event, Claudia would host the Church of the Pancake, an irreverent celebration of the beloved breakfast food complete with sermons, hymns, and guest speakers.

She brought her curatorial energy with her to the West Bank for the Zombie Pub Crawl, connecting the event with the local businesses and instilling some connectedness. The weird thing is, the streets of the West Bank at the onset of the COVID-19 crisis felt more like a real zombie apocalypse than the pub crawl ever did. During the first weeks of Minnesota's stay-at-home order, with restaurants and bars shut down, the once busy streets of Cedar Avenue were much quieter than usual. The thought of visiting a packed restaurant—much less a district packed with thousands of zombies drenched in fake blood and dancing to Girl Talk—still seems like a faraway dream.

What will spaces be like when we gather again?

How will events unfold, and how will people come together to find community—perhaps a little differently than before?

› On her connection to the West Bank...

"The West Bank is easily ... my second-favorite neighborhood in Minneapolis!" Claudia laughs. I know her first favorite is Northeast, where she lives, and do my best to only be mildly offended.

Claudia's Cedar-Riverside life began long before the zombie crawl. She lived at Middlebrook Hall during her time at the U of M and fell in love with the neighborhood.

"We used to eat at Hard Times—that was our go-to stop," she remembers.

A Milwaukee transplant, she loved the community of the West Bank.

"It's a punk rock neighborhood—and I include the refugee populations that live there. They are punk rock, too! With the West Bank hippies and entrepreneurs that are creating cool spaces, it's just such a fantastic neighborhood."

› On the nightlife...

Claudia agrees with other West Bankers I talked to that the nightlife here has evolved over the years.

"I think it's still a punk rock community ... but I think about Triple Rock, too. That venue not being there anymore, it's such a loss. It was an anchor as both a venue and a destination, bringing people into the neighborhood.

"The West Bank feels like a smaller neighborhood than most other places that are sprawled out. Because it has these natural boundaries, it's just so compact. Maybe that's why they haven't had huge condo developments—there's no unused space in that area."

› On what remains the same . . .

"Everything is so walkable, and people are out and about. It has a different feeling than any other community. The spirit of that continues on the West Bank, whether it's the old-school stuff that was there twenty years ago or the vibe that's there now."

› On what she imagines for the future . . .

"I think that whatever happens, the West Bank will remain interconnected."

Be the Change

› ABDI MUKHTAR

> **"** West Bank is my home, my number one! . . . The West Bank feels like one big family. **"**

I came to know Abdirahman Mukhtar through my community outreach work on the West Bank. Abdi is a Somali American whose love for the Cedar-Riverside community runs deep. He's the founder of *Tusmo Times*, the first Somali American newspaper, and over the years he has worked for a variety of West Bank organizations, including Brian Coyle Center, and even helped with outreach for the West Bank Business Association!

He resides on the West Bank with his wife and kids, but his notion of care (*daryeel*, in Somali) for family extends to the greater community. He is the founder of Daryeel Youth, a youth outreach effort that he and his family lead on Friday nights, offering food and drink to youth experiencing homelessness in the neighborhood.

When it comes to the ethos "be the change you want to see in the world," folks like Abdi model it well.

A few weeks into the COVID shutdown, he is working from home; his job at the Minneapolis Parks and Recreation Board has changed in scope. When I check in, Abdi and his wife are home and safe with their beautiful new baby. He is in good spirits.

"We are blessed, honestly," he tells me, smiling. "I was planning on taking a leave from work. By the time

Jamie and Abdi

this whole thing started, we had the baby. Staying home for both me and my wife in a way is a blessing—but it's also a lot. She's a small business owner; this is a hard time for her. But even if we want to complain, a lot of people have a much worse situation.

"I've been thinking about the young people right now because I don't do the Friday nights anymore. Metro Transit [buses] and the trains—they eliminated 40 percent of their services. The young people that are on the streets, especially those that are homeless, that's their main transportation to move around. And they will not say it out loud, but everyone is afraid.

"When I get groceries, I try to check up on them. This is a 'new normal' for them, too. I told them there are new shelters and people are welcoming them in better than before."

› On his connection to the West Bank...

"West Bank is my home, my number one!" Abdi says, his face lighting up. "I've lived on the West Bank more than I lived in my native country. This is where my kids were born. I've done a lot of my professional work and my volunteer work—my growth as a person, as a professional—it took place

93

on the West Bank. When I first came to this country twenty years ago, I came here."

› On changes in the neighborhood . . .

"The biggest way, honestly, is housing. A lot of families moved out of the neighborhood because they don't have access to four-bedroom and three-bedroom apartments or houses. So a lot of families that lived in the West Bank moved to other areas.

"Another way the West Bank has changed—the turnover. The people that work here. Whether it's nonprofits or teaching, people come and go.

"Politically, the election of Abdi Warsame was a big change. I think the East Africans getting involved in local politics, that was a huge change. He was the first Somali American elected to city council! He opened doors for a lot of people running for office."

› On food . . .

"I remember eating at Sahara," Abdi recalls, fondly remembering the restaurant that once occupied the space that's now Baarakallah.

› On what remains the same . . .

"I think the relationship between people and professionals has stayed the same. The West Bank feels like one big family, and that has stayed the same. That's why I raise my family here, that's why I live in this neighborhood. Because not only me but my whole family is getting that family feeling."

› On the neighborhood culture . . .

Abdi pauses before responding.

"Historically, this neighborhood has been a welcoming neighborhood. But it kept the same because of that unique history. So, early, with the number of Oromo families moving in, we began having restaurants where Oromo women could open their own businesses. It's a change, but also it's the American dream for new immigrants continuing in the neighborhood.

"I miss Bedlam Theatre," he says, looking nostalgically out his window. "There are few places like Bedlam that exist. A lot of funding for young people has changed, too. And I think some of the issues we deal with are from those changes. Like the rent increases and the housing disparities. A lot of the seniors that grew up in the neighborhood are going. We've lost some of the old-timers that people knew on the West Bank."

› On the nightlife . . .

"I don't see as many college students as I used to see. Before, it used to be more young people from the colleges and universities. I think there's still some of that—you know, they come to the Cedar Cultural and Palmer's. But with the addition of Cedar Cultural Center's Midnimo project, it attracted a different group to come at night to the neighborhood."

› On his "West Bank story" . . .

"West Bank is a home away from home. I am a West Bank story!" Abdi says emphatically, grinning from ear to ear. "I feel this is my home. Only in 2016, when the election campaign was happening for Donald Trump, rhetoric and more Islamophobia followed. That's the only time I ever felt like an outsider. But other than that, my West Bank story is really feeling like this is home.

"A West Bank story could also be my work with Daryeel—being out there every Friday, with the youth. I only took a break because of social distancing, but I miss it."

› On what he imagines for the future . . .

"I think I'm afraid of gentrification," he says slowly. "Because of the lack of affordable housing and how the city is changing. But at the same time, I'm excited with the new initiatives—the recreation center project with Fairview and thinking about that. It's highly needed. I'm hopeful, but at the same time I'm afraid of displacement for residents and businesses, too." He pauses again to think before continuing on.

"I'm thinking about the declining programs for young people. That's also created a new challenge. We have a high number of seniors in the neighborhood, and we don't talk about that a lot. And because of what we have right now, with the pandemic, I think it's so important that we take care of our elders.

"I worry about the businesses, too. There are a few efforts taking place, but I don't know if that's reaching to everyone—that's the challenge. A lot of them really don't know how to navigate the system. Some of them have some challenges getting loans, too."

The last time Abdi saw a tall bike was at an Open Streets Minneapolis event before the pandemic.

West Bank Rides

What's a great way to get around and a great way to get to know a neighborhood? By bike!

In spite of the through traffic on Cedar Avenue, the West Bank is known for being a bike-friendly district, largely because of the businesses and the culture. Plenty of bike racks, bike-friendly businesses, and seasonal stations for our local bike-share system, Nice Ride, mean bikes are a regular feature of our little district. But I realized not all the residents were comfortable on a bike, and many guests still drove into the district.

In 2014, we started hosting annual rides for folks to get to know the area better and/or get comfortable on a bike. For the first year, we hosted pit stops around the neighborhood, including pop-up galleries, a mobile dance party, and a bike track for kids in the neighborhood to practice riding. We partnered with the restaurants and venues in the district, many of which had recently added or were in the process of adding additional bike parking. SPOKES, a nonprofit that boosts biking and other outdoor activities, hosted the ride. The organization's volunteers helped size and fit helmets and get kids comfortable riding.

One year, we worked in conjunction with other cultural districts to host events all along the Green Line light rail route, featuring artists, events, and musicians at each stop and throughout the path of the ride. Heart and Soul Drum Academy led workshops, local artist Jon Reynolds created custom letterpress for the neighborhood, and Altered Esthetics gallery hosted a pop-up at the Acadia café.

The already bike-friendly West Bank became a little bit more and more so each year. We added new bike racks, some sponsored by the business association and some paid for by businesses. Slowing down traffic as we did on Cedar Avenue made it safer for cyclists to get around. We encouraged businesses to participate in programs like Bike Benefits, offering discounts to cyclists and those who took public transport to the district.

We also helped sponsor resident activities for children, like the annual bike giveaway, in which kids from the neighborhood would get a free bike and helmet. Nurturing a love of cycling young was especially critical in a district where a low rate of car ownership was the norm. The Cedar-Riverside/West Bank Safety Center worked with the kids to help them remember to lock up their bikes and, of course, wear their helmets.

Plus, who doesn't enjoy seeing a kid taking off on a bike for their first time? The joy of cycling—it's like watching love take flight.

After a few years of operating programs and events like this from my closet-sized office, we received an invitation from the Southern Theater to move. Going through their own turbulent transition as a result of some problematic decisions around funding in years prior, they had recently downsized staff. Some office space on their first floor had become available at a cost comparable to what WBBA was paying—but for twice the room! The association made plans to move.

At this time, my colleague and longtime Minneapolis friend Lucas was helping with communications and marketing. He joined me at the new office, and together we repainted the pinkish walls to a light gray, the door bright red to match our logo. We worked to clean up the space and its vacated desks, shifting file cabinets and depressing office remnants of the Southern's former staff. Moving furniture around to expose and clean up spiderwebs (and other things), I pulled out a small rolling cabinet. As I pulled it away from the wall, a small red envelope fell out. In it were two perfectly shiny quarters.

Learning to ride

I took the envelope to Damon Runnals, the Southern's executive director, who laughed. "Gary, our last executive director, left these all over the building tucked into corners here and there. It's supposed to bring good luck," he said. "I, uh . . . I don't think it worked."

Living on the West Bank

The West Bank is a great place to visit and a fascinating place to live, with every different type of housing you can imagine. You will find a cooperatively owned housing community, long- and short-term apartments, a series of high-rises, and a small and dwindling number of single-family homes. There are Airbnb rentals, housing that caters to the student demographic, and a four-star hotel. While there are new market-rate apartments popping up along the edges of the district, many historic housing options remain.

The Holtz

The Holtzermann Building is located right on Cedar Avenue. The site of Al-Karama mall, the West Bank Grocery, and Al-Karama Cedar Square on the first floor and apartments above, it's been home to countless West Bankers—particularly artists.

Holtzermann is right in the heart of the neighborhood. With its aged red-brick exterior, the historic building stands tall and bright. The secure front doors are located in between the businesses' storefronts. My friend Marie, a resident manager, gave me a tour of the building a few years ago to be featured on the district website.

Upon entering, you are greeted with a small staircase and spacious hallways. (If you have ever attempted to move a bed or couch within an apartment building, you know that wide hallways are something to look for. "*Pivot!*") The units themselves are scattered generously, with only a few units per hall. The whole building has a nice, quiet atmosphere, in peaceful contrast to the busy street outside. Some of the units have interior décor features such as exposed red brick and tin ceilings, giving each apartment an artistic feel.

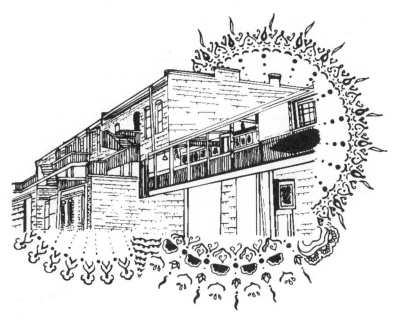

The Holtzermann

Some other interesting aspects of the building are found out back. Connected by a grand web of stairs and porches and accessible to all residents, the "backyard" of the building contains three gardens and a massive, sheltered storage area for bikes. This inter-web design also allows for residents to go from one end of the building to the other with ease. The Holtz, unlike the other newer buildings, fully encompasses the unique character of the West Bank neighborhood in its design, history, views, and feel.

Riverside Plaza

Riverside Plaza opened in 1973 and was originally dubbed Cedar Village. This massive development project was preceded by blocks and blocks of houses, which were razed for its construction. A brutalist-style apartment complex, it boasts six buildings, many of which are simply named with letters, and 1,303 residential units. The original plans were for more than 12,000 units in a unique attempt at in-city density; the structure that was built is still substantial in scale and scope, not unlike large buildings common in other high-density cities. Many folks from all over the state will recognize the iconic towers, their concrete walls, and the multicolored panels of red, yellow, white, and blue that pepper the exteriors of the apartments. The complex includes the Cedar Riverside Community School, its own grocery store, a playground, and several nonprofits.

It's not just locally famous but also TV famous, as shots of Riverside Plaza were used in *The Mary Tyler Moore Show* as the site of her new apartment in the television show's sixth season. In 2016, the neighborhood shut down a proposal by HBO to film its series *Mogadishu, Minnesota* in the district. A common target of misperception, the community was wary of outsiders exploiting the neighborhood and its residents.

Coastal Connections

› MARK VALDEZ

I met Mark Valdez a few years into my tenure with the WBBA. We connected over the still-new idea of "creative placemaking," the Mixed Blood Theatre's role on the West Bank, and our shared Southern California roots. He is a director, writer, and producer based in Los Angeles—about ten minutes from my old place! (Or an hour in traffic.)

> **I've never, ever felt unwelcome on the West Bank. It's one of my favorite neighborhoods in the Twin Cities.**

Mark's work focuses on art and social justice, and it has garnered him a variety of prestigious local and national awards. I knew none of this when I met him. His artistry is humble and reflective, inspired by a respect for community, genuine self-awareness, and a desire for continued creative growth and

Mark Valdez

learning. Because he popped back and forth between Los Angeles and Minneapolis, I appreciated our meetings when they could occur.

› On his connection to the West Bank . . .

"I live in California, but I've been working with Mixed Blood since 2006—I've been going up there every year for the past fourteen years.

"The work I've done at Mixed Blood varies. It started out as directing, but then it evolved to a thought partner in creative placemaking. My presence at the theater has changed over the past six years, also, and I've been more present and aware of the neighborhood. Trying to be a contributor to the neighborhood rather than popping in for specific projects."

Mixed Blood Theatre

› On food...

"Hard Times Cafe has been reliable. Dilla's Ethiopian has been good. In the last few years, I've made it a point to go into the various Somali places. I do miss Afro Deli, though!

"For me, it's like—I was often looking for quick. And cheap. Things are very affordable on the West Bank, but you can't always get in and out as quickly. To enjoy your meal, you want to stop for a little bit."

› On changes in the neighborhood...

"Oh my goodness, it's a different neighborhood. The first project I did in 2006, I felt like there was a strong Hmong [and general] Asian American presence on the West Bank. It didn't feel as active [as it does now], though I was there in February and March for the very first time, and everything in the Cities is a little more shut down in the winter. But even that summer, it felt a little bit more isolated.

"By 2010-ish, something felt different. The activity at Brian Coyle felt more robust, families were hanging out at the park and felt more present. Felt like more businesses engaged. It started to feel more like a neighborhood.

"I would be curious to learn when the East African community felt more settled. They had been there awhile already, I know. But now, it just feels like they're thriving. It feels like the neighborhood has an understanding of its political power, voice, and agency—and sense of determination for what the neighborhood wants to be.

"The work that the WBBA was doing and the earlier neighborhood council work—something was working, something was taking root. My sense now is that it all feels a little more like there's a class of leaders that are rising. They are saying, 'Where do we want to go?' And there are more diverging opinions because there are more leaders involved.

"There's also a generation that has come through the West Bank and moved on. I think about how the neighborhood will continue to evolve, especially as more people move in. What is the culture going to look like?"

› On what remains the same . . .

"It feels like a defined community. The West Bank feels like the West Bank, and you know you're not in Uptown or the Powderhorn neighborhood. Some of the other neighborhoods just feel like, honestly, white Minnesota. West Bank just feels different. You're in a community. It feels global. It's always felt that way. It feels textured and interesting, and it hasn't lost that. It's not at all pretentious, and very down-to-earth, and welcoming. I've never, ever felt unwelcome on the West Bank. It's one of my favorite neighborhoods in the Twin Cities. It feels rich—culturally rich—and vibrant."

› On the neighborhood culture . . .

"I feel like this neighborhood has just kind of been a gateway community for immigrants. That's part of the history of the West Bank. That has given it its culture. Like New Orleans—it has layers, it has got texture.

"For so much of its history, it has been ignored by the city, it has been ignored by the community at large, so it's been able to retain those textures. But as downtown spreads and grows and the university grows and spreads and Seven Corners grows and spreads, it all starts to encroach on the West Bank.

"I've been more aware of culture shifting in the last five years with housing developments, with more Minnesotan middle-class-and-higher presence starting to come into the neighborhood. Because of the bars, there have always been people coming out to the area. But now, they are moving in, and as the 515 building thinks about expanding their housing, it's interesting to think about how culture is starting to shift. It feels less insular than it used to. And now, it's in conversation with Minneapolis in a way it didn't feel like it was before. But in doing so—in opening up your borders—you're opening yourself up to change. It certainly feels like it's changing.

"And the other thing that's important is the political awakening of the East African community cannot be stressed enough. With the understanding of political power, you can assert yourself. You can demand things. You can ask for things. Like when the community ran out K'naan."

In 2016, demonstrators from the neighborhood protested HBO's *Mogadishu, Minnesota* project. K'naan, a Somali rapper and spoken-word artist who was behind the series, came for a free performance to help promote the show. The performance ended early as a result of the demonstration, and eventually HBO canceled the production.

"It was like they said, 'We know who we are, and we know how we want to be represented, and if you can't abide by that, get out.' That kind of assertion and power is relatively new. What happens with that kind of power, I'm fascinated by it. The kids that are now graduating high school—so much work has been done to establish autonomy and community.

"And it must be said, it happened because the city overlooked the neighborhood. The city ignored it. The city did not do its job in its racism. Let's also be clear about how problems happened. We can celebrate the West Bank culture, but it's only as resilient as it is because people had to fend for themselves, because in many ways the city abandoned them. And now that the land that it's on has increased in value, now people are caring, people are paying attention. That's racism—that's all that that is."

› On the nightlife and social dynamics ...

"I would go to Viking Bar—it was pretty low-key. I remember when I first came, I loved that bar, and it was one of my favorites. I'm not as much one for the Palmer's and Nomad crowd, partly because it's very hetero. As a queer person, I didn't find those spaces as comfortable. As I came in, I felt like these are straight spaces. After a certain level ... they give way into sort of a hetero drunk bar culture. I was always mindful and didn't hang out there as much. Or, on the other end, it's hetero East African. So, as a Latino, as a queer man, I didn't feel those were spaces for me. So that part of life there was not something I was ever taking much part in. Viking Bar was low-key, and there weren't as many people there also—so that helped.

"The West Bank is just not as queer-friendly as it could be. For all of its great diversity, there's some growth there to be had."

As much as I love the West Bank, I've seen this side of it, too. Mark elaborated on the complexity of this dynamic, the intersection of a variety of gender, cultural, and relational identities:

"A sad memory I have is this one time I had an early call. It was very early in the morning, and a young woman was also coming down in the elevator. She carried this shame with her, and she said, 'I don't know what happened, but I snuck out.' I was the first human being she encountered. I tried to be as helpful as I could be, not being from the area or knowing what resources were available, but she was hesitant. There are all sorts of gender norms and biases wrapped up in an already traumatic situation.

"We're human beings, and we contradict ourselves all the time. We hold multiple realities. If you take a few steps back, these are some of the challenges in Minnesota and one of the things we have to confront as a neighborhood if we're going to become a healthier community."

We talk a bit more about the resources that would be needed for culturally informed safety services and help. One of the most pressing concerns is dealing with the opioid crisis—being able to manage addiction without shame and stigma so people have their community support network is critically important.

› On his "West Bank story"...

"Some of my favorite memories are so simple. Standing outside of Mixed Blood flying kites—Mixed Blood staff brought them outside to fly, and people would walk by and join. It started off with kids flying, but then parents wanted to fly. I remember a man talking about growing up in Somalia and fond memories of flying a kite there. He asked to take the kite home with him, and he was just so happy.

"Another time we took out remote-control cars to the park, and kids were just lining up. They were all so excited to play with them.

"And Bihi—I run into Bihi all the time. He's everywhere; it's almost a joke! You're walking down Cedar Avenue, and *there he is*! Then you go somewhere else for lunch, and *there he is*! It's like Where's Waldo!

"A few years ago, I would just walk the neighborhood. I thought, you know, I am a guest in this community, and I need to make myself present, visible. So I would just go for a walk and do laps around the neighborhood after lunch and go for regular walks. After a few weeks, people started to say hello. A few weeks after that, people would ask questions and start conversations. There's this sense of people looking out for the community and paying attention. When they started to see me as a community member and wanted to engage me, I appreciated that."

› On what he imagines for the future...

"I think there are two ways to answer that: 'What do I hope?' and 'What do I think?'

"I think the future will be a much more racially diverse neighborhood as long as the Towers remain there. I think an immigrant and/or East African presence will continue on the West Bank. But I think the economic reality is, one way or another, Fine Associates are going to build something new on that lot they have remaining, and it's going to be market-rate housing.

"We'll probably see more development, more high-density housing on Riverside that will invite a different racial demographic. In time, the East

African identity will diminish some with those changes. What I would *like* to see, my hope, is that we know that that's coming—how can we intervene in ways that help mitigate displacement and alienation and help prevent mistakes? We know how this scenario plays out. There is no mystery. The playbook is written. How do we counter these economic forces to preserve culture, to help people who want to stay here, to preserve that texture? There's a way to mitigate it, and I hope the neighborhood can organize itself enough to do that.

"But somebody has to steward that conversation. By the time the community feels like they need to have that conversation, it's too late. People are thinking about it—there's just a lot of need right now, and there are things that are more immediately urgent. But in this moment, when the economy is going to collapse, properties are going to go to commercial developers. How do the nonprofit, community-based, mission-driven developers come in so that they can say, 'Yes! We're going to have housing, but what does it look like, and who is it for?'

"The Fine Associates and private developers of the world are looking for money. They want to rent to richer audiences . . . it's in their personal interest to develop, because that's where the money is."

"True," I agree. "And that's something we're actively working against, that displacement. But—my friend has a phrase she's been using in our creative work: 'a refusal to move at the speed of capitalism.' I subscribe to that when it comes to the creative process. It's so important to have a good process. But the market moves fast, and those with resources can move faster."

"Right," Mark says. "Some of that has to do with policy. The boxes you have to check will always make them unsustainable in terms of affordability. The other thing to think about: the mixed-income requirements for the housing are temporary! Once that window is gone, it's gone!"

"One hundred percent!" I agree. "That's what I'm trying to help with for some of our local projects. When it's only a temporary commitment to affordability, in the end you've just subsidized the giant property of another wealthy developer who no longer has to abide by that value."

"Absolutely. The West Bank/Cedar-Riverside, specifically, is at a moment. Where is its power, and where does it want to assert it? How do you build enough community will and understanding for the factions to come together and say, 'It's in our collective best interest to think about that right now'?"

"I think those wheels are in motion," I respond. "That's part of why I moved to Minnesota; it's part of why I got so involved with the Northeast Arts District. That action was in place for preservation. And there's gentrification in Northeast happening now, but can you imagine what it would have been like if we didn't have coalitions of nonprofits and artists working to buy their properties and open affordable studios?"

"The same thing is going to happen in Cedar-Riverside," Mark says. "And it's likely going to take an outside group to help push that conversation along. To take the punches for coming in as an outsider, but get a conversation going. That section where the Love Power Church is. That's just screaming to be torn down."

"You're right. I think there may be some historic protection to that space. But there have been five or six failed initiatives in the past eight years, just that I know of."

"Some of it will get torn down for high-density housing. I'm sure of it. And don't get me wrong—I'm for high-density housing, but we need to make sure that doesn't come at the cost of displacing the East African community."

Mark has seen tall bikes in New Orleans, Seattle, and Minneapolis—but never in Los Angeles. He's seen fewer and fewer in Minneapolis over the past years.

Sparks

There's an unbridled joy that comes with bonding and connecting with another spirit. It can give way to a spontaneity in relationships. Like brief romances, they can spark and then taper off as life continues to shift and evolve at a dizzying pace. The embers of these friendships can reignite years later, their light and warmth coming back to life with the breath of memory.

When I was in my early twenties in California, I met my friend Colleen at a Halloween Haunt event, where I was working as a makeup artist and she as a masked monster. We bonded with joy over *The Nightmare before Christmas* and Halloween, our mutual love of both being part of what kept us returning to our annual event year after year.

One year, we decided that after the Haunt ended, we'd hit up New Orleans. We saved our paychecks to purchase two round-trip flights and researched where we'd stay, what we'd do, where we'd go. This was to be our first trip out of state without parents—a Big Deal, and the coolest place to go for it. Not quite the big party type, we planned to go in November, when it would still be fun but slightly less chaotic than during Mardi Gras.

I adored Colleen. She was all Halloween all the time, even when we weren't at work—long dresses and long hair, both pitch-black. She lived about fifteen minutes away from me with her grandmother and pet bunny, and her spirit was simultaneously calm and fun. Introverts find each other even before we know we're introverts, I think.

Halloween drew near, our annual event almost coming to a close— but that was okay, because we had our trip to look forward to! We had been doing research online before our evening shifts at work, sharing thoughts and ideas with each other later from across the makeup chairs in our dingy warehouse.

I walked to the warehouse one afternoon, fans blasting loudly as I passed the giant metal doors. Costumes from the night before hung in racks along the far wall, slightly less sweaty after being air-dried overnight. As I approached my makeup chair, a friend took me aside, pulling me by my hand toward the bathroom.

"Did you hear about Colleen?" he asked. My heart skipped a beat. "Her grandmother called in to work today. She fell asleep on her way home from work last night. Her car hit a tree. She's okay, but she's pretty banged up, and she's going to be in the hospital for a while." My stomach sank, bottoming out along with my heart.

The following day, a few uncostumed monster friends and I piled into my car and headed to Long Beach Memorial. Colleen, whose frame was even more waifish than my own, lay in bed covered in white and blue blankets. As she saw us walk in, she sat up and smiled, then looked my way and hoarsely whispered an apology that she had zero need to offer, though the disappointment was mutual: "I'm so sorry about our trip."

Our friends and I did what we could to take the edge off a bad situation, bringing her soft fruits and yogurt to offset the hospital's abysmal kitchen offerings. We'd go before work when we could and bring stories from Haunt—gossip, relationships, and all the latest news. (None of it was actually important, but it was oh so dramatic at the time.)

When the big day finally came for her to return home, she asked for our company, and of course we obliged. Her grandmother was working, so we stayed together at her house, sprawled along the soft living room carpet while the bunny hopped around peacefully. A soft, friendly rabbit the size of a small housecat, it padded over, cuddling in next to Colleen. Everybody was grateful for her to be home.

Years later, I finally had the opportunity to head to New Orleans to attend the National Main Streets Conference. So pregnant I had to get special permission from my doctor to travel, I also took Nick—just in case. We added a few days to the front and back ends of the conference for more time to explore the city. It was spring, before the thickest part of the heat set in. I attended the conference during the day, while Nick rolled around New Orleans on a rented bike.

We both fell in love with the city immediately—the soul, the art, the music. We had the good fortune to be there during French Quarter Fest, and the streets were lined with additional pop-up shops.

My days were consumed with learning, and our nights were consumed with exploring. We hit up all the touristy spaces and explored the many cultural centers. At the recommendation of a friend, we got tickets to a show at a venue called Snug Harbor. We walked around Frenchmen Street beforehand, spending some time at the Frenchmen art market. In an empty city-owned lot tucked between two clubs, artists had organized to fill the space with activity. It was a brightly lit market with joyful lights strung from side to side.

As we walked through the stalls, the ground gritty beneath our feet, I saw artwork of a familiar style: Curt Fleck, one of the artists who participated in the first West Bank Art Crawl, had a booth in a far corner. I excitedly smiled and reintroduced myself, and we chatted about Minneapolis, New Orleans, Palmer's, and art.

Frenchmen Art Market, New Orleans

Nick and I meandered over to the venue when the show was about to start. The moment felt magical and perfect. As the band began to play, I felt the warmth of happiness flood my system—there are few things better than to be immersed in the sound of live music. The band played jazz into the late evening while I sat in a dreamlike state, soaking it all in. I knew this would be our last trip without kids and our freewheeling nights of music would be fewer and further between.

Suddenly, there was a small popping sound, and the room went black around us. The crowd murmured, concerned, phones flickering as people turned on their lights to make sense of the room. In the near-total darkness, the band piped up again, connecting via sound to continue their song almost seamlessly. Phones flickered back to dark, and we sat, in awe and appreciation, as the band completed its set. At the end, phones emerged once more, highlighting a dimly lit but wholly enthusiastic standing ovation for the miracle band that had played through the darkness.

The days of our trip flipped too-quickly by, and I continued learning through the Main Streets Conference. As I moved from session to session, I took notes, jotting down bits of inspiration to take back to the West Bank. But when it came to the field of creative placemaking, I couldn't help but think we were already doing such great work in the Twin Cities. Between the Springboard for the Arts Irrigate program, the cultural districts partnerships, and more, the community was leading in exciting, creative ways. I took back a lot of learning and inspiration from New Orleans as well as a confidence boost. The whole cohort of travelers left feeling excited—we were definitely on the right path.

Creative Genius

› SCOTT ARTLEY

Scott Artley is one of my dearest friends and colleagues. We first met at an event at Intermedia Arts during an antiestablishment break-out session led by Erik Takeshita, a local champion for creative placemaking. We then worked together on a variety of projects, both West Bank and not.

> **"There's a history of creative activity on the West Bank that could *not* happen anywhere else."**

Scott is a brilliant curator of space and a gatherer of community. He helped with the graceful sunset of Patrick's Cabaret and helped lead events at Madame of the Arts, a queer community art space. He is a fierce advocate for accessibility and safe spaces for the queer community.

All of this to say he's one of my heroes, and I love him. Can I gush?

› On his connection to the West Bank...

"When I moved to Minneapolis, I had transferred from a school on the East Coast to the U of M. I'm from Minnesota, so there's lots of reasons going into it. I won't pretend I didn't move for a boy! I had an apartment in Marcy-Holmes.

"I was trying to figure out what I was going to do with my extracurricular time. I got assigned to go do a review of Balls Cabaret, and I had no idea what it was. I went to it—rode my bike—and saw this weird art community at midnight putting on some stuff. It included one person who wound up being my German teacher. It was just this good encapsulation of all the reasons why I moved back to Minnesota.

"I recognized the arts community we have here was special. Having been on the East Coast, there was a lot of Big Arts. I couldn't see the grassroots, close-to-the-bone kind of work that I was interested in. Balls felt like this informal sharing of works in progress, or people babbling on stage, or an excellent storytelling performance that was well polished. That was a good reintroduction to what the arts community in Minnesota could offer me.

Scott and his mom on the West Bank

"That was my literal first time on the West Bank—as an adult, anyway. I think a long time ago, I may have gone to a show by In the Heart of the Beast based on 'On the Day You Were Born' with my mother.

"After that, I got an internship at the Southern with Kate Nordstrum. The Southern used be a much different organization—I was there just as the artistic director was let go. It was interesting to be at an arts organization in crisis. Now it feels like I've only been with arts organizations in crisis! Seeing it up close was this amazing education. The board chair/interim director at the time [Steve Barberio] was like, 'Who are you? Why are you here?' And he pointed his finger at me and said, 'You are going to learn so much.'

"I interned at the Southern for a year, and then I got my first job out of college, and that was at Mixed Blood Theatre. I was the development associate. I almost got another job back at the Southern, but Mixed Blood offered me work that was more interesting. This was the darkest days of the 2008 recession. The 'easy recession' of our lifetime."

(We laugh-cried at this thought.)

"I was interested in the neighborhood and curious about it. I got this neighborhood engagement program funding. Initially it was just $1,500 to market Mixed Blood shows to the neighborhood, printing posters and handbills. Instead of doing printed things, I said, 'Let's hire people.' We hired three Somali liaisons and did engagement. And it was like 'What would it be like to actually engage the community?' And then I was like 'Ohhhhh, this is everything I'm into.'

"I've been interested in things that make me uncomfortable, which is a lot, as somebody that is anxious all the time. I went to this open house at Dar Al-Hijrah, next to Palmer's. I was anxious about that—it was so different from my life at the time. But every time I've done something like that, it's been so rewarding. I've since tried to do something like that all the time.

"That being said, I would never do skydiving."

› On food...

"I went to the Wienery a lot! I went to Jimmy John's a lot, actually, and Afro Deli. And I went to Bobby and Steve's probably more than all of this combined because it was exactly my favorite song away. And I'd get a sandwich and I'd go back." Bobby and Steve's is a gas station with an attached grocery and convenience store on the outer edge of the West Bank.

"Sometimes I would eat in my car. I was so emotional when I was working at Mixed Blood. I would cry and get angry. I would get into fights with board members. It's kind of a good thing I was there during a recession because I'm pretty sure I should have been fired. I know I was doing incredible work, though, and that probably boosted my job security. I was twenty-three! And I was in charge of raising $1.5 million, and I had no idea what I was doing.

"I tried to go to the Med Deli a lot, but I don't think they had ... hours. I would show up, and they'd always be closed. And then Acadia was a go-to meeting spot. I went to Mapps a lot. In fact, there was a moment when we had school matinees at Mixed Blood, so we'd all have to go work somewhere else. So I'd go to Mapps and drink a big coffee and get an enormous Costco muffin."

› On changes in the neighborhood . . .

"All of the DIY arts venues—Bedlam, 400 Bar. Even the People's Center Theater . . ."

In the early '70s, the People's Center Theater, located in the People's Center Clinics & Services facility, was home to At the Foot of the Mountain, the longest-running women's theater company in the United States. The theater closed around 2015.

"It's not the same arts magnet that it used to be. The things that happen at the Cedar are not as much what I'm into, and I guess that's true of Mixed Blood, too. The stuff they do is not really my jam. I love the DIY aesthetic that was so prevalent on the West Bank. The number of DIY spaces—1419 and West Bank Social Club and Medusa—those were the places where I spent my twenties. They're gone now, and they are gone from the city in general. That whole layer of venues and that whole layer of the art world is gone.

"Wait." Scott pauses. "Is it just that I'm old now?" We laugh.

"No, I don't think it's just you," I say. "With the economy and the cost of rent increasing, there just aren't as many of those dingy little spaces available."

"That's the thing that makes me the most scared for Minneapolis. And it's because of Minneapolis's prosperity. At the time I enjoyed those things as much as I did, it was 2006 and 2008 . . . those spaces were not going to be yanked up by developers then. Prosperity is such a euphemism for gentrification. What it really means is capital investment, one kind of wealth that so often displaces how culture already makes us rich. I'm all for a much more robust and well-rounded view of what prosperity is."

› On what remains the same . . .

"When I was working at Mixed Blood and I was working the neighborhood program, I would do walking meetings. Somebody once said, 'I just feel like I'm not even in Minnesota right now.' And they were right. The West Bank is so densely populated, it's so diverse. I get this sense of a global village that feels surprising for a place like Minnesota. So just thinking about the West Bank's history as an enclave for the newest immigrants—that has stayed the same. Because it was an area that was so disinvested for so long, the residents had to come up with their own prosperity and it makes for a richer environment. Different ways of valuing, infrastructure, and how we use it."

› On the neighborhood culture . . .

"I've seen the city treat [Cedar-Riverside] more and more like 'Little Mogadishu' exclusively. I'm worried about the concentration of a district becoming ghettoized rather than becoming a gateway to all the cultures that are currently present in the neighborhood."

› On his "West Bank story" . . .

"One time, some friends and I went to Mixed Blood to hang out, and from there we walked to Medusa. My friends kept being like 'There's nothing down here!' and I said, 'Just you wait.' We turned the corner, and there's the Medusa, an old car mechanic's turned into a punk music venue. We get in. Throughout the night, there's a party called Pegasus—this is a precursor to Madame. There was a roving party that then went through the West Bank. People were in wild costumes.

"There's people lip-synching, there's people dancing to a DJ set, a group of friends called themselves Muscle Twitch and performed a dance piece

Jamie and Scott at a queer dance party on Halloween. (Jamie was nine months pregnant with a disco ball for my belly, her costume was "a party"; Scott was . . . you figure it out!)

much like their name. And throughout the night, there were drag queens walking around collecting beer cans—you'd put them in the shopping cart. Then, they lip-synched to [Lady Gaga's] 'Paparazzi'—*until you love me, papa-paparazzi*—while tossing the beer cans at the audience. That could *not* happen anywhere else.

"Part of the reason that we made Madame is that Pegasus got thrown out of Bedlam. Something involving baby oil and glitter and how we weren't allowed to have either of those things. Then we went to Medusa, and then we had to find our own venue where we could have baby oil and glitter."

› On what he imagines for the future . . .

When I ask Scott what he thinks is ahead for the West Bank, the first thing he mentions is infill—things like lidding the freeway as a base for other projects, such as parks and housing.

"The West Bank already seems so dense, and the reality is it's kind of this island of density, yet there's a lot of empty space around it. All the stuff around the highways. I think there's going to be infrastructure changes as it relates to transportation. I can just see . . . it's the place where the two light rail lines meet. So all of those roads to the Washington Avenue Bridge—I don't think those are going to be there forever.

"I think there's gonna be less of a focus on the arts. And maybe that's okay. I just see the city moving in the direction of making it 'Little Somalia' and branding it only that way. The whole cultural districts thing is interesting. What was cool to me when I was hanging out there: there was punks walking around with students walking around with people going to prayers on Friday. That's what's so rad about it. It would be sad to lose diversity, especially in the name of diversity."

Scott isn't sure when precisely he last saw somebody on a tall bike. But he once saw Fancy Ray[8] *on a penny-farthing. "I thought to myself, now my life's complete."*

---

8. Fancy Ray McCloney is a Minneapolis-based comedian and advertising icon.

Music Festival Take IV

The 2013 West Bank Music Festival marked year two for me at the organization and year four of the festival. As before, we ran it with a committee of bar and venue owners, making decisions collectively. Everybody helped with one aspect or another, and I handled the admin and organizing.

I felt solid about this year's festival. We had gotten an earlier start on planning, which meant we had a little more breathing room for our outreach, marketing, and logistics. More time for booking meant better odds of a good headliner, too. I structured the logistics so that all major event decisions and contracts would be completed well before two months ahead of the fest and those last two months, which overlapped my maternity leave in part, would be left for promotions and marketing. I also felt like this year, we had more of a team—with a part-time communications staff person, two interns, and, of course, the committee itself.

There is nothing cheap about throwing a festival in the city of Minneapolis. In addition to paying for bands, contractors, stage and equipment rental, and porta potties, there's also the cost of event permits. A typical festival will need several: at minimum you'll need an event permit and amplified noise permit. Add tents and you'll need a "membranous structure" permit, a fire permit, and more. Each has a cost associated with it. An "expansion of premises" liquor permit is pricey and comes with additional constraints, such as a city policy that, until 2020, required hiring off-duty police officers. Any street closure ramps up that figure considerably, as off-duty officers are also required at each intersection. It's very easy to scale from "community event" to "giant-ass expensive production," and we had certainly reached the threshold for the latter.

While we didn't have major grant funding this year, we hoped the early start would give us a boost with sponsorship and fundraising. The bars and venues were already considered hosting sponsors thanks to their help with planning and promotion, which left me to fundraise largely outside of the neighborhood. And, while I may be an adequate grant writer, I'm a terrible salesperson. I tried to hire a dedicated person for sales, but the first one I found was hired away to another full-time gig two weeks after starting, and the second trailed off.

As the months rolled by, other festival logistics and planning went well. We booked an amazing headliner, Minneapolis rapper Brother Ali, with the help of a new booking agent who had been referred to us. We continued to work on booking for the main stage, which would be at the northernmost tip of Cedar Avenue, as well as a community stage for the other end of the avenue. We reserved porta potties, procured extra trash cans, and commissioned new designs for festival shirts and posters. We worked again with local alt-weekly *City Pages* as a main ad sponsor for the event. As we met and planned, my belly grew and grew. My due date was six weeks before the fest. Plenty of time!

But we were still short of some of our sponsorship goals. In part due to the continued growth of summer festivals over the years, traditional sponsors were getting spread thin, which meant they were contributing half or less of what they had to us in years past. Concerned about the cost of a larger festival when paired with the minimized income, I got together with the booking agent to think through some options. We came up with a compromise: hold the festival in the parking lots instead of the street, not unlike what Cedarfest used to do. It would drop our costs to 25 percent of what they would be if we shut the street down, due to the security and permitting costs around street closures.

We brought our plan up with the committee: a festival with a slightly more limited footprint. Still more than enough room to cover the expected attendance and two stages, on two of the city-owned parking lots, which we could rent for nearly free. We'd need a parking plan for attendees and staff, but that was doable with all the ramps within walking distance. Unfortunately, the idea was shot down. In spite of the added expense, the committee was committed to the vision of a street festival—wide-open stages, attendees floating from bar to bar with beer in hand.

Little by little, the event expenses increased. The city bumped us to the next attendance level and pay scale for event permits; this required us to add additional off-duty MPD officers, which cost a hefty-for-us figure of $50 an hour. This was the single largest nonmusician expense of the event. But with each mounting expense, the committee wanted to keep scale. "Don't worry!" was the prevailing sentiment. "We have an awesome headliner—all the expenses will be made up on the day of the event, and then some!"

Contract advances and permit expenses tapped out our reserves and maxed our line of credit. My due date fast approaching and powerless to override the committee decision, I hoped they were right.

Sacred Spaces

On Cedar Avenue, where Dania Hall once stood, there remains a vacant grassy lot. This area across the street from Cedar Cultural Center is a long rectangle, a conspicuously open and empty space in an otherwise packed neighborhood. It's currently outlined by a tall fence in the back, the long white edge of a building on one side, the bocce courts at Part Wolf on the other side, and a broken, gated fence lining the front. Wind blows freely into the lot, carrying with it bits of paper and other trash that collect along the edge of the wall and the back fence, adorned by the spikes at the very tip top.

At the front of this space is an obelisk. Graced by a mosaic on all sides, it uses pictures to share community stories and values.

Built in 1886 as a social space for Society Dania, Dania Hall became a gathering

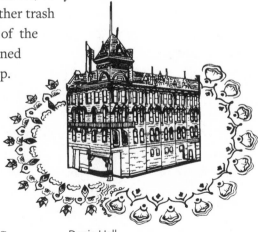

Dania Hall

place for many immigrants in the community. A beautiful tall building with a large theater and music hall in its grand main room, it was a vestige of a former time. It withstood the West Bank's evolution into the bohemian era, though the '60s and '70s saw the space plagued by infrastructure problems.

While it remained standing for many years despite multiple fires, a final, extensive blaze in 2000 wiped it out completely. The neighborhood mourned the loss of its beautiful communing space and commemorated Da-

The historic tied building at 1500 South Sixth Street

nia with posters, the obelisk, and a promise to make positive community use of the location for anything that comes next.

When talk of what should happen with Dania comes up, it seems like collective goosebumps rise for the community, and the hair on the backs of everyone's necks stands on end. When one business owner pitched the idea of turning it into a parking lot, they were met with a protest, complete with picket signs.

A solution very nearly arrived around 2012, when a local developer began work in another part of the neighborhood. A historic "tied house" stood in the way of its new construction plans. (A tied house refers to a saloon that was "tied" to a particular beer company, only serving that company's beer. Often, the interior—from the tin ceilings to the tiles— would have a consistent design.) The concept was to use rollers to move the tied building to the Dania Hall lot, making use of the space and keeping the historic building in the neighborhood. The developer would sell it to a local nonprofit for a nominal fee, and the building would just have to be moved. A panel held off the bulldozing long enough for the nonprofit in mind to do the math on the purchase of the lot and transport of the building. The cost? Just shy of half a million dollars, not including any interior repair once moved.

None of the local organizations could swing it. In the end, the building was razed.

What are the spaces you love? Have they been there for some time, or are they new? What makes them homey to you, or comfortable? Like a family settling into a home and breathing life into the space, I think buildings retain a palpable energy when they've been occupied by so many people over years and years.

Are buildings happier when their space is used? When a building is empty, does it sit like a worried parent, waiting for its children to return? And when we tear a building to the ground to make way for another space—even one that arguably makes better use of the location—what of that building's energy? Does it dissipate into the air as the demolition occurs, or does it settle into the ground where it once stood? And if people make a place, what energy do they bring, and leave, as they interact with the environment around them?

Dania Hall was a sacred space for the community, and a space for comfort and camaraderie. What will go in its place is still to be determined—but it should certainly be something special.

Pizza and Root Beer

The West Bank ladies and I continued our regular nights out during my pregnancy, hitting up bars and restaurants throughout the city. About a month or so before my due date, we had an afternoon happy hour at Psycho Suzi's, a tiki bar along the Mississippi River very close to our house in Northeast Minneapolis. I wandered (well, waddled) onto the patio, tired from feeling too hot and too pregnant. Only this time it was my lady friends who got there early, bringing with them balloons and bags of baby goodies. Surprise! We toasted to our soon-to-be West Bank baby.

West Bank love. It's the realest.

My due date came and went, and with each passing day my anxiety would tick up. The closer we came to the induction deadline, the more my heart would race, hoping for a labor as natural as possible. I also was aware of the responsibility that awaited me on the other end of the labor and delivery—not just the responsibility of a newborn, but an event to manifest as well.

Everything was in order for the festival. The budget, though a bit larger than my comfort level, was at least firmed up in a near-final state with checks and deposits sent for musicians, equipment, stages, and other festival necessities. Marketing was underway, thanks in large part to *City Pages* and its team as well as a few other partnerships.

The only thing I couldn't cross off my checklist was having the baby!

As both events loomed closer, I kept at it. Everything was all planned at home, everything ready to go at work. Having heard horror stories of extra-painful labors, I did everything I could to avoid induction. And I was terrified of having a c-section, figuring (in at least some degree of naïveté) that I could still run a festival as a new parent, but it would be much harder if I had a "C."

Nick and I took lots of waddling walks, and I did everything I could to encourage a "natural" state of relaxation to get the oxytocin flowing. I used some gift cards I'd gotten for prenatal massage, one of them a pressure-point massage said to help with natural labor induction. At a doctor's appointment a week and a half past my due date, I watched the monitor as it pulsed the rhythm of my baby's heartbeat. I was comforted by the fact that the baby seemed healthy. "Can you feel that?" the nurse asked me as I watched the gentle beating. She pointed to the screen. "You're having minor contractions. Could be Braxton Hicks, but they are pretty consistent. Far apart at this point, but noticeable."

The following Friday morning, I went for my final prenatal massage, a late-term one they only allow for those at least thirty-seven weeks along. When I confided I wasn't working with a doula even though I had wanted to, the massage therapist, also a doula herself, talked me through some exercises and things to be aware of. "Don't be scared to advocate for yourself," she reminded me. The Twin Cities birth community was a small one, and she of course knew my midwife. "Your midwife will do the same. She's one of the best." I felt comforted.

I went home and brought up my contraction timer app, keeping track of the ever-increasing waves of tightening I felt. They were still very far apart and very subtle, but noticeable and quite regular. Nick came home, and we decided to walk to Grumpy's Northeast for a pizza dinner.

As we sat and ate, my contractions took a stronger turn. Maybe it was the Heggies pizza? Owner Pat Dwyer came over to chat and say hello as usual, though about what precisely I couldn't tell you, because as he talked another wave came over

Actual list of things to do from my 2013 weekly planner (I tried to will it into happening. It didn't work.)

me. This time, it being noticeably more painful, I grabbed the edge of the table as we talked. I passed my husband a look, and we settled up the tab as Pat continued to banter. After one or two more contractions, I was sincerely worried that my water would break all over the flecked floor of our beloved bar.

The walk home was a bit more intense than the walk over, and I had to pause a few times, bracing myself on Nick as each wave of contractions passed. I labored at home as long as I could until, as per the advice of our teachers, the contractions had gotten close enough and the pain intense enough to feel as though it was time. I will spare the reader the sordid details of my labor story, but our daughter Madeline was born healthy and happy—two weeks past my due date but one day before induction.

The Day of Arrival

I took two full weeks off to heal. No work calls, no emails, and I held to my boundaries. Instead I nursed and walked gently around our home in a confused, sleep-deprived daze. I ate food with one hand while holding the baby with the other, and I cried because my husband unwittingly ate the last piece of pizza, the very last piece, the one with the fresh basil on it, the one I had been thinking about all day.

With festival marketing already underway and everything in order, I started attending meetings again about two weeks after Maddy was born. I did this slowly at first, as I could easily do most of my work from home at that point.

We had a few last meetings of the festival committee, for which both Nick and Madeline joined me. I worked on both healing and building up strength, as I knew the day of the festival would have me running more than I would be otherwise.

As a gift from my family and absolute godsend, my niece Natalie flew out for the week of the festival. A teenager who was naturally gifted with small kids and babies, she

Kermit, Nick, and baby Maddy

wanted to come help with meals the day of the festival and to bond with her little cousin. At four weeks old, Madeline was just a little lump of baby, her personality not quite yet emerging and simply content to be around people. She wasn't taking a bottle, so I had the good fortune of being still her single food source—which meant less pumping (pro) but a greater need for my body (con).

When the festival weekend arrived, things shifted into high gear. We were as good at organization as the Fyre Festival was bad at it, ready with volunteer orientation checklists, logistics sheets, and coolers stocked with sunblock and ice. Luckily, because I had some staff in addition to the festival planning team, we could split up the day between us. I, up at the crack of dawn with a newborn anyway, would kick things off in the a.m.; Scott, Raven, and David would close things out.

Closed for the evening, the Cedar Cultural Center offered our team and the musicians its greenroom as an indoor artist space. Our manager had also set up a "greenroom" tent stocked with amenities. We might not be fancy, but the West Bank has hospitality! The Cedar's space was closer to the center of the action than my office—and it was a perfect spot for my niece to hang out with the baby when she wasn't out and about in the festival proper.

I started the day feeling organized. The weather was perfect, slated for 80 and sunny. I headed to the festival alone, with Nick and Natalie planning to meet me on-site a bit later with the baby. Tents and stages were set up, sound tested, food prepped.

This year we had booked the Brass Messengers, a Minneapolis band "formed from the annual rubble of the Heart of the Beast MayDay Parade and Ceremony," as the group's website puts it, to kick off the event. They broke out in song on Cedar Avenue, marching the ever-increasing crowd of festival participants up to the main stage. We had also hired local stilt-walking group Chicks on Sticks to walk through the crowd, blowing bubbles and spreading joy.

The weather couldn't have been more perfect, and the crowd was excited and friendly. As I passed back and forth through the tents and venues, I would check in with my niece, give the baby a snuggle and a meal, and continue with the day's activities. There were a few minor emergencies, such as when a volunteer left the beer truck for a moment to go to the bathroom and came back to find a small crowd helping themselves to a pint or two. It was quickly resolved, as somebody stepped in, but a fun beer-flavored shopping spree in the meantime, I'm sure.

As the day turned into evening, the music continued on. Folks danced in the street near the community stage before heading back up Cedar to catch the main acts. Brother Ali, who at one time played regularly on the West Bank at the Red Sea, shared the stage with the dancers who had appeared in his "Mourning in America" video. An all-female, all-Muslim team founded by Amirah Sackett, they were known as We're Muslim, Don't Panic.

Once the evening turned into night, I began my slow trek back home to meet up with my family. As the rest of my team queued up to take the evening shift, we agreed: it had been a very good festival. Attendance, however, wasn't quite the stunner we had hoped. We estimated the crowd had been about 3,200—an increase of 10 percent from the year prior, but the committee had hoped to at least double the previous number. "Welp," one of the bar owners said, "let's at least hope they bought a lot of beer."

They didn't. The festival, though logistically nearly seamless, was a

Chicks on Sticks, West Bank Music Festival, 2013

huge cash loss for the West Bank Business Association. After all beer and ticket sales were done, after all artists and vendors were paid, the event lost the org $25,000. The biggest non-artist expense: the cost of shutting down the street, the permits, and the required security, both private and off-duty officers.

The board met to discuss the fate of the festival—and my position. Some (okay, one board member) advocated for terminating me. "I personally would like to see Jamie fired" were, I think, his exact words. Other board members went to bat for me, noting that not only had I tried to raise flags in terms of rising costs and expenses without the sponsorship to back it, but how would the remaining staff and board be able to dig themselves out of a hole if they let go of the grant writer and fundraiser for the organization?

In the end, we settled on a 75 percent furlough to help save on staff costs while we reworked our budget and implemented a new fundraising policy. This included my full-time role as well as our other part-time help. I lobbied for the board to implement new accounting policies that would give me some executive control over spending decisions and allow me to pull the plug on expenditures when key milestones were not met. I also recommended instituting a policy that we only use our line of credit when we had grant income to offset the expenses. It had never been intended to be used like a

Brother Ali

credit card—it was only a line of credit to be used when we were waiting on our grant reimbursements.

That the festival had been a financial loss also was a catalyst for our org to rethink all those unanswered questions and conflicts posed the year prior. With two hundred businesses in the district we were responsible for helping, was focusing 80 percent of our staff capacity on one financially draining event the best way to serve the West Bank? The bars had a great night, but the event nearly killed our organization. As we worked our way out of a sea of debt, we rethought our operating model, those business priorities that had been clearly laid out, and the future of our organization.

During Cedarfest's heyday, summer festivals were few and far between. But since then, there had come to be several each weekend in the Twin Cities region. Even with a great headliner and a sunny day, there was a limit to how many people we could draw. There was also the element of audience—the West Bank Music Festival was largely a destination event, and not necessarily a community-based event, even with the community stage.

As we asked ourselves the hard questions about what a community event would look like in our ever-evolving district, we began to make decisions about the strategic use of our organizational resources. I thought back to a piece of nonprofit advice that someone had given me years prior: "If a program had a good run but is no longer viable, celebrate it. But then—be done."

These days, many event organizers, venues, and cultural districts are seriously rethinking their events and activities as a result of COVID-19 while also struggling with the loss of tourism revenue and event proceeds. I wonder what events will look like as we reshape them to scale—and whether they will emerge after the pandemic serving their immediate communities with more tenacity than before.

Transition

I want to talk about the phenomenon that is the reentry into the world after labor. In my case, the urgency of the festival masked a lot of this simultaneously slow and too-fast transition.

Madeline was born as the hot stickiness of summer in Minnesota settled in for its annual visit. I don't think it was gray outside, but that's how I remember it: gray all around. Nobody in the house was sleeping through the night, and to say I was exhausted would be an understatement. Nick, the baby, and I were just beginning to find our groove after her arrival.

As I caught up with a friend over the phone, she asked how I was doing with the new addition to our family. New-mom stress, sore nipples, labor. As the topic turned to work, which I was to return to in just a few weeks' time, I confided in her: "I don't know how I'm going to do it—I'm barely able to get through a day at home without losing my mind." The idea of going back to work seemed overwhelming, if not impossible. My vague veneer of put-togetherness, thin as air, was dissipating. I thought of the months ahead, bustling around the office with my stitches still healing, and all I could do was weep.

Working for a small nonprofit whose programming revolved around an annual event didn't give me much leeway when it came to my schedule. But despite it being so daunting initially, it gradually became my new rhythm, and one morning I loaded Madeline into a baby carrier for our longest day yet.

Though not every day had festival-level energy, nearly perpetual to-getherness was a theme for Maddy and me throughout the first year of her life. Unable to afford full-time care, Nick and I took advantage of my flexible work schedule and made the best of a tough-but-could-have-been-worse situation. I got the bigger, more important chunks of work done during naptimes, after bedtime, and around any and all available edges. I was able to bring Madeline with me to most of my meetings and outreach opportunities, and she soaked up the attention—or slept. Fortunately for everyone, Madeline was a very easygoing baby. Unfortunately for me, I had precious little time for anything else. The advice "sleep when the baby sleeps" was laughable. As Madeline grew older and more mobile, Nick and I found a home daycare we could both afford and trust, and we eased in one day at a time, working our way up to full-time by age two.

That chapter of our lives now seems like a lifetime ago. The transition from postpartum back into reality can be brutal, and the working world puts new moms through the wringer. This is particularly true in the States, and for many others like me who work for or own small businesses. Is it a trauma or an achievement, an awful badge of honor? I look back to pictures of myself during that time, and I see clearly the gaunt, exhausted look to my face. But even with a photo in front of me showing the extent of my fatigue, I still feel that tinge of guilt: "Don't complain—it could have been worse." Isn't that the case for so many women looking back on any hardship?

Baby Maddy holding Jamie's hand

I'm certainly not alone in returning too early to the workplace. According to a report from *In These Times*, one in four American women return to work within two weeks of having a baby. Two weeks! That's before our bodies have had a chance to repair—before our stitches have healed, before our fluid and hormone levels have rebalanced, and certainly before many of us are fully emotionally and physically ready to add full-time work back to our daily menu. Most of us, however, don't have a choice.

I am lucky. I may have gone back to work soon, but at least I was able to take my daughter with me. Many women can't. I had a crib next to my desk and a private-ish office. Our business district has a lot of small businesses where people also bring their kids to work. A perk, but also a necessity. When Madeline was born, the price tag for full-time infant care ran several hundred dollars more than our monthly mortgage. So she came with me.

Cookies from a friend

There's a growing body of research showing the benefits of allowing babies in the office. As corporate America looks to more cost-effective benefit structures, higher-ups are increasingly considering this option as a way to keep working moms engaged. If it becomes more common, it will be interesting to find out the long-term effects baby-in-office policies have on moms and children, not to mention families as a whole and the other people in the office. A side-by-side comparison of these policies versus extended or federally sponsored maternity and paternity leave would be an informative research project. But maternity *and* paternity leave? We'd have to go outside the States for most of that data.

Overall, the benefits of bringing my daughter to work, for me, outweighed the cons. By waiting to start daycare and easing in gradually, I was able to pump less and breastfeed longer. Madeline was a healthy baby, and our sick days were few and far between. I was able to avoid some working-mom guilt . . . some. Somehow moms find a way to feel guilty about things no matter what, don't we?

That first year was a hard transition, but we came out of it gradually. Sitters were hard to find, in part due to the financial reality as well as a limitation of our very small babysitter network, yet to be established. One of our first outings was, appropriately enough, back to the West Bank to see one of my favorite bands: Dengue Fever. As Nick and I headed to the Cedar Cultural Center for this rare night out, I felt both excitement and more of that guilt. New-mom feels are complicated. But all was put to ease when I arrived. Somebody had told the staff it was my birthday, and my friend Sage left cookies for me at the ticket table. The Cedar's assistant event director, Michael Lord, was working the bar and gave me a big hug and a birthday stout. As the band started and the warm waves of music unfolded around me, I felt centered and calm.

The Wienery and Edna's Park

I t's not just the location. It's the people.

Pat and KJ of the Wienery are two of my favorite West Bankers. I first met Pat when Nick took me to the Wienery for breakfast one morning early in our relationship. He swore the hash browns were the best in the Twin Cities—and he was right. Pat is one of the friendliest guys you'll ever meet, and you're lucky if you catch him behind the counter with time for conversation. The time will fly by as you find yourself in an animated and captivating discussion that could span politics, capitalism, kids, and home improvement, all within a single visit. And KJ is one of the smartest people I've ever met in real life. She joined the West Bank Business Association team after working as a program evaluator for the Office of the Legislative Auditor. (And, for the written record, hiring her was one of the best decisions I've ever made.)

The Wienery is a little diner right on Cedar Avenue that serves hot dogs, as you might have gathered from the name, as well as burgers, fresh-cut fries, and hearty breakfast food. The space is long and narrow, with a clear view from the counter to the kitchen in the back. Small tables line the wall. Along the back of the counter are jail wristbands—if you're emerging from an overnight, Pat will feed you your first meal out free of charge. (But you can't be a creep.) Once featured on the Guy Fieri show *Diners, Drive-Ins and Dives* as a "dive," the Wienery has great grub at a very affordable price. Prior to being the Wienery, it was Edna's, and next to Edna's is what's known now as Edna's Park.

A few years into my tenure at the WBBA, neighborhood cleanups were still a part of our regular drill. One cleanup day, I went from my office to the basement, grabbing my rolling cart and a bin full of supplies. I would be meeting a crew of kids at Edna's Park for the day's effort.

I rolled my wobbly cart down Cedar Avenue, a box of graffiti wipes stacked precariously on top of the Rubbermaid bin. My old bungee cord had snapped and I hadn't yet replaced it, so I took every bump with a deep breath, hoping my awkward load wouldn't topple. I made it to the park with only one or two close calls.

I arrived a few minutes before our scheduled meeting time, but Jennifer Weber and the kids were already there.

"Okay," Coach Weber said, laughing, setting her hand on my shoulder. "The kids want to know who Edna is. And what she did 'to have such a horrible park named after her'—no swings or anything!"

You see, Edna's Park is not really a park the way kids would view it—it's a grassy area that sits in between two buildings and their corner businesses, the Wienery on one side and Samiya Clothing Store on the other. An unpaved alleyway of sorts also known locally as "the cut," it widens from a roughly twenty-foot point along Cedar Avenue into a larger, open space behind. The restaurant has doors from the kitchen area that lead out the back, overlooking Edna's Park. Edna lived behind the diner in a house right in the center of this area.

The park is surrounded by other businesses on the two remaining sides as well—a halal store and restaurant on the side that faces Riverside Plaza and more shops and restaurants across Cedar Avenue. A long, blank brick wall runs alongside one edge, practically begging for a neighborhood mural. Though the lot is owned by one local development company, maintenance for it is the responsibility of another, leaving it in a gray area that has often led to neglect. This is why we would often base our cleanups in this space, starting in Edna's Park and spreading out to other spots in the neighborhood.

Over time, we added amenities like benches and plants, continuing our regular cleanups as we could. But it was neighborhood residents who helped maintain the space with more continued success, adding flowers and helping haul away trash regularly so it wouldn't build up too heavily over time.

Planting Seeds of Joy

› JENNIFER WEBER

> **That's what I really love about the neighborhood. It's that joy. It's there, it permeates everything.**

I met Jennifer Weber through our work with the Brian Coyle Center and seeing each other pop up at endless events and activities for the community. Jennifer, or Coach Weber as the kids and almost everyone else calls her, is a beacon of awesomeness for the West Bank.

After raising three of her own kids, she decided to go back to college. She chose Augsburg University, in large part because of its clear and demonstrated commitment to community. She took her teaching skills to Cedar Riverside Community School, where she worked first as an aide and then as a behavioral specialist.

Some people are just so graceful at parenting. They have a natural way with people, especially young people—like they can see the potential in everyone. Jennifer is like that. And as our friendship grew, conversations about programs turned to conversations about our own families. She would give me great insight on parenting and the things Nick and I were struggling with.

Jennifer "Coach" Weber and kids from the Cedar Riverside Community School

› On her connection to the West Bank ...

"I started as a student at Augsburg—I got a scholarship to go back to college. At Augsburg, I was triple majoring. I knew what I wanted to be when I grew up.

"I did day school, night school, all school! I got convinced to be on student government. I got involved with the Augsburg Indigenous Student Association. I was super, super involved at Augsburg. I knew Ricky White—he was director of the Cedar Riverside Community School at that point. I worked at Anoka-Hennepin Indian Education, and I said, 'Hey, can I come over to the school? I can do whatever you need me to do. Classes in the morning, classes at night. I want to stay in the neighborhood—put me to work!' That was supposed to be six weeks, but I stayed for ten years!

"I started with sports after I was done with service learning. I did three kinds of service learning that year, each for six to eight weeks. Then Ricky said, 'Instead of you coming and volunteering, would you want to just work here?' Then he convinced me! I ran a basketball clinic and said, 'You know what this school really needs? It needs sports.'

"It just got started that way. The kids would see us all playing soccer and say, 'We want to play soccer.' And a lot of it was just so much relationship building. The more that I knew the kids from the school, the more I knew the families. I was there in the evenings when the families were more available, so I got to know a lot more people in the neighborhood than the teachers typically get to."

› On food ...

"I started off going to the places that the Augsburg students would frequent. Then it started to be more of the other restaurants—businesses that are further down onto Cedar. Afro Deli was the go-to place when it was on the corner. Mapps was always a go-to spot for coffee and to visit; it was just a hub where everybody came.

"Cedar Avenue can be kind of a barrier. People will come to it but don't generally go past it from the neighborhood. And conversely, you don't often see Augsburg students or U of M students being on the west side of Cedar.

"You don't see a lot of the residents or people venturing over unless they're going to West Bank Grocery. I would even have a hard time getting people to go to the People's Center. When we'd switch meetings from People's Center to Coyle and back, we saw a 50 percent drop in attendance."

› On changes in the neighborhood ...

"I think that it's opened up more, the West Bank in general. But I don't know if it's better or worse for opening up more. I didn't frequent the Cedar and 400 Bar. My daughter loved being down in the neighborhood. The Towers were pretty isolated for a really long time. I think it's probably the light rail that brought more traffic through, and the new stadium—you'll see a lot of Vikings people coming through the neighborhood on game days.

"I saw it as very insulated; the neighborhood kept to itself and did its own thing. But now it's the children of the first immigrants, and they know their way around, they know what's happening, they know much more about the world outside the Towers, so it adds a layer of exploration."

› On what remains the same ...

"The way the community relies on each other. Just like, right now, it's what the community has always been about. It's about helping each other, when the going gets tough. There's so many people that are the staples of the community, and if somebody passes on, there's a love and support for them. It doesn't matter who you are or what you believe in—if you're one of those people from the neighborhood, we're going to help out any way we can. That's the beauty of the neighborhood and the part I fell in love with. It goes back to being a small town in a very large city. I grew up in a small town—if the farmer had something happen, everybody chipped in until he could do the chores, until the family was well again."

⟩ On the neighborhood culture...

"The kids are more Americanized than ever," Jennifer says.

"For better or for worse?" I joke, and she laughs.

"There's a tugging of the traditions and the elders—they are proud of where their family has come from. But so many of the kids, they go back home on those visits, and that's when they decide they want to make their way in America.

"I'm always interested when kids come back two, three years after going back to Somalia. This is their home. They imprinted here. Same with language—even if you don't think they are listening, they are. They soak it all in, the language, the culture.

"Right now, there's a shift in the businesses that is tied to the residents. I do wish the graffiti would stop. I don't know how to get it to stop—it drives me up the wall."

⟩ On her "West Bank story"...

"Oh my gosh. There's so many things that can only happen in Cedar-Riverside. You know what's a great story? That plastic bag project!" She laughs. For an art project, kids from the neighborhood strung up plastic bags from the trees—to create an awareness and conversation about the plastic ban. "That's the first time the plastic bag ban was gonna go through. The kids were like, 'Yeah, we're tired of plastic bags floating through the neighborhood.' Then that's what they voted to do! Then we started getting calls: 'There's bags hanging in the trees!'

"And the park itself, the kids kept asking about Edna. They would say, 'Who is she? Is she some terrible person to have this awful park with no play equipment named after her?' And then they'd say, 'If I die and you name something after me, it better be something better than Edna's Park!'"

Jennifer laughs, then pauses.

"I really would give money to help make Edna's Park beautified in a mean-ingful way that would be lasting."

› On what she imagines for the future . . .

"I imagine that it stays as an opportunity hub for more people to own small businesses and to get their start. The American dream is, if you're coming to America—this is where all immigrants have come. This is a hub and a place where, even back into the times of the mills, people came to make a life for themselves.

"And you know, starting your own business . . . you can be your own boss and have your own freedom, but you work twice as hard. But to be able to have a place where you can start a business and get it off the ground—I hope that that stays possible and that the gentrification does not come in and overtake what makes the community what it is.

"So many of the people live here and work here and make their life here. It goes back to Afro Deli: [Abdirahman Kahin] had his business on the West Bank, and now he's got spots all over. What if some of those other restaurants could have those types of opportunities? It's a place to start with people that support you.

"There's a lot of turnover in the neighborhood that happens . . . but there's beauty about the neighborhood. Maybe it's the eternal optimism—like what I love about kids. There's that same eternal optimism that lives in the neighborhood.

"To plant the garden, I have to have hope for the future. That's always what happens in Cedar. You're going to be there to see these things grow. I'm waiting on the garden to come in. Even among things that are hard and could break the spirit of people with less fortitude than people on the West Bank. They move on and find joy and humor."

"That's what I really love about the neighborhood. It's that joy. It's there, it permeates everything. And once you're in, you're family—you can't get away even if you try."

The last time Jennifer saw a tall bike was as she was walking to Augsburg for basketball practice. She says the kids in the neighborhood always want to figure out a way to try one and want to talk to whoever is riding them.

This Isn't the Front Yard— It's the Back Alley

L et's revisit the map of the neighborhood, shall we? A sambusa-shaped wedge with freeways on two sides and a river on the third. Cutting through the neighborhood is Cedar Avenue, not only a commercial corridor but also a freeway through-pass. The freeways in the neighborhood don't connect, and the county adjusted to this problem in urban planning by directing traffic (that is—trucks, cars, and SUVs) from one freeway through Cedar Avenue to the other. Combining a commercial corridor with a "freeway alternative" makes for a very . . . interesting experiment in pedestrian safety and urban planning.

For guests to the district, Cedar Avenue is often the entry point. Most people coming in to attend a show at one of the West Bank's venues would find their way to Cedar first, then head for parking somewhere off the main strip. City planning documents including the "Cedar Riverside Small Area Plan" included prioritization of the commercial corridor as part of the district's growth.

How did this play out in funding and policy decisions? The city of Minneapolis has some great programs, like the Great Streets business improvement district grants as well as façade grant funds—a business can receive a matching grant to improve windows, storefronts, and siding. That pool of grants, however, mainly funds the corridor-facing improvements in what felt to me like a Wild West model of storefront improvement.

Focusing on the corridor was an effort to boost the resources to the business (i.e., tax-generating) portion of the neighborhood. But what did the residents think about that, and what was their viewpoint? For the neighborhood, it was a no-brainer. With more people accessing the businesses on foot from local buildings and high-rises, it only made sense to make the businesses approachable and welcoming from all sides.

Over time, we watched as several businesses along Cedar Avenue turned over, transitioning from white-owned businesses to businesses owned and operated by those from the East African community in the neighborhood. Instead of opening their doors along Cedar Avenue and participating in the commercial corridor, some moved their main doors to the residential side instead. The businesses would tilt toward the preferences of the pedestrian residents of the neighborhood instead of the primarily car-driving guests.

Some of our board members were understandably frustrated when this happened, especially in the case of businesses with storefronts or street-facing businesses along Cedar. It was not good for other businesses to have a neighbor store with seemingly shuttered doors, they said. "It makes it look like the corridor has vacancies, and eyes on the street are better for safety." While they weren't wrong about eyes on the street, I came to see things a little differently, and gradually my perspective of the neighborhood began to shift.

You see, on the other side of Riverside Plaza is a beautiful park— Currie Park. Kids would play in the playground while aunties and uncles watched from the side. Older kids played soccer in the fields until late in the evening when the sun would set over the Minneapolis skyline. The park, not the commercial corridor, was the front yard for the neighborhood. What seemed like back-door access points for car commuters was front-door access for pedestrian patrons.

The evolution of the spaces made sense for residents, but the shift from destination retail- and entertainment-oriented spaces to other purposes shifted the neighborhood energy. We began looking at ways to incorporate 360-degree design principles into neighborhood improvements. Half of West Bank residents did not own cars, compared to 27 percent in other parts of the city. We continued to look at ways to make the West Bank more pedestrian friendly, designed well on all fronts.

Generosity in the Days of Furlough

ate in November 2013, a few months after our budget-bursting festival, an email hit my inbox from a woman named Kathy Mouacheupao. She introduced herself as the new cultural districts coordinator at the Local Initiatives Support Corporation (LISC). Still downtrodden from my recent furlough and meticulously rationing my precious windows of time, I brushed off her initial meeting request. "I've been downsized," I explained in an email, "and the board is greatly reducing my hours." I offered to set her up with somebody from my board to meet instead, as per their direction.

Within what seemed like minutes of sending that response, I got a call from my previous LISC contact, Erik Takeshita. "What's up, Jamie? What's going on?" he asked empathetically, and I told him the saga of the festival, explaining our current position. I could practically hear him nodding over the phone. "Well," he said, "try to see if you can figure out a time to meet with Kathy, even if it's brief. And if you need me to talk to somebody on your board to explain, let me know—I'm happy to do that. She may be able to help, especially through this transition."

Within a week, Kathy and I had a meeting on the calendar. Madeline joined us, babbling from the crib as we talked excitedly about everything from cultural districts to websites. Continuing our research from the year prior, a cohort of cultural districts would be meeting regularly. The WBBA was invited to join.

The Local Initiatives Support Corporation is "one of the largest organizations supporting projects to revitalize communities and bring greater economic opportunity to residents," and the local LISC office works to "provide capital, strategy and know-how to our Twin Cities community development partners." I knew of LISC through my prior work in Northeast Minneapolis, where it helped provide loan funding for an artist housing project. I reconnected with the organization early on during my time with the business association, brainstorming with its staff about the creative assets along the upcoming Green Line light rail route.

That brainstorming session, led with the support of community organizer Amelia Brown, pinpointed that up and down the pathway for the Green Line, there existed a chain of cultural districts. This was unique, and quite remarkable. In San Francisco, the Bay Area Rapid Transportation (BART) system links a series of districts—financial, business, downtown. Every district along the Green Line was home to a vibrant cultural community, each strikingly different in its history and composition.

After my talk with Kathy, the WBBA joined the cohort of cultural districts, and for the next four years, LISC provided us with capacity-building support. It awarded us $40,000 for the first year of funding—enough to bring me out of furlough and move us a step toward growing the organization. The work also connected us to other districts along the Green Line struggling with similar issues: business retention, cultural preservation, and creative placemaking.

I was grateful for Erik's and Kathy's time and generosity. Anyone else could have ignored my downtrodden board-redirection email without a passing thought. But they both took the extra time to connect and hear what was happening at the organization, and they were even willing to go to the board to help advocate for my time in this realm.

The funding and pathway had fortuitous timing for the association. It allowed us to sustain our momentum by increasing my hours and funding additional program work and staff time. It also opened the doors to other funding opportunities, which brought another wave of grant resources to the neighborhood and to our work.

Controlled Burns and New Growth

P ixels and places.

A drama nerd through high school, I started out in college with the intention of majoring in theater, switching briefly to the "more employable" major of graphic design. It was the '90s, after all, and websites were all the rage. I had been crafting HTML sites filled with rotating graphics for years, so why not make a career out of it? I spent hours learning about pixels and fonts for a smart career option. But as my classes progressed, I thought, "Do I want to do this forever?" While taking my college classes, I was also working at a small family business. I made my way through different jobs as I filled in for folks at the office on maternity leave or out for other reasons, tackling everything from accounting to shipping/receiving and HR in the best hands-on, baptism-by-fire training ever. I designed concept sheets and drawings for the salespeople and even started a basic, borderline embarrassingly bad website for the company.

But—as a career? I was unsure. What if I decided to do something else and had no other useful skills besides graphic design? And what if my future clients all wanted to use Papyrus font, and as I acquiesced to their obscenely poor design choices my body turned into ash and the wind slowly blew away the dust of my remains? It wasn't worth the risk.

After contemplating, I switched majors one last time: to philosophy with a minor in art. I joined a tiny department of thoughtful colleagues and mentors I'm still in touch with to this day. I ran through logic models and learned the elements and principles of design. I continued working in Photoshop and Illustrator on my own, outside the classroom setting.

One of the pieces of advice I give my students and interns now is to have an internship or do some volunteering or part-time work in your field of choice, if you're able to, before you commit to a major. It's helpful to at least try the job one wants to do before committing a huge pile of money and time for the degree. For the U of M leadership minors who worked with the WBBA, I tried to incorporate their chosen line of work into their internship experience so they had both hands-on experience and résumé-building opportunities.

I'm grateful that I switched, that philosophy instilled in me a greater ability to dig deep no matter what field I go into. Art parallels that curiosity, a balance to think creatively. To date, I have not had a job in which I've not applied both. On the West Bank, working at the intersection of art, culture, and community, I found them inextricably connected.

After the WBBA's budget crisis, we rolled out of the furlough time methodically, with capacity-building support first from LISC Twin Cities and then from other funders, such as the McKnight Foundation. We revisited the priorities our business community had outlined. With retention being the top priority for a majority of our businesses, we began to think about how we could help, given our rather modest resources and staff capacity. We settled on a strategy that involved three core aspects:

1. External: market the area and all its great restaurants, venues, and spaces
2. Internal: build the capacity of the businesses within the district so they are more resilient to changes such as cost of goods and rent increases or policy changes
3. Regional: have a hands-on role in the policy issues coming from downtown that affect our district

We set out a new, less event-focused plan for the organization. Instead of spending most of my time planning and running a one-day festival, I would shift gears toward building and providing a technical assistance platform for businesses. With restaurants in need of websites, retail spaces in need of signs and promotion, and venues in need of marketing, there was no shortage of ongoing help needed. This would be more consistent help than a one-day festival could provide.

We didn't abandon events entirely, though. We created an events committee and materials to support the events in the district that were already occurring—of which there were many! From Palmfest to the Global Roots music festival and more, there was plenty we could already draw on that would boost district visibility and cross-pollination among the businesses within the district.

And the design chops I gained during those first years of college came in handy. I had improved my skills over the years just for fun and freelance and was able to build websites and help with design work for the small businesses. Between that background and the development gig I abandoned post-Manchester, I was well positioned to help with marketing and branding for the businesses and the district, too. I was lucky to have landed myself in a role that used all my haphazardly gained skills—from drama nerdery to waitressing to graphic design.

Growth was slow but steady at first, as over the months and years businesses became more aware of how we could help. We crafted a menu of service options based on what we could provide internally, making sure we weren't duplicating services already available from our partner non-profits that offered technical assistance like financing. We worked with the city to provide pro bono technical assistance to small businesses and microentrepreneurs that could use an extra boost. Over time, it became not only one of our core and consistent revenue streams, but also a demonstrable value we were bringing to the district. We grew program services to the extent I was able to bring on additional staff members, adding to our expertise and available services.

As a retention support mechanism, it worked. We saw turnover for businesses in the neighborhood shrink. We tried to be very careful and specific in how we put out marketing. Instead of glitzy ad campaigns that tried to make the district out to be something it was not, we focused on personal stories and narratives. With most businesses being locally owned, the stories and selections were unique and compelling. Further, we wanted to connect businesses with audiences that were truly their people. With everything from our website to the district brochure, we tried to represent the community as it actually was.

As you travel, do you ever think about the design of the place you're in? The menu, the restaurant logo, their awning? The hand-painted signs, even the vinyl map in a parking lot? Pixel by pixel or stroke by stroke, somebody designed and created that for you.

Check out the built design of a neighborhood, but the vibe of it, too. Any marketing that may have led you there. Did it feel like you were sold something that the place didn't deliver? Did you feel like you experienced what you set out to experience?

As much as I may not have thought graphic artistry would be the be-all-end-all career choice for me when I was studying it, I certainly underestimated its utility in having a community impact. We're all young once and love Papyrus at some point, I guess.

Artists, from poster designers to muralists, help make the world a beautiful place.

Politics Is What We Do

› CAM GORDON

C am Gordon is the real deal. I first met Cam after I took my position with the West Bank Business Association. He was not my home neighborhood council member, but he came to feel like one thanks to his steady presence and reliability in communication and leadership. He is a member of the Green Party of Minnesota and has been a consistent advocate for neighborhood needs in housing, community-led development, and ethical processes in a political landscape tinged with dramatic politicking.

> " The West Bank was home to some of the nation's first co-ops. . . . There's lots of potential with that model. "

As the late Paul Wellstone once said, "Politics is not predictions and politics is not observations. Politics is what we do. Politics is what we do, politics is what we create, by what we work for, by what we hope for and what we dare to imagine." One

Cam Gordon

of the things I appreciate about Cam is that he always made sure there was a seat for me. In conversations about the universities that would impact West Bank businesses, he made sure to invite me to join. He and his equally collaborative aide Robin Garwood did their best to keep the West Bank at the table—even though we could be a feisty neighborhood to work with.

> ## On his connection to the West Bank . . .

"I lived on the West Bank, on South Sixth Street, before 1977. I lived in two different old buildings and duplexes on that block during my time there, and I probably moved out in the early '80s.

"I did some work subsequently as a community organizer for the Blue Goose housing cooperative before I ran for office. I was also a community organizer for Seward Towers. I was the West Bank councilperson from 2006 to 2010 until the redistricting; now I only serve a component of the district."

Around 2012, our ward underwent a big redistricting process, which split the West Bank district into two. At the time, folks said it could be either good or bad: either the West Bank would get ignored or we would then have two council members that could go to bat for us. We landed somewhere in the middle of these possibilities. While the redistricting divided up some business districts into two parts, many advocated for the divide as a way to have a more representative city council in the years to come. True to promise, the subsequent election saw the first Somali American elected to Minneapolis City Council, Abdi Warsame.

> ## On changes in the neighborhood . . .

"You know, the neighborhood has changed dramatically since my time there. Over the years, it's gone through shifts of populations while keeping some stability in the mix. There's definitely some long-term West Bankers still there. But back in the '70s, there was a big push against a redevelopment plan that resulted in Riverside Plaza and the condos on Seven Corners.

"When I moved in, there was a big fight to preserve Riverside Café [now Acadia], lots of single-family homes and duplexes that had been slated for demo. There was redevelopment from Heller and the University of Minnesota, which tried to—and did—expand their West Bank campus. There used to be a hardware store on Riverside and the block I and Willie Murphy lived on. There was even a bar. Richter's drugstore was there also. I think they were still on when I moved in. But there was a big drug and alternative music scene. Lots of college-aged students.

"Also, there were immigrants coming into the public housing. There was an isolated Korean immigrant population. When the Vietnam War ended, there was an influx of Vietnamese immigrants as well as Cambodian and Lao refugees.

"The East African community started to come over during the time I was living in the Longfellow neighborhood. There was a standoff at one point and kind of a victory when the West Bank Community Development Corporation was created because the people that protested won, and there was a very innovative structuring to preserve affordable housing in the area. The CDC was leasing land from the city, and there was lots of organizing that went on. That whole block—where Riverside Café [was]—was saved by the CDC and the community.

"I was on the fringe of those protests. We actually had some gigs in Dania Hall and the Southern Theater—which was the Palace at the time. I remember when they door-knocked, I was a resident out of college and found it so interesting."

› On what remains the same . . .

"I think there's been a push to keep it local. I think that there's even a Starbucks and a Jimmy John's at all is a little strange, given how hard the neighborhood has pushed for local.

"I think there's some property holders who have a certain theory and ethic that has to do with grassroots and small business. Peter Dodge[9] has to be some sort of player in this. Rod Johnson is the same way. I think in the '70s he was operating Midwest Mountaineering out of his apartment—he started off as a microentrepreneur. He's sort of like Peter Dodge in that way, with the mindset that independently owned business is the way to go. People would come out fiercely to save local businesses on the West Bank, even then.

"I got there before they made Currie Park, and I remember I had friends that lived over there. I remember protesting the Metrodome. It was a feeble little protest. When the freeway came in, cutting off the West Bank from downtown and then Seward, must have been huge." Cam is referring here to the I-94 and I-35 freeways, whose controversial construction plowed through neighborhoods, destroying communities and connections.[10]

"And the West Bank has often been ignored," he continues. It was always seen by the Big Money folks as a run-down part of the city that wasn't going to bring much money—probably even more so as it got additionally cut off and isolated.

"By Mixed Blood, there were a couple of old houses that were left. The university also was coming in from the other side. The incoming development probably helped people fight even harder to save what they could. The community will rise up and fight for their local places.

Artist Ifrah Mansour at the Southern Theater, performing an excerpt from *How to Have Fun in a Civil War*

---

9. Peter Dodge is a property owner who owns several key buildings in the Cedar-Riverside neighborhood.

10. The history of the freeway projects throughout the Twin Cities is a part of local history that still impacts communities. In St. Paul, the I-94 project specifically demolished historically Black neighborhoods, and a current effort is underway to commemorate and rebuild the Rondo community it displaced.

"I think the West Bank is still a very diverse community. I think it's still kind of a college neighborhood, with the universities and dorms present. There's staff, faculty, and alumni that love the West Bank.

"It's consistently been an immigrant resettlement and transitional place besides the students. In many ways it looks the same: there are still lots of independent businesses. That the theater district has survived, that's pretty impressive."

› On what he imagines for the future . . .

"I have a pretty big nightmare about it. What I would love to see is the smaller independent businesses thriving—I can imagine that working out. I would like it if we had a historic district, but because of the libertarian property owners, that might be tough.

"I sometimes worry about people buying the buildings and putting up these Stadium Village–style 'ticky-tacky boxes.' We will see how this recession pans out, but it might come to that—look at how east of downtown is. Maybe we'd do a land bridge. Lot A will get developed, then maybe the Holtz would come down. Then Palmer's comes down. I mean, that's the nightmare. That level of loss.

"The West Bank was home to some of the nation's first co-ops. So if we can help some of those businesses become cooperative owners, there's lots of potential with that model."

› On his "West Bank story" . . .

"You know, there's so much that has happened over the years. I think of things like the family that kept their house that Augsburg wanted to buy. Augsburg just waited for decades—they waited from house to house to slowly scoop them up one by one. The institutions have this life that goes on forever and are waiting to sneak in and devour the little pieces when they get a chance. But by waiting, they are doing it in a more humane way, I guess.

"When I was living on the West Bank, the block where I lived was full of houses. Later, when I was on the council, I saw people worried about their houses getting taken. Back in the '70s, the fledgling CDC was beating back against the giant institutions. Then, as the years slowly rolled around, the perception shifted—that the CDC was a monster, and that Tim was a devil and all he wanted to do was line his pockets with money, and that the CDC was letting the cooperatives die." Tim Mungavan is the longtime director of the West Bank CDC, a champion for the neighborhood, especially in the late '70s and '80s.

"It's strange how as the narrative evolves," Cam muses, "the good guys can become the perceived bad guys—whether or not that's actually the case."

Cam saw a tall bike just yesterday on a group ride, two friends along for a larger group ride. He also saw Per Hanson, president and founder of the Black Label Bike Club, on a tall bike a few days ago—two sightings in a week.

Visions and Illusions

As we worked with our local businesses, we also worked closely with other neighboring districts and nonprofits. We shared lessons learned, tools like human resources guides and employee manuals, ideas. There are a variety of antidisplacement and retention strategies districts can use, and many of us were going through similar problems. As organizations, we were working on building our capacity and working with businesses to bolster their income and increase profitability. Most businesses were renting, but a few were able to buy their own buildings as a stabilizing factor in mitigating business displacement.

Downsides of the ownership model, of course, include the expense and lack of flexibility if a location change is needed. But if a business is owner-occupied in a cultural district, that can help secure footing and mitigate some risk of displacement.

The West Bank Business Association faced the same problem itself. Our ability to have a footprint in the neighborhood was not guaranteed— what was the long-term role of the association in an entrepreneurial environment? We recognized the importance of arts and culture in our district, but what of others? The arts and cultural fabric of the district was not certain either. To explore an idea, I talked it over with staff, a few businesses, our committee members, and then our executive committee.

I drew up a plan, a concept sketch, and a presentation. I gathered quotes and estimates. And then, I pitched to the executive committee the idea of establishing a multiuse, multilevel center for business incubation, retail, and a continued footprint for the West Bank Business Association in the West Bank district.

The goals would be multifaceted: to secure a footprint for our organization; provide a hub for small-business incubation and development; build a more sustainable nongrant revenue stream for the business association; create a permanent home for the arts; and provide community-oriented use of a city-owned parcel with strong emotional connections to the community. Not only did this align with our mission, but it also aligned with the city of Minneapolis's long-term plans and the Cedar Riverside Small Area Plan that had been established for our district.

In crafting a three- to five-year vision, I saw the center filling a vacant space and serving as an incubation space for new businesses. Our programs felt like they were bursting at the seams, and capacity growth was an option.

The response from the executive team at the time was tolerant, but lackluster. While there was potential in the idea, they felt the board members had their hands full operating their own businesses. While they deemed it a future possibility, the timing and composition were not quite right—particularly not for a fairly conservative, risk-averse board that had no desire for anything even close to a capital campaign, especially not terribly long after a pretty scary debt crisis.

I was disappointed, but it was still healthy to keep the big picture in mind, to take a step back and look from a distance. It's hard to have the balcony view when you're in the day-to-day, but keeping those future possibilities in mind constantly inspired and informed my work.

A Bird's-Eye View

When I was visiting Minneapolis for the first time, in 2003, my friend Chris drove me around and showed me the sights. As we headed to Minnehaha Falls, we saw workers testing the Blue Line along Hiawatha Avenue. "That's our new light rail!" he said excitedly. "It's opening soon." The Blue Line would connect downtown Minneapolis to Bloomington and the Minneapolis–St. Paul International Airport, a part of the region's long-term sustainability and economic development strategy.

Ten years later, I would find myself a Minneapolis resident in the thick of planning for the opening of the region's second light rail route, the Green Line. I had moved to Minneapolis from Los Angeles the same year of that visit with Chris, in search of a new adventure in a more affordable area of the country. Drawn to the city's literary and creative community, I opened a nonprofit gallery in Northeast Minneapolis, a story I go into in more depth in my first book, *It's Never Going to Work*. (It did work, for a time.)

The Green Line would connect downtown Minneapolis to downtown St. Paul, joining the two cities. Rather than following the freeway, as originally planned, the light rail would roll along University Avenue. The hope was that it would trigger economic development along the corridor, being a boost to those businesses and an amenity for residents and commuters.

The West Bank was one of only two neighborhoods to have a stop for both Green Line and Blue Line trains. The Blue Line's station is on Sixth Street, tucked along the freeway side of the neighborhood. The Green Line got a stop right on Cedar Avenue. The advent of the second light

A view of the West Bank from the roof of the Courtyard hotel, 2013

rail station meant an additional infrastructure boost and another access point for the many residents.

The Green Line runs through not just one or two but a series of cultural districts, a unique feature of the train's route and a testament to the cultural tapestry of the Twin Cities. Early in 2014, the districts gathered together to plan coordinated celebrations for the opening, with local committees planning individual events. Each cultural district had something special planned, and I needed to get some aerial photos of the West Bank.

The general manager of our local hotel happened to be on our board and part of our hospitality efforts for guests to the neighborhood. I asked whether I could take some shots of the neighborhood from an upper floor, and he did me one better, offering me the roof of the hotel to safely snap some photos.

One gray afternoon, I headed over to the hotel to meet up. We made our way to the roof via the elevator and a service ladder, and he showed me around and guided me on where it would be safe to walk. The roof was far more interesting than I would have imagined! With rocks for drainage, plants, and a walkway, it was not unlike a hidden courtyard. On one side, the hotel's head chef kept a series of beehives, using the honey in his recipes and signature desserts.

As we circled back around to the front of the building, he asked, "So—how long do you need? Half hour or so okay?"

"That should be plenty!" I said cheerfully.

"All righty then," he said, beginning his descent down the ladder and back into the hotel, peeping his head back out once more before closing the hatch.

For opening day, we on the West Bank decided to highlight the neighborhood's businesses and community members. We invited community leaders, local leaders, and other residents to be among those to take the inaugural trip on the train to St. Paul and back again. And, of course, Madeline came for a bit, too.

Jamie and Maddy at the light rail opening, 2014

We invited restaurants and nonprofits to set up tables in a parking lot adjacent to the station reserved for the festivities, and we invited artists from West Bank venues to perform. The Oromia Youth Association performed traditional Oromo dancing, and Marimba Africa played as well. The day culminated with West Bankers Cadillac Kolstad and the Union Suits performing as a strong storm rolled into the Cities, blowing tents and canopies out of our hands as we hastily tried to secure them.

While it was an exciting event for the neighborhood, the advent of the light rail was not without challenges. After five years of construction, including street resurfacing, sidewalk renovation, and track laying, our small businesses were struggling. While the light rail promised to bring in additional customers, that did little to alleviate the stress on parking and access in the midst of the process. We did what we could to support businesses during this time, and we collaborated on efforts to help guide retention and recovery. The Central Corridor Funders Collaborative was a body of grantmakers and other funders committed to supporting the districts up and down the Green Line, and nonprofits throughout the region rallied to help. While we saw promising retention rates in our district, other areas, like University Avenue, were much harder hit by the construction process.

Springboard for the Arts, a nonprofit organization whose mission is to support working artists, launched its Irrigate program. Springboard worked with artists to host pop-ups, events, and activities to support businesses along the Green Line during construction, seeding efforts to stitch arts into economic development and recovery.

The Central Corridor Funders Collaborative worked with local non-profits to provide forgivable loan assistance to area businesses, providing funds to get them through the slow spots of revenue when the construction prevented income generation. These proved to be so helpful that the concept would pop up again during future construction projects.

With so many businesses in the district, the need was certainly greater than our small nonprofit could fulfill, but we did as much as we were able to prioritize retention and help businesses stay in business. We were largely successful with these efforts, reducing the turnover rates in the neighborhood considerably and helping businesses remain in place.

A Crash Course on the West Bank

Our district has many bars, music venues, and theaters, and artists, actors, and musicians are cornerstones of our creative economy. While businesses were generally accepting of the neighboring performance spaces, not all drew the correlation between the creative economy and their bottom line. But surveys, research, and traceable restaurant activity repeatedly demonstrated the impact the venues and cultural organizations had on the restaurants' and bars' earnings.

The WBBA did what it could to highlight this connection and nurture those relationships. In 2013, we hosted the first West Bank Arts Foundry, a full day of learning for artists, business owners, and arts enthusiasts on the West Bank. It aimed to connect Twin Cities artists with local business owners and create more opportunities for artistic endeavors in the neighborhood.

A year or so later, my colleague Damon messaged me about a week-long opening at the Southern Theater that fall. "Unfortunately, one of our groups had to back out. Could the WBBA use the space?" he asked.

It was a tight turnaround, but we took a stab at something new that expanded on the Arts Foundry concept, the West Bank Crash Course. The hope was to craft a series of workshops that would give folks an avenue to learn a new skill or something about the neighborhood while encouraging partnerships among the businesses. We also wanted to continue building the skills of artists and musicians, the "creative enterprises" in our business district.

Osman Ali, founder of the Somali Museum of Minnesota, presenting "A History of the Somali People"

We hosted a full week of events, including workshops and informative walking tours. The event was a great entry point for students just getting started at the universities, a good introduction for businesses, and an accessible learning point for niche topics related to the district. We also hosted bike rides, neighborhood cleanups, and happy hours. Still uncommon for local conferences today and even less common at the time, we made it a point to pay all speakers an honorarium for their time. (More of this, please!)

For the cycling community, we hosted workshops on roadside basics and bike repair as well as a crash course on winter cycling. Friday's sessions were all about music, with information on sound recording and promotions. In what would become an annual tradition, Wednesday featured a storytelling session on the patio of Palmer's—where all good stories happen anyway. The second year, we would dive deeper into skills building for musicians, with a daylong event that culminated in a live celebration of women in Minnesota music.

The Crash Course was a hit among attendees, with survey respondents reporting that they learned something useful or helpful and 90 percent saying they learned something new about the district. It successfully promoted crossover between venues, and an overwhelming majority of attendees said it positively influenced their perception of the West Bank.

We continued to host the Crash Course series, each year putting a slightly new spin on it based on the shifting needs of the business community and interests of the West Bank audience. The weeklong intro was a success year after year, achieved many of the goals we had for the district, and was a lot less draining on the organization financially than was the Music Festival.

Angels Among Us

February 23, 2012—A welcome email

Welcome, Jamie! I didn't get a chance to introduce myself. I'm Eunice Eckerly, the Trinity member who spoke to the changing of our ward lines. I try to be a nonviolent peace activist and have lived in the neighborhood and attended Trinity for about forty years, so I'm dedicated to our West Bank area and diversity. I certainly will go with whatever happens, but it does worry me that we don't become a society (again!) of "us" and "them." I worked at the Urban Coalition, a diversity organization back in the '70s and have been dedicated to an integrated society with equality for all most all my life, and Trinity works for that too, which is why I'm glad to be a member there.

I am impressed with all these efforts and was with your introductory speech. If there is any way I can help, just let me know! I'm here with you and for you—and for all of us! Thanks again, and welcome!

—Eunice Eckerly

Mary Laurel and Eunice

It can seem like people who walk the walk are few and far between, but I count Eunice Eckerly among them. Eunice was a WBBA board member representing the local Trinity Lutheran church. (Don't let the traditional-sounding name fool you; Trinity folks are pretty radical.)

A longtime West Bank resident, she was highly engaged in the community—and she was a fierce advocate for the neighborhood. She was the happy, cheerful voice on the bus ready to strike up a conversation with anybody interested, excitedly talking about a new West Bank restaurant or activity. She was also a champion of the WBBA and of the active role she and other board members played in the community.

Eunice was a regular fixture in social events and activities. Whenever we had a storytelling session, she would join, sharing stories about the neighborhood's past and her time coming to the district years ago.

Over the years, Eunice's health declined, though her passion did not. In 2018, she moved from her home on the West Bank into Augustana Health Care Center, a senior living facility. I know she missed the neighborhood tremendously, and many of us tried to visit her as often as possible. As we did, our conversations while she was in care were similar to what they had been before: West Bank news, excitement, and, of course, the latest gossip!

Eunice passed away December 18, 2018, but her enthusiastic spirit and dedication to the West Bank/Cedar-Riverside community live on.

Interfaith

Another thing to love about the West Bank: our religious diversity and mutual respect. In precious few neighborhoods can one experience true interfaith relationships and conversations.

Representatives of Dar Al-Hijrah Mosque, the Common Table / Cedar Commons of Augsburg College, and Trinity Lutheran Congregation came together regularly for conversations and shared learning. The goal was, in part, for attendees to learn about the faiths of their neighbors. But it was about far more than hearing or reading information we could get from Wikipedia.

Interfaith, which took place at Common Table's community space, was also about building relationships. For several years, the leaders and folks from each congregation would come together and get to know one another, hear one another's stories, and . . . become friends! The group present would reflect on what was happening in the world and on how one's faith or nonfaith experience informs them. The meeting on the second Tuesday of the month included a meal, and at all others Somali tea was served.

What may have seemed revolutionary to folks outside the area was community as usual for the West Bank. Other congregations asked Pastor Jane of Trinity Lutheran to speak to them about the interfaith effort and how everyone could be better neighbors to one another. But it didn't seem innovative at the time—just communicating and respectful dialogue across faiths.

As Pastor Jane would say, "Sometimes a big part of the work is just showing up and being present."

In 2017, I had the opportunity to kindle a West Bank–style iteration of the night market in New Orleans I loved so much that incorporated this spirit of interfaith respect. That year, the Northern Spark event fell during the Muslim holy month of Ramadan. Northern Spark, coordinated by the nonprofit Northern Lights.mn, is an overnight arts festival that moves locations annually throughout the Twin Cities—this lucky year, it came to the West Bank, and the organizers invited us to participate. Wanting to be mindful of the holy day, we rolled plans for Ramadan into the festivities for the evening. Northern Lights.mn partnered with Minnesota Interfaith Power & Light to host an iftar, the meal eaten by Muslims to break their daily fast during Ramadan, as part of Northern Spark.

While the West Bank is known for its diversity, the community has found itself the occasional target of hate thanks to its density and high profile. That year, a small fringe group organized an anti-Muslim event at the state capitol. The unwelcoming sentiment was heard loud and clear. There were racial and religious underpinnings to the anti-Muslim event, and what was worse, it, too, was held during Ramadan—the same day as Northern Spark.

Local imams and other community members decided to combat the hate of the event at the capitol with a gesture of loving-kindness in our neighborhood. People and organizations joined together to scale up the community iftar to include a wide host of community partners, among them the Minnesota chapter of the Council on American-Islamic Relations. In response to hate, the West Bank did what it does best—it connected, collaborated, and mobilized love. The love on the West Bank is never more evident than in times of crisis. Floods, fires, and emergencies can be heartbreaking—but for our neighborhood, they bring out the best. That was evident at this moment. Pregnant with Nick's and my second child, I was grateful for the warm community that enveloped me, for our family, and for the kindness of the neighborhood that radiated.

During the day, my colleague Khadijah and I set up tents and prepared for our overnight festivities. She and I had worked together for several years on the West Bank and collaborated on creative initiatives for Cedar Avenue. She's a cofounder and the director of the Soomaal House

The West Bank Night Market

of Art, which is, in its own words, "a Minnesota-based Somali art collective that provides studio space, studio critiques, artistic community, mentorships for younger Somali artists, and an annual exhibition space with educational programming." Ninety-degree heat and lots of wind made for a tough setup. As the sun began to set and the temperatures dropped slightly, the streets gradually closed for the celebration.

The crowd was calm and full of love as the sun set on Cedar Avenue. Earlier that day, perhaps twenty or thirty anti-Muslim protestors had stood outside the capitol. But now, hundreds from outside the neighborhood stood alongside thousands of residents in solidarity. Local restaurants supplied thousands of sambusa, dates, and other easy-to-hold foods. After a poetic adhan (call to prayer) from the roof near the Cedar Community Plaza, the nearby locally owned restaurant Gandhi Mahal offered a full meal.

As the Ramadan iftar festivities slowed down, Northern Spark ramped up. Local artist Ifrah Mansour set up an aqal—a Somali nomadic hut—and invited people to share space. In the open Dania Hall lot, we had our gift market. We worked with artists to give gifts like paintings, screen prints, poetry, and music. I hosted a plant booth, where I gave away hundreds of seedlings in little pots I had planted and grown over the month prior. Thousands of tiny plants, prints, and journals were distributed in a market that exchanged no currency.

The Dania Hall lot, usually dark and empty at this time, was alive with light and activity. At about 2:00 a.m., I went to the office and lay on my back on the couch, my pregnant belly tired from the day. "Am I too old for this?" I wondered.

No—but maybe too pregnant.

Here Comes a Regular:

› ANGIE COURCHAINE

Angie Courchaine is a visual artist, an aerial artist, and a cofounder of Pinwheel Arts and Movement Studio. When we kicked off our "Here Comes a Regular" feature on the West Bank blog years ago, which highlighted local friends, Angie was the first West Banker on the docket.

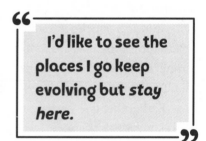

> I'd like to see the places I go keep evolving but *stay here.*

› On their connection to the West Bank . . .

A West Bank resident for over a decade, Angie went to school at the University of Minnesota, where they lived in Middlebrook Hall before heading to West Bank proper. Angie spent much of their social time at the old Bedlam Theatre (the second Bedlam) and 1419—another arts collective on Washington Avenue.

› On changes in the neighborhood...

Angie Courchaine

While Angie feels the West Bank changing in numerous ways, they first think of the creative spaces.

"I've seen at least five underground art and theater venues close—two within three months of me moving here! Four were underground, radical spaces. They were a big part of the reason why I moved here. Since then, two different bars on the street have closed as well. We have the Southern and Mixed Blood, but they aren't as experimental as those other spaces were."

But there are positives, too. Angie notes that some of the businesses that have changed hands are now owned by East Africans connected to the neighborhood.

"Dilla's used to be Baldy's BBQ,[11] and now it's this awesome Ethiopian restaurant," Angie says. "In a way, that's been encouraging. Every time one of those places closed, I was worried it was going to be a Starbucks. Even if things that I enjoyed are displaced, I'm not mad about what filled in."

They notice that there are definitely a lot more new apartments popping up on the borders, along the light rail, and near Fifteenth and Riverside. With those new apartments, they see more residents from higher income demographics—though Angie doesn't always see them around. "I don't know where they're hanging out, but I guess it's not the neighborhood places." Angie's own apartment complex has become more racially diverse over the years, but they note it still seems to be maintaining its vibe as a place for poor and queer artists and students.

---

11. Prior to Baldy's, it was K-Wok, which Dan Prozinski references in his interview.

› On their "West Bank story"...

When Angie thinks of uniquely West Bank things, they think of the Ten Minute Play Festival. An annual event hosted by Bedlam Theatre, the festival (also known as 10×10) was always full of new works—of all kinds charming, creative, boring, and often ridiculous.

"I remember one time they needed help pushing this bike-covered wagon thing from . . . maybe from the Ivy building [in the Seward/Longfellow neighborhood] over to Mixed Blood. It didn't have wheels, had stuff duct-taped around the wheels. I remember pushing that back and, like, a million tall-bikers passed us on the way."

And safety? Not really a problem.

"I've always felt fine walking down the street even at three in the morning," Angie says. "There would always be somebody else that I know, probably multiple somebodies. It's a huge neighborhood in that way—there's more people living in this neighborhood than the whole city I came from. Everybody has their own circles for sure, but I see a lot of the same people. Seeing Big John[12] used to always help me feel safe."

› On what they imagine for the future...

"I'd like to see the places I go keep evolving but stay here. I understand things probably will change hands at some point. I'd like to see what happened with the businesses before. I think it would be good if the African community got better representation in the neighborhood. I also hope it remains an affordable place for me to live—I'm hoping artists like me are able to afford to keep living here."

When did Angie last see somebody on a tall bike? "Right outside my window. A day or two ago."

---

12. 'Big' John Duhart, a bouncer at Palmer's for over two decades, passed away in early 2020.

Art on Cedar Avenue

When you drive quickly through a neighborhood, you miss so much. The feel of different types of sidewalk underneath your feet. The bumps of tree grates on your shoe as you trip over the edge of the iron, lifted up by thirsty overgrown roots. Looking around as you move about a neighborhood on foot or on bike enables you to take in much more than you can through the window of a car at high speed.

When I began my career so long ago, art and business seemed like separate enterprises to many, but I'm convinced they are inextricable for healthy local economies. According to the City of Minneapolis's Creative Vitality Index, creative sales pump nearly $5 *billion* into the city's economy annually—more than nine times the amount of its sports sector revenues. With photographers, musicians, singers, writers, authors, graphic designers, fine artists, and more, the city is rich with creators and creatively minded individuals.

Supporting a livable, creative Minnesota is a value residents share. In 2008, the state's voters passed the Clean Water, Land and Legacy Amendment, which directs a percentage of sales tax to arts and environmental initiatives—meaning our economy feeds our creative and environmental health, quite literally.

Perhaps not surprisingly given my background, I worked continually with visual artists in my West Bank work. There is a strong visual arts presence here, and it became an increasingly visible part of the landscape. Businesses and creators added new murals and sculptures with regularity. Phil Vandervaart, the preeminent hand-painted sign artist in Minneapolis, was behind several gorgeous and iconic signs on the West Bank—on the Hard Times storefront, at the Wienery, and at the Cedar Cultural Center, to name but a few.

"Walkability" is a measure of how safe and comfortable a neighborhood feels for pedestrians moving about. We did what we could to increase the walkability of the district, not just for guests of the area but for people who live there as well. With eight thousand residents, only half of whom have cars, pedestrian and public modes of moving are the norm. And even for those driving to and from the neighborhood—well, drivers are pedestrians too at some point on their journey, even if it's just from their car to their destination. Slowing things down on Cedar Avenue was one thing. Nurturing the creative aspects of our district was another.

West Bank artist David Witt at the West Bank Art Crawl

In 2012, we held the first West Bank Art Crawl. We matched up artists with local venues and hosted a pop-up gallery tour on what would otherwise have been a slow evening for the district. Curt Fleck—the Minneapolis artist who spent half the year here and half in Louisiana, where I ran into him at the Frenchmen night market—showed his bottle-cap fish at Palmer's Bar.

David Witt, a local artist well known for rock and music posters, set up shop at the Triple Rock. As we were getting his show ready, taking down some of the beer signs to make room for art, we found an old Triple Rock poster taped to the wall behind them. The designer for the poster? David, of course! Little signs from the universe like that made me feel as though we were on the right track.

From that first "crawl" we moved on to pop-ups in key locations along the avenue, where we hoped they'd both provide an aesthetic functionality and serve as a deterrent for graffiti and trash. When we conducted our area cleanups, we tracked where we removed trash and graffiti. "Hot spots" indicated good candidates for some environmental design—physical improvements used to deter future instances. Over the course of a few years, we tested things out with the goal of creating a more permanent visual arts presence along Cedar Avenue.

Our eventual goal was to create an "arts walk" along Cedar. Installations would celebrate the cultural heritage of the West Bank and elements of what made our neighborhood special. Well-executed, place-based installations could also celebrate the businesses and venues that make the West Bank unique.

We never secured any of the very large-scale grants we applied for, and instead we made progress bit by bit to move our goals along. In 2015, we hosted a series of pop-up art installations in conjunction with the neighborhood's Earth Day celebration and cleanup. We worked with our partners at Brian Coyle to build a community garden and with local artists to host a Little Free Library, place pop-up mini murals along Cedar Avenue, create an herb garden, and install an interactive mural on the Southern Theater.

In the spring of 2016, we hosted another series of art pop-ups, calling the effort Station to Station. Working with local artists and crafters, we showcased works and ideas that reflected our neighborhood's rich cultural heritage as an immigrant community and a destination for music and theater.

We received a lot of local support from those who knew the WBBA's work and the neighborhood well. The city of Minneapolis contributed, as did the University of Minnesota's Good Neighbor Fund. We worked with art teacher Brianna Jo Lee and students from Cedar Riverside Community School on a project for the neighborhood: the students created prints inspired by family fabrics and patterns, learning block printing as part of the process, and we scanned in the prints and used them to decorate the utility boxes in the district. These art pieces, created by young residents of the neighborhood, added a beautification element to the avenue while also deterring graffiti. And it was a great lesson for the kids in applied geometry—who says the arts can't also be practical?

A city grant enabled us to work with West Bank resident Phil Kelly and several of his artist friends to create wood benches and a walkway for Edna's Park. We hosted another cleanup there and planted some resilient daylilies; the benches are still intact and usable today.

While we never received the huge infusion of funds we would have needed to make our wildest dreams a reality, we chipped away at our goals over the years. Visual arts in a variety of manifestations has made Cedar Avenue a more pedestrian-friendly street for all who live, learn, work, and visit the West Bank.

Creative Energies

› ALLEN CHRISTIAN

Allen Christian is a working artist and the founder of the House of Balls gallery in Minneapolis. An eclectic sculptor who works largely in recycled materials and metals, he is another cornerstone in the Minneapolis art community, participating in events from the ArtCar Parade to the annual Ice Shanty projects. He is also always helping out in the community, through mentorships, cleanups, and serving on the WBBA board.

> " The West Bank is one of the few places left in Minneapolis that still have their own sense of history. "

I catch up with Allen at his studio a few weeks into the COVID-19 pandemic. He has just bid farewell to a local inebriated guest—the guest, whom neither of us know, stopped by the House of Balls with a piece of meat from an undisclosed location. Allen, the ultimate host, fired up the grill so the guy could cook his lunch.

Allen Christian

Our conversation runs the traditional spread of our mutual passions: art, community, and (of course) the West Bank. House of Balls can be tricky to find, but once you know about it, you'll appreciate the creative oasis it is. The Blue Line light rail cuts diagonally through the neighborhood, and the gallery's entry point is tucked away into the back corner of the district. Across the rails you'll find what looks like an empty dead-end street, but it's actually home to a small apartment building and the House of Balls.

Prior to its current iteration, the space was the Medusa, an underground punk club featuring music, dancing, and community. When it closed, the neighborhood worried apartments would be the building's fate—like the Haçienda in Manchester, made famous in the days of New Order and the Happy Mondays only to become apartments. Imagine how relieved we were when it was not a fancy developer but instead a local artist who bought it. Imagine how relieved *I* was when the artist joined our board! Hooray for creative camaraderie.

Allen says he's doing okay, all things considered, and we talk about the pandemic situation at hand. The West Bank is unusually chill, and we were both worried about the businesses.

"You know," he says, "I'm hoping I might be able to get the area real cleaned up while everything is so quiet." Another West Banker who leads by example, Allen often helps clean up areas beyond his building. It's not rare to see him blocks away from the House of Balls with a trash grabber and a couple of trash bags, removing litter and bottles from the grassy areas that surround Riverside Plaza.

› On his connection to the West Bank . . .

A longtime Minneapolis artist, Allen came to the neighborhood for food and festivities before opening the House of Balls.

"One of the best memories I have of the West Bank is when Obama was elected. I remember driving down Cedar Avenue after the results were announced. I had a different art car then called *Harry Balls*," Allen recalls, laughing. "My wife Mary Jane and I were downtown; Keith Ellison was also downtown and having a party at the event center. We got to the truck and drove down to the West Bank. As we got up to Palmer's, the street was just packed, everyone celebrating. Everyone was out on the streets. Tons of

WBBA board meeting at House of Balls

people from the Somali community, and it was this blissful chaos. Everyone was in the street, everyone was honking, people were rolling across the hood of the truck, all in love and fun."

› On changes in the neighborhood . . .

Allen points to big development like the 515 on Currie Park. This large building adjacent to Riverside Plaza includes both market-rate and affordable units as well as mixed-use space on the ground floor.

"Developments like that have literally changed the landscape of the neighborhood," he says.

› On what he imagines for the future . . .

"When I think about the future of the West Bank, my hope is that to some degree development stops, and there's not the same kind of development that the power brokers right now have been running. It has all been about creating these structures that all look the same, and they're the same all over the country. There's a sense of lost identity in that kind of development. The West Bank is one of the few places left in Minneapolis that still have their own sense of history.

"I envision the West Bank as economically vibrant—we're all in it together. Together we're stronger, as we are when we keep what makes our community unique. Development should express the soul of the neighborhood."

Allen has hosted some of the West Bank Business Association's board meetings. We would sit at the long table outside his studio, conducting business in the fresh air. The trees of the courtyard provided shade from the afternoon sun. As we voted on minutes and discussed business, we could hear the sounds of the Blue Line trains passing back and forth along the tracks. The West Bank, we were reminded, was its own little island. But we were—and are—ever connected.

Allen saw somebody on a tall bike just last week.

On Cultural Districts

My trips to New Orleans and other charismatic spaces often left me wondering: What is it people love about a place? The architecture? History? Food? Arts? The "authenticity"?

In my work with neighborhoods and communities, my goal is to support them and bring out their best. From Northeast Minneapolis to the West Bank, this has centered largely on what are known as arts districts or cultural districts—the "destination" areas that draw people to gallery crawls, festivals, restaurants. But why are we so drawn to them, and what makes them so compelling?

The West Bank, though quite different in history, geography, and landscape, is like New Orleans in that its shows, restaurants, and events are a draw. It is a destination for entertainment, music, and more. Neighborhoods like these also have a special energy, something other spaces can't easily replicate in an authentic way. Cultural districts are a demonstration of a community's values lived fully. We love them and are drawn to them because they are rare and beautiful examples of our best lived selves. Even when we live in a great cultural district ourselves, we pop over to others to visit, eat, see dance, theater, and art.

Gentrification is a common word in economic and community development—but it's not a term without nuance. For some, gentrification is simple change as economies and cities evolve and develop. For others, it is representative of a painful process, as it articulates the displacement of people from a place against their desire to stay. As community organizers, we work against the negative impacts of gentrification. The process is painful because it pushes out the buildings and the people that breathe life into a district. It's like watching the slow death of a cherished friend. It's particularly damaging to those who build a district and then lose access to the very community where they found connection. It's critical we do all we can to preserve and protect the ones we have held up and nurture the development of more.

In the end, however, we shouldn't aspire for every city to have a designated cultural or creative district—rather, we should aspire for every neighborhood to be a cultural or creative district. Each neighborhood should have access points for residents to connect to their roots, their culture, to fulfill their creative inclinations. Every human has a history of cultural and generational wisdom from which to draw. Many have generational trauma from which to heal. Building better, more creative communities and helping people find this within themselves is a key. If we help draw out what's naturally present in an area, we will have more resilient neighborhoods, more closely knit communities, healthier economies, and happier citizens.

That is part of what makes the West Bank so beautiful and fascinating to me. Not only is it a district full of culture and places that resonate with so many people, but it has evolved to meet the continually changing needs and composition of its community.

Fast Friendships

› ABDURRAHMAN MAHMUD

My friend Abdu emigrated from Somalia in 2015. He's had an exciting time in the States so far, working in community outreach for health awareness. His work has been critical, particularly around the AIDS epidemic in Africa. His experience both here and abroad has given him understanding in the areas of health, water, sanitation and hygiene, humanitarian assistance, protection, human rights, food security, livelihood, community-driven development initiatives, and more.

> **The West Bank community is innovative and resilient. No other neighborhood has all the things the West Bank has.**

In 2010, he joined international nongovernmental organizations and United Nations–funded programs in the Horn of Africa and Yemen region, serving as a coordinator for a number of projects. His travels eventually landed him in Minnesota, where he has developed a great reputation for working with nonprofit organizations and adeptly managing a number of projects. Now, he serves as a project coordinator at the West Bank Business Association and the Lake Street Council. He is also the founder of Twinist, which helps immigrant job seekers and businesses connect.

Abdu is a storyteller—charismatic and witty, with a great sense of humor. I came to know him first through his work with Mixed Blood Theatre. We worked together on community projects for

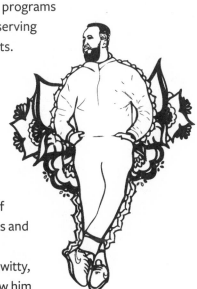

Abdurrahman Mahmud

Springboard for the Arts and People's Center, creating pop-up events and programs for the West Bank that built connections between the healthcare clinic and the residents. From there, he joined the WBBA team directly to help us part-time as we worked to support West Bank businesses.

› On his connection to the West Bank...

Sisco Omar, Abdullahi Sheikh, and baby at the Connecting Community in Cedar-Riverside event

"What first brought me to Cedar-Riverside was the community itself—the community connection that I have is to the West Bank/Cedar-Riverside first. A lot of families that I know live in the area, a lot of people that I know run businesses in the neighborhood, a lot of friends that I have live or hang out in the neighborhood.

"When I first started to work with the West Bank, I was with the Aliveness Project. My work was to educate the East African community about HIV and do some community awareness raising and education program testing.

"Cedar-Riverside is known as a hub of the East African community—anywhere in the world. It carries the name of Little Mogadishu elsewhere. I was doing a lot of work in the West Bank, with Mixed Blood and West Bank Business Association. But my connection got deeper and deeper every day—whenever I started a new program, new job, new engagement work, my relationships would continue to expand. I never lived in the neighborhood; I live in Whittier, Minneapolis. But I know nothing about Whittier. I can say my neighborhood is the West Bank. You know, we just spend the night, the places that we live.

"You know, in Africa, I used to work with a lot of expats to educate and train them on how to work with African organizations and African communities.

176

And now, coming to America, I became the African expat to help American organizations understand African communities here." Abdu laughs. "The work that I do is really making simple connections, sharing the understanding that I have about the community, and that's been really helpful for the organizations that I work with."

› On food . . .

"There's three places I can say! It depends to what kind of flavor I want. If I need a Somali dish, I go to Alle Aamin—that's the restaurant that is run by three women owners. They are the nightlife of Cedar-Riverside. If I want Oromo-style or Ethiopian food, I go to Dilla's. If I want an American dish, I go to Hard Times. These are the three favorite restaurants [where] I wish to spend time."

› On changes in the neighborhood . . .

"People think I've been here for a long time because of the work that I do, but I can only talk about the past five years. Most of the issues that are happening right now, they existed when I came. People are struggling. People come and go, and business owners change frequently. Community organizers come and go. But the housing issue is not yet solved—there's no economic opportunity yet sparked in the neighborhood. There's no big change I can see yet.

"We are also still in the pandemic. Maybe a year from now, we can say, 'These are the visible changes from that event.' But still in the middle of the COVID pandemic, there are a lot of challenges. The Cedar-Riverside area lost many to COVID already.

"Cedar-Riverside is the most dense neighborhood when it comes to housing and available green spaces in the neighborhood. It is one of the most dense neighborhoods in the whole state of Minnesota. So, in a condition like that, community transmission of COVID or any other contagious disease is big. Folks in the neighborhood are susceptible because people are living in tiny apartments.

"And a lot of businesses lost revenue—I worry some businesses will close. Hopefully, we will see something positive at the end of the pandemic. But we still are in the middle, and people are struggling. People have challenges, and people are trying to survive. But"—he pauses—"people are resilient."

› On what remains the same . . .

"Economically, people are still struggling. And some families depend on social welfare, but many are truck drivers or have labor jobs or service jobs like driving a taxi, or things like that. They work hard. When you add up all these things, you feel this community's resilience.

"The community and the people—they are innovative, they find ways to generate revenue. People are trying to counter and fill the gap of social services. That just tells you the community is resilient. That word carries a lot of meaning. It's amazing! I mean—you can see a family that came to the United States fifteen or twenty years ago. Both parents struggled to provide for the family and help their kids succeed.

"Some youth are on the street, and that is tragic. But when you look at the kids that are doing well—going to college, succeeding, buying a house— the numbers are a big thing. All the elders in the neighborhood, they tell you their kids are university graduates. Their kids are married. And if you understand where that family came from, how they sustained, tried to succeed and give their kids a better life, that's the picture of Cedar-Riverside."

At that point the discussion turns briefly to his parents, my immigrant parents, and the hope of Coming to America. So many people come to find a better future for their kids. I think that's one of many reasons I find myself connected to Cedar-Riverside, and that uniquely American immigrant story.

"And now," he says, "people stay in Cedar-Riverside, they stay in the same place, they don't want to move out. The kids help support them, they don't want to move out, they love it here. Imagine the father of Ilhan Omar—he never moved out of M building.

"With the elders in the neighborhood, their children want them to move, but they say, 'Why would I move to a suburban space when I cannot drive, where I don't know the people? Here I have restaurants, cafés, my mosque. I can walk to People's Center. If I want to go to downtown or Mall of America, I can ride the train.' They can afford to live in another space, but it doesn't matter—they love this space.

"What other neighborhood has all this? No other neighborhood has all these things," Abdu concludes affectionately.

› On the nightlife . . .

"The Somali way of nightlife is for people to come, chat, drink tea or drinks other than alcohol, and chat about politics and the neighborhood. Not just in the neighborhood, but in the country, in the world, back home, this is the place that is like that. Cedar-Riverside is where to go when you need late gatherings at the restaurants and coffee shops. Elsewhere, they close at midnight. Here, there is late-night gathering and community. People think nightlife and they think bars and music, but the West Bank is more than that."

› On his "West Bank story" . . .

Abdu smiles.

"Cedar-Riverside is the only place you can come 2:00 a.m. and find all kinds of Somali food. I mean, that's the *only* place. Even in Africa, I can say that. It's unique. Like this—Alle Aamin, the restaurant owned by the girls. Even when I go to Nairobi, after 11:00 p.m. or midnight, you can't find food. Cedar-Riverside is the only place!"

› On what he imagines for the future . . .

"The West Bank is a diverse space where a lot of communities live together side by side. They work together to achieve a common goal. Collaboration is great—they use the word specifically, and it's strengthening that unique and diverse neighborhood. That's something that's unique.

"One other thing that I would like to happen in the future is the equity when it comes to the home ownership in the area." The racial disparities in terms of both property rental and residential rental are much higher on the West Bank than the national average. I can only agree with Abdu that moving those figures in the direction of ownership is ideal.[13]

Abdu last saw somebody on a tall bike at a block party in Cedar-Riverside.

West Bank Family Dinners

"I don't like to refer to my coworkers as my 'work family,'" my colleague Jenny said to me one day. "It normalizes toxic behavior that shouldn't be okay at a job."

"True," I responded. "But those toxic behaviors shouldn't be okay in a family, either."

"Facts. But you can't fire a boss, and you can't fire your mom."

"Point taken. You do have to admit you probably spend more time with your coworkers than you do with your family."

"Yeah," Jenny conceded. "But still not family."

Finer points aside, I think there's something to be said about the bonds we make with our "work families"—whether or not we refer to them as such. Working on the West Bank felt very much like a village of new cousins, aunties, and uncles, all the more critical for me because I was living so far away from my own relatives. While it was not without its challenges, I loved bringing my kids with me to work. I loved that, after they went on to daycare, if I showed up to work without them I would be jokingly scolded by those who probably preferred to see my kids over me. How lucky was I to earn a living where I could bring my full self to the

13. As of 2019, 84.5 percent of those in the 55454 zip code rented their living space, according to Minnesota Compass. This is a 50 percent higher rental rate than the national average.

office and not have to hide any portion of it? Not that I could have done that well, even if I wanted to . . .

I'd spend weekends making our family's curries and other specialties. During the week, we had plenty of Somali and Ethiopian fare. Holidays give families moments to celebrate together, and the West Bank had moments like that as well. The WBBA's annual business holiday party was one such occasion, and the multicultural dinner event was another. The latter, held each year at Brian Coyle, was a free evening celebration of the community and an opportunity to share a meal with fellow West Bank residents in communion. Catered by the restaurants in the neighborhood, it also gave folks a chance to sample the local selection.

Friends hug in Cedar-Riverside

Each year, we'd pack the gym, pulling tons of tables from storage to set up a gymnasium-sized dining room with rows and rows of tables from end to end. A final, longer row of tables would spread along the far side of the wall to be lined for paper plates and utensils, food, and refreshments: water and, of course, Somali tea.

There would be entertainment and activities from the youth, like spoken word and poetry readings. Oromia Youth dancers performed traditional dancing, leaving the music on after they were done for all the kids to continue dancing throughout the evening. Sometimes Nick would join; other times it would just be Madeline, me, and the rest of our West Bank family.

As I wrote in *It's Never Going to Work*, terrible coworkers can make a decent job unbearable, but a great job combined with wonderful colleagues is without rival. Never did I feel that sentiment more than during events like the multicultural dinner at Brian Coyle.

Ghosts and Muses

› ANDREA SWENSSON

I first met Andrea on the patio of Palmer's in 2012. What was supposed to be a pretty brief interview for the West Bank Music Festival turned into a much longer enjoyable conversation about the West Bank, music, and other nerdery. We've stayed in touch over the years through our work supporting women in the Minnesota music industry—on the West Bank and beyond.

> **West Bank is for locals.**

Andrea Swensson

Both writers, we bonded over the awkward necessities of blending in with the normals, a sometimes painful process exacerbated by the fog of parenthood. Andrea is one of my favorite writers, in part because I love her process and the style of writing it produces. She combs through archives and records and the various bits and pieces history leaves for us to view. She weaves them together with eloquence, bringing a depth of understanding few surface-level authors ever reach.

› On her connection to the West Bank . . .

"I first came around in college. As a person who works in music, it's one of those corridors that I always found myself on, but never at the same place. There were so many venues.

"I went to Hard Times in college a lot in the late '90s. They let you smoke cigarettes there!" She laughs. "I often needed a place to go in the middle of the night and write. I loved that. That's around when I saw my first shows at the Triple Rock and 400 Bar. I spent my teen years in Apple Valley, my friends and I going to Sunday-night dance parties and Cheapo like nerds. 'We're in Uptown, guys! Wow!'"

› On changes in the neighborhood . . .

"I feel like from a music standpoint, it has lost a lot of the venues, big landmark ones for the rock community. I've not yet been to Part Wolf, but it seemed for a while we were losing all these spaces, and the places for up-and-coming music were disappearing, which was disappointing.

"One thing I think is great is the East African community is so much more visible now than it once was. There are more restaurants, 400 Bar is a community space now. That's just a very visible change."

Our conversation turns once more to art and writing, and the fine line between creation and obsession.

"When the 400 Bar closed," she said, "I went nuts and interviewed sixteen artists for a 116-year history of the bar. Nobody told me to do that. Sometimes you just become obsessed. I made it into an hour-long audio documentary. It felt like it was something that was needed."

"That was a beautiful piece. It felt like an appropriate and respectful eulogy to a very special space."

"Thank you. It was fun to write. It needed to be written. I feel like that's a part of the West Bank, too. Like, when you travel to a different city you go to the spot with character. The West Bank is that spot. If you were trying to show someone a lot of stuff in one visit, you could try to go here, here, or here or you could just take them to the West Bank and they could experience a bunch of stuff all together.

"It almost feels like a small town within the city in that way. It's dense, it's eclectic, there's so many characters, and you feel like you're going to run into people you know. It has so much character and history and depth in that way. Sadly, I wonder if we're going to lose a lot of that."

› On what remains the same . . .

"The vibe of the West Bank is that it's so welcoming to radical people and anyone that's outside the norm. That has remained consistent throughout. There's still West Bankers from the Koerner, Ray & Glover and Willie Murphy days. They are still interwoven with punk rock and the underground hip-hop scene at the Red Sea. There's just this cool, underground alternative vibe to it. The community has been able to cultivate it because it doesn't have one prevailing scene or group of people that own it. It's so eclectic, so it feels inclusive in that way—it belongs to everyone."

› On the neighborhood culture . . .

"The East African community is so much more visible and also engrained in every aspect of that area now. It feels very international in a way that other parts of the city don't. And losing some of those predominantly white spaces has an upside. It doesn't feel quite so starkly segregated in the way it sometimes would when you were going out to those places years ago."

› On the nightlife . . .

"It always felt very unpredictable. Not in a bad way—just, you never knew what was going to happen. I was pretty young at that point, in my late teens and early twenties. I never felt unsafe. It never felt like 'Oh, I'm going to get mugged,' but it definitely had a vibe of 'You never know what's gonna happen on the West Bank!'

"The West Bank just has a vibrancy to it that other places don't. If you go downtown, you see a lot of people that don't live in the city—people are going there to get shitfaced and take a cab back to Minnetonka. But the West Bank feels like it's for people who live there or live nearby. It feels like you kind of have to know what it is, and you have to get to know what's there to want to hang out there, you know? West Bank is for locals."

› On her "West Bank story" ...

"The ghost story, of course!" We both laugh as we immediately recall the time we had a close encounter with ghosts at the Southern Theater. "The other that came to mind is sitting on the patio of Palmer's Bar and getting to know Lisa Hammer. I wasn't doing an interview at that time, but it just turned into a three-hour-long hang."

Lisa Hammer at Palmer's, holding court

"Like ours," I recall.

"Totally! And that was Palmer's, too."

"That's what Palmer's patio does."

"Right? It's just so ... perfect. Everyone just seemed like they knew each other and hung out there every day. It was such a beautiful group of people, and Lisa was so welcoming and awesome and open. She was, like, *presiding* over the patio and making sure everyone was happy. It felt like you could stay there forever."

› On what she imagines for the future ...

"I guess I appreciated more of the history of it going through the article I wrote for the 400 Bar and realizing it's always been an important space for immigrant communities. And now such a big East African population lives there. I guess in my mind it's a place where people coming here can feel welcome and share their traditions and cultures with the rest of Minneapolis in a way that isn't marginalizing and feels authentic and respectful. It's an important part of that community, and I just hope that is always at the heart of it. That the West Bank is a place where people feel welcome."

Andrea's husband once found a pink tall bike abandoned in an alley. He would ride it around the big room of the carriage house where they used to live, making circles around the piano while Andrea played.

Good Ghosts

P atio season in Minnesota is great. As the snow melts and temperatures climb, the tables and chairs appear overnight. Minnesotans run outside on the first 60-degree day in shorts and flip-flops, ready to Frisbee.

Andrea and I met for drinks one afternoon in 2015, this time at Republic at Seven Corners. Happy hours at pubs and restaurants are packed with the aficionados of spring, a well-needed boost for Minnesotans' vitamin D levels and businesses' bottom lines. West Bank patio crowds thicken up again in the later evening as theaters and venues release their audiences from shows and concerts.

We sat on the patio and discussed women in music, the Minnesota music scene, West Bank history, and writing. We talked and talked until it was nearing bar close and the crowd around us slowed. Our conversation turned to the Southern, just steps away from where we were sitting.

"I have a confession," Andrea said quietly, leaning in. "I've never actually been to the Southern."

"What?!" I shouted.

"I was supposed to go a few times, but I feel like stuff kept coming up. I was supposed to go the other week, even, and the show got canceled."

"Let's go!" I proclaimed, tossing my napkin onto my abandoned plate. "We can go now—do you wanna?!"

"Um, *yes!*" she exclaimed.

The Southern Theater, by the way, is totally haunted. Old neighborhoods have old ghosts. I punched in my door code and unlocked the deadbolt. Even though we had the keys for entry, and my office was the first door on the right, it felt quite like we were sneaking in.

I showed Andrea our little front office and some of the music memorabilia I had collected from the neighborhood. We went on a mini tour, walking through the first level and then heading upstairs. I hit the theater lights to spotlight the beautiful historic arches, a stunning time capsule one would never expect from the building's otherwise nondescript façade. After I shut down the lights, we went back to the lobby.

We were standing at the counter and continuing our chat when we heard—not subtly—the sound of a child laughing from upstairs. As we perked up our ears, the sound was followed immediately by a door slamming. Having just been through the building ourselves, we knew not a soul was up there. At least, no living soul. At that moment, what felt like a giant cobweb hit my face, and we both screamed and ran toward the front door, shrieking and laughing. We got outside, wide-eyed, still laughing hysterically in a mix of fear and amusement.

"What the heck was that?" Andrea said.

"I have no idea," I replied. When we bravely went back in to investigate, the doors were exactly as we had left them upstairs. I locked up the building and we headed out, walking together to our cars lest any creepy spirit attempt to follow us home.

As I returned to my office the following morning, I remember my hair standing on end just a little bit. Whoever the ghosts were, I just hoped they were nice. And that they stayed asleep during the day!

A West Bank Story

› DAN PROZINSKI

I officially met Dan Prozinski through his board work at the West Bank Business Association—but, though I didn't realize it, in very Twin Cities fashion we knew each other via a different channel as well. My husband, Nick, a musician, knew Dan through Willie's guitar shop in St. Paul, and we had run into one another at various gatherings in the music community.

> **" The West Bank has been a place I can be creative and live at the same time. It's perfect. "**

Dan is a graphic designer, musician, and inventor. His Harparatus, a patented creation born out of his own need for a better tool for singing and playing harmonica, does away with the traditional neck rack and allows a musician to play harmonica from a microphone stand instead.

As is West Bank fashion, we came to be as much friends as we were colleagues, and I got to know his family as well. His daughters would join him as he came to area cleanups and, as they grew older, were our first babysitters before they went on to college. I appreciated Dan's perspective as a longtime West Bank resident and local business owner, running his graphic design enterprise from the West Bank for years. In addition, he's a Minneapolis history buff, so I knew I had to interview him for this project.

› On his connection to the West Bank . . .

"Ohhhh . . . I was coming here in the late '70s to experience the music. I had a love for the neighborhood. And in my young adult years, I was looking for a place that I could be creative and live at the same time. I ended up

Dan and Chester (photo taken by Marsha)

on Seven Corners, renting an apartment above a recording studio. I came here and I never left!

"When I saw Samuelson's came up for sale, my fiancée, Sue, and I fell in love with the place. The old Samuelson's building became my work studio, my graphic design studio, my music studio. And then, we had kids—and our family lives here, we raised our girls here. It's a live/work space. It's perfect."

› On food . . .

"Before I was married, I used to go up the street to the outdoor grill at the Cabooze for a chicken breast sandwich and a beer. But later, with Sue and the girls and I, our favorite was the K-Wok, a great mix of Asian fusion foods. That woman could cook! Otherwise, the foods around here haven't changed a lot."

› On changes in the neighborhood . . .

"Just in the residential population, the hippies are gone, there's not as many students living here. I think it's more new-citizen families. That's a big change, but the nightlife seems to still be the same. It's not maybe always

Samuelson's Confectionery (image courtesy Minnesota Historical Society)

as local, like the Viking Bar used to be local—maybe Palmer's is still largely a local crowd.

"A big change was some of the retail. The hippie retail, the Depth of Fields and those types of places.

"Our number of live venues is certainly down. The ones that survive are still popular. I hope they can hang on—I think there's a demand for it, if we can get beyond COVID."

› On what remains the same . . .

"The diversity, and that it still feels like an exciting place to be. You know, the connections here are so great. This isn't a reflection of the neighborhood composition per se, but I like being able to get anywhere easily from here. North, south, east, west—it's easy to get anywhere from here. The institutional presence has stayed largely the same, too."

› On the neighborhood culture...

"That's hard for me to answer because I don't get out as much as I used to! There are still West Bankers hanging out at Palmer's and Hard Times. I feel like they're my kin. There's not as much in the way of art stores, craft stores—none of that remains. Restaurants and theaters are the most consistent things we have."

We discuss the history of Seven Corners, how the Southern used to be more active than it is now, and Balls Cabaret's long-standing run in the area.

› On his "West Bank story"...

"Oh, this is a good one," Dan says excitedly. "I thought about this—I think you'll appreciate this one.

"So a while back, I lived above where Surrinder's office is now. It wasn't his office at the time—it had been a recording studio, but it was vacant. My band was playing at the 400 one night. I had to drive down because I had all my gear.

"On my way to the show, I saw this giant dog—this big schnauzer running free. And my neighbor above the pawn shop had a giant schnauzer, so I assumed it was his dog, and I was able to coax him into my car. So now I had my guitar and the gear and there's this giant schnauzer that I had to leave in the car while we did the gig, but it's a cool night and it's better than leaving the dog to run down Washington Avenue. So afterwards, we were having a big party back at my place, all of us up on the roof with this giant dog, since my neighbor wasn't home yet.

Dan Prozinski at the 2015 West Bank Vision

"And that's the first night I met my wife, Sue. We're all partying with this giant schnauzer. And it turned out Sue's childhood pet was a giant schnauzer named Josh. He died in her arms at the vet's office, and she grieved for him terribly. And here I am, I'm this guy that saved this dog.

"Well, I finally got ahold of my neighbor. And I said, 'Hey, I've got your dog,' and he said, 'What are you talking about, man? My dog's right here!'

"So—I've got this dog and I'm wondering . . . whose dog is this?!

"Schnauzers were still pretty rare, and my neighbor contacted his breeder, and his breeder knew who the owner was. We got ahold of the owner—apparently the dog took off and he hadn't been able to find him. He was so grateful.

"But . . . yeah. That's how I met my wife. We're a West Bank story."

› On what he imagines for the future . . .

"I imagine a little inner-city neighborhood island that is timeless. It retains its quirky nature, its arts component. I would love to see our parking lots developed into something for the community. If they want to encourage homeowners, you could have a series of live/work spaces that were like townhomes, perhaps with first floors that worked both as a person's studio and as their retail space.

"If they're going to develop the 1400 block of Washington Avenue, with its old brick storefronts, the area around Byerlys and Nye's in Northeast Minneapolis is a good example to follow: save the shops and build something behind it. Maybe micro housing, or micro apartments, if done right. I love the history here, and I value the lessons we can learn from it. I'm inspired by it, by the hard work and the lives that came before us. I like to see the better parts of history preserved in what comes next.

"Did you know just one block east of here, where the U of M now has a wildflower garden, there used to be a grade school called the Peabody School? It was a beautiful little brick castle. And down Fifteenth behind me? There was a beautiful public library, churches, and a synagogue. It's just—all gone. Gone. To think that Samuelson's girls, they were born and raised here. They just had to skip down the block to go to church and school. I would want people to know that those types of communities, built whole for the people who lived there . . . they worked before, and they can work again."

As we wrap up our chat, I simultaneously feel pangs of nostalgia imagining the neighborhood as it once was and optimism for the future.

The last time Dan saw somebody on a tall bike was between the law school and the ball field, right near the riverbanks, near where the Bohemian Flats once were. A small group of folks were biking toward the Mississippi River. One of them was on a tall bike.

Hiding in Plain Sight

I made my way toward the Mississippi, turning toward an out-of-the-way parking lot close to the River Road. At the far end, I walked beyond the concrete supports and found myself standing underneath the Tenth Avenue Bridge.

A hundred years ago, the surrounding area was known as Bohemian Flats, a collection of shanties that made their peace with the river. The community shared resources and space until, over time, the city cleared the flats for development and reclamation of the riverbeds for public use.

By 1963, Bohemian Flats was completely gone. Decades later, in the late '90s, an avid cyclist, artist, and West Banker named Chester brought their spirit with him. Over the course of two decades, Chester built his home—from bedroom to kitchen—underneath the secure footing of the Tenth Avenue bridge.

Chester on a bike during the West Bank Ride

This home under the bridge was a magical space not unlike a time capsule from a different era. As my late friend Daniel Polnau said at the time, "It's like this place had a charm over it. It's incredible it has remained this way for so long." Dan was a character, an artist and puppeteer who passed away before his time.

Chester himself passed away in 2018, and his partner, Marsha, passed away not long after. Although the dwelling had previously been protected and exempted from the restrictions and displacement that besieged other encampments, the city was now planning to remove it. We had a few things to do before that happened. A public commemoration for the couple was scheduled, but one chilly morning before that, a few West Bankers gathered to commemorate them quietly in their home, to share stories, and to help preserve some of their things for history. I'm grateful to Cameron Gordon, Allen Christian, and local author Mary Jane LaVigne for conducting the cleanup and preservation with such care.

Most of what I did that morning was listen. Honestly, a lot of my job is to listen. That day, I listened to other folks who knew Chester as they shared their stories and talked about how they knew him and Marsha. When it was my turn, what I shared was this: as long as I'd known the West Bank, I'd known Chester, and he was as much a part of this neighborhood for me as had been anything else. It was hard for me to imagine the West Bank without him, and in many ways I never will. When I think about institutions that make up the tapestry of our neighborhood, Chester was a cornerstone.

When I coordinated the first West Bank ride in 2014, we had a pretty small attendance, but the people who came to the event were a broad mix: guests, business owners and staff, residents. Including Chester. I saw that he joined the ride, going from stop to stop, creating drawings along the way. I spoke with him briefly outside the Acadia, and his presence, to me, was a sign that we were on the right path with the work we were doing for the West Bank. We were aiming for inclusivity for the people and businesses that make up the fabric of this community—our events should be for everyone.

All around us are people we touch directly: our friends and family, our colleagues, our neighbors. But there are people we affect indirectly. I've heard friends and community members describe themselves as feeling "invisible." Left out. Unwelcome at certain events and activities. I've made a concerted effort to see where my knowledge gaps are. I have had some cringe-worthy moments when I've missed the mark considerably. I continue to try to improve in this regard, and it's a constant, nonlinear learning process.

As the group of us helped gather some of Chester's artwork for preservation, as well as books that Mary Jane LaVigne thoughtfully saved for Little Free Libraries, I found a postcard hanging in one of his image galleries. It was from one of Altered Esthetics' first Bike Art shows, from ten or more years prior—one of the first art shows I organized. Chester had taken the postcard from the exhibit and added it to his carefully curated collection of art, posters, and other mementos. I was simply floored.

This was a year I struggled tremendously with self-worth and imposter syndrome. A lot of my peers were feeling this way, too, and while I hated to see other people I admired having those same painful self-doubts, it did help me not to feel so alone. This was a year when I

A Chester original at one of our West Bank Ride booths

did a lot of reevaluation, self-checks, and even some affirmations to help offset those feelings.

But finding that postcard in Chester and Marsha's home, from an event over ten years ago—to know that I impacted somebody in a positive way—felt like a little star falling from the universe to let me know that I was doing okay. In this work, on this path.

The next week, I had a different opportunity: to hear my friend Joan Vorderbruggen speak about ethical redevelopment. One thing she said in her presentation especially resonated with me: "I've asked myself if I could pick up the passion I feel about this work and put it in another place, and the answer is . . . no. Not quite in the same way."

The West Bank Business Association's mission is this: "WBBA exists to engage the business community in the responsible economic development of the West Bank district while preserving the unique character and heritage of the Cedar-Riverside area." I did my best to help fulfill that mission and to bring my whole self to it.

 # Sunbeams

› MICHELLE KWAN

Michelle is one of my favorite people to work with on the West Bank—sunny, cheerful, and upbeat, even when the going gets rough. Michelle grew up on the West Bank, above the Keefer Court Bakery and Cafe. The Kwan family is a fixture of the neighborhood, and Keefer Court is a cornerstone space.

> **The West Bank is my home! It's my playground. It's what raised me to be the person I am today.**

I'm able to connect with Michelle as things gradually began to reopen for the summer, to see how both she and Keefer Court are doing.

"How are you doing?" I ask.

"I'm doing good in terms of the neighborhood. The neighborhood is really strong. Even with the current situation, we're in a good place in terms of stability. There could always be more resources, and more help. But watching the community come together—both businesses and residents—has been very uplifting. That sense of community, I've always believed in it. But during the protests and even during COVID, it just shows we are there for each other."

› On her connection to the West Bank...

"Well, the West Bank is my home! It's my playground. It's what raised me to be the person I am today. Growing up on Cedar-Riverside shaped me to be who I am. I had a slightly different take than the rest of my siblings growing up here, but I feel like I embrace the neighborhood. The diversity has been something I've held on to and appreciated. It just shows connectivity

Jamie and Michelle cutting the ribbon at the new mural, 2019

and community, and an ever-changing climate to what cultures are like in America.

"I grew up in one of the most culturally and economically diverse neighborhoods, and it gives me a lot of hope for refugees and the diversity, culture, and integration within our communities. I love it. I love the West Bank. I love Cedar-Riverside, and I hope to continue to see it grow for the communities that are there."

› On food...

"What's your favorite spot for lunch, other than Keefer Court, of course?" I ask. Michelle laughs.

"So it all depends on the time frame—the restaurants have changed so much," she says. "When I was little, next door to us used to be a place called Perfume River, a Vietnamese restaurant. As a kid, I used to *love* going next door. I'd ask my parents for a couple dollars to walk over and get spring rolls. I did that up until I was eight or nine, when they closed.

"After that, as I got a little bit older I would go over to the Wienery—this is before KJ and Pat bought it. I remember one day walking down the block. Perhaps my parents didn't know I was going down the street." She laughs again, and pauses. "You know, I didn't see it the way they did; I just walked around the neighborhood. 'This is what people do, they walk around their neighborhood!' I ventured over to the Wienery. I grew up in Chicago a bit, and the Chicago hot dog was my jam!

"As an adult I appreciate Dilla and the Red Sea. I mean, I *really* enjoy Dilla's food. I kind of have this 'Oh my god this food is so good!' I love it there; I'll keep going back. That's one of the things I love about West Bank restaurants. All these restaurants have been there for ages, and it's just kind of like—you don't know about it. But when you go to it, you're like, 'This is what the West Bank is all about!' These hidden-gem restaurants. They aren't all over social media, you're not reading about it in blogs, it's just a delicious restaurant and you don't get to try it when you're at the trendy places.

"Also, where Malabari is—that used to be a Korean restaurant called Korea House. We'd go there as a family. That was probably the only restaurant I can remember [where] we as a family would go together to eat. . . . It was amazing. That's one of the things, now as an adult, I can appreciate. There's a huge East African community now. Growing up, that community was so different. It was full of Korean and Vietnamese communities, and the restaurants reflected that. But as the years went along, there was that cultural shift and the restaurants changed to reflect that."

› On changes in the neighborhood . . .

"Culturally, things have changed, and the demographic that is thriving right now in the community. When I grew up, there was a lot of Asian refugees in the neighborhood. I remember one summer I came home and started school, and we started seeing new people. We weren't exposed to the Muslim community much as kids until then. Seeing the physical changes in terms of different demographics of people and learning about this community and understanding who they were, why they were coming to Minneapolis, and understanding the differences—that was interesting to experience as a young kid.

"Growing up, there was at first a huge hippie community and even bikers. People were in the neighborhood on a daily basis, the tall-bike grungy crew, punk rockers at Triple Rock, bikers at Cabooze. Hard Times still brings in the tall-bike crew, but it's not as prevalent.

"People grew up and out of the neighborhood. Growing up, we had a lot of Vietnamese friends—they are older than me. The common thread was 'We got jobs, and we're moving the family out of the neighborhood.' They eventually bought their own homes. That has historically been the American dream for immigrants. Their parents come with literally nothing, the kids build on that and move into a home. They are having this 'American life' as everybody sees it as. But believing that it does work, they don't have to stay in poverty. I'm not saying West Bank is poverty, only that the neighborhood is the starting point for many families. People have a sense of pride for the neighborhood and come back later. That's the best part: when they come back to show their kids around. I remember a family came in and told me, 'I remember there used to be arcade games in the hallway. I broke the window and had to tell your parents.'"

› On what remains the same . . .

"We consistently have outreach in the neighborhood and a sense of connection. This comes from the work people are doing. People like you—you are doing a lot in the neighborhood. You tried to revamp Cedarfest. I remember coming back from my time in China and getting more involved.

"I just feel like there's consistently people in the neighborhood that are trying to continue to unite the neighborhood and keep us connected instead of segregating us. There was definitely a point in time where there started to be a bit of the divide because of the cultural differences, but having community members and the associations to get us together and coexist with events and meetings—it is so helpful.

"Like, the West Bank Night Market was awesome. That's something I noticed, being a part of the community development. Participating in that led to other things, the neighborhood community people coming out and inviting us to the different activities that were going on. With different business and property owners reaching out and coming in to introduce themselves and support our business, that's always been strong within the neighborhood."

› On the neighborhood culture . . .

"I think it's a tough time right now. It's a high-density neighborhood. I think the neighborhood gets a bad rap in terms of crime and drug rates—that's been difficult for the community because from the outside, people look at the community differently.

"One of the things that I appreciate was the youth group that was involved in the night watch. We sit here and a lot of people talk about how bad the neighborhood has been for the kids and all the troublemakers, but it's like—these youth. I think the cultural shift has been different, but I think we're not supporting youth enough in the community. That has a lot to do with the outside perspective of Cedar-Riverside. I sometimes hear negative things from outsiders who don't know the community, and what they see. That's just not what it's like when you live here.

"Also, one of the changes I've noticed that makes me smile: the amount of Somali representatives that are running for office. Especially in this specific neighborhood. It's because people care so much—they grew up here, they know what changes need to happen."

› On the nightlife . . .

"Oh, Cedar was popping! To have the Red Sea bar at the end of our block and 400 Bar across the street, Acadia, Nomad, and Palmer's on one side, Viking Bar, Republic, Triple Rock—it was *loud* on Cedar!" Michelle laughs. "On Friday and Saturday, our walls would shake. You could hear the bass from the Red Sea.

"When Triple Rock used to be Blondie's, you could hear the Harley-Davidsons—but it was like music to my ears. It was my lullaby to put me to sleep. I moved to Florida to work at Disney World one summer and I heard crickets, and I couldn't sleep at *all*." She laughs again. "I missed the bass and motorcycles!

"It was also super busy. I remember in high school, I couldn't come home between midnight and 1:30 because the cul-de-sac was *packed*, and I couldn't drive into our driveway. There were just so many people with cars trying to leave at bar time.

"There would be times when shootings would happen, too. I remember one year on July 4th, my mom was at home with her friends playing mah-jongg and the real fireworks went off. Then around 12:30, we heard what we thought were fireworks and we looked out the window—and it was a shooting. And at the time, I was surprised something like that would happen. Every once in a while, things would happen. But it was so rare. It never made me scared of the neighborhood. I never was fearful to go outside at night. My friend lived in Dinkytown; I would take the city bus home, before I had a car, and walk back. I was aware of my surroundings but never scared. . . .

"I traveled a bunch, too, and I trust my instinct. I think that's a part of why I appreciate the neighborhood and see the neighborhood in perhaps a different light than my family. I did hang out in the neighborhood—I explored and felt more comfortable."

› On her "West Bank story" . . .

"One of the earlier stories I can think about is—I must have been six or seven years old. I was hanging out at the roundabout behind our block. I had just learned how to ride a bicycle, and I was painting my bike with paint and a toothbrush. At one point the back door was open to the Red Sea. I remember riding around and peeking in. The bartender saw me and said, 'You want some pineapple juice?' And so I popped up and was sitting at the bar, drinking pineapple juice. You know, only on the West Bank could a six-year-old walk into a bar and get pineapple juice! Well, maybe that happens in other neighborhoods and small towns where the family knows the bar.

"The other thing is only on the West Bank can you check out 400 Bar and check out super grungy music and then head over to Nomad and hear this other genre and jump over to Palmer's and hear bluegrassy music and go to Triple Rock and get super punk music. The diversity is not just in who lives here but in the music venues, too."

› On what she imagines for the future ...

"That one's hard. It's very uncertain. The first thing I think of is with what happened this past year and that building they were trying to build." Michelle is referencing a city-led development behind the Keefer Court building. "That kind of gave me some uncertainty. What is this neighborhood going to look like, and how will it change for better and for worse?

"Also, I wonder about the sustainability of the businesses. The pharmacy recently closed down—Ross Westbank Pharmacy has always been there; they were also good family friends. That was an era that's slowly starting to disappear." Ross Westbank Pharmacy was one of the few family-owned pharmacies left in Minneapolis. It closed only a few years ago.

"I think COVID has been hard on the businesses, especially in terms of the bars, the long-standing businesses who have been there for a while. What does this change mean for our businesses? Midwest Mountaineering has been doing great—they'll have the support because of the type of businesses they have and that people come to them. Some of us that are smaller, it depends on the climate and the economy, how things are going.

"I don't know what lies ahead for the future of Cedar-Riverside. Keefer Court, we're uncertain of where things are going to go for us. How long do we see ourselves on the West Bank? How much longer can we sustain our presence? Especially if property taxes keep going up so much. I've been trying to wrap my head around it, but we've been on the West Bank for almost four decades! We've made our stake with the community and Minneapolis. As my dad put it, change opens up opportunity. If we were to close, then somebody else could have what we've had the opportunity to do for decades—it would open up another opportunity for somebody else. It could be a blessing for us, too. If somebody wants space and wants to do good about it, that's something we could be a part of and help make that happen."

"That's true," I respond. "And a much more positive way to look at it. To have a hand in shaping that—that would be good. I mean, could you imagine a McDonald's on this intersection?"

"Oh, no," Michelle says. "Something like a chain store on the intersection would totally change the neighborhood. Honestly, I think if Hard Times goes, I think that's when the neighborhood would see a drastic change."

The last time Michelle saw somebody on a tall bike was just the other day, a few blocks from the West Bank at the Seward Café, a worker-owned cooperative. She was waiting in line, and an older gentleman with long white hair came in on a tall bike. She recognized him but couldn't quite place where from.

"There was just this familiarity to him," she says. "Ten years ago, that's all it was, all over—tall bikes. Guys and girls riding around the Cedar-Riverside neighborhood. I can't remember the last time I saw somebody other than last week. I don't see them as much anymore."

Cornerstones

ome neighborhood cornerstones are monumental—like Riverside Plaza gracing nearly every view of the West Bank. Others are more subtle, yet no less fundamental to the neighborhood's composition—this is the case with Keefer Court Bakery and Cafe. Owned and operated by the Kwan family since 1983, Keefer Court is a Chinese bakery and restaurant right at the intersection of Cedar and Riverside avenues. A long, narrow building, it runs along Riverside, with a storefront popping out onto Cedar. Sunny and Paulina own the restaurant and raised their children in the apartments upstairs, the family and restaurant ever present in the community as the landscape shifted around them.

In the days when Madeline was coming with me to work, sometimes we'd head to Keefer Court before going home. We'd sit in the little café across from each other and share some chicken fried rice, Madeline playing with her chopsticks before moving along to fistfuls of rice, toddler-style.

Keefer Court was quietly involved in neighborhood activities, setting up a booth with buns and baked goods at the music festival and joining us for the night market. Michelle even served on our board for some time, continuing the trend among West Bank businesses of helping guide the organization. Eventually, her parents began to think about retirement. They wanted to keep the business in the family, and it came to rest with Michelle, the youngest. As she planned for this transition, she trained in the various roles at the restaurant, getting a good picture of the nature of the business and how its operations ticked. It reminded me of my experience years ago with Marie's, where I had the best managers.

In 2019, one day of our West Bank Crash Course workshops focused on climate change and our district being part of Minneapolis's Green Zones Initiative. We discussed the concept of food sovereignty and how climate change connects to communities like ours. We learned about aquaponics, mass transit, and walkable neighborhoods. "Why do I need a car?" one resident contributed. "I can take the light rail anywhere I need to go or walk to the store." Though some businesses still relied on car traffic, it did seem the neighborhood was on the precipice of change.

Louis Alemayehu, a local leader in this effort as well as a spoken-word artist, cohosted one of the sessions. He was among those who spoke about food sovereignty:

> Small, local businesses play an essential role in the food security of a neighborhood and also can be sites for a creation of food justice and food-justice initiatives. It's a matter of how business owners want to be in relationship with a neighborhood: if they want to be in a neighborhood to extract wealth from it or if they want to be in a neighborhood to contribute to its vitality. Part of businesses leading the charge in food security and food-justice work is to help make communities sustainable.

Small businesses often bear the brunt of policy changes, shifts in the economy, and crises of many kinds. New governmental requirements, rent increases, and supply-chain woes for food and goods often have a harder impact on small businesses. We knew West Bank businesses in our district would be affected by a variety of incoming policy shifts, and we aimed to start preparing them before it became an emergency.

The light rail infrastructure was a blessing we had that other districts didn't, but we wanted to get businesses set up for other things as well—like recycling, composting, and encouraging pedestrian, cycling, and transit-oriented traffic. All were part of helping our district's economy, but also part of preparing us for climate change and what it might bring to the district.

Louis said, "There's going to be a lot of pain whether we want it or not, but there's also a lot of opportunities. Whatever the new world is going to be, it's either going to come through us or over us."

Especially in recent years, Keefer Court has worked to prepare for the inevitable changes. The West Bank is great about leaning in to its strengths and its values. Small, local, fiercely independent, and ever prepared for what comes next.

The Little Night Market That Could

The West Bank Night Market that happened during Northern Spark was more than a display of neighborhood togetherness. It also activated a long-vacant space that was the very definition of underutilized. Dania Hall was still an empty lot, Al-Karama Cedar Square to one side and the Nomad's bocce courts to the other. It was a tricky space during late evenings, when traffic from bars was picking up—the open, dark area was a safety concern for both those coming to visit and those living in the district. However, when activated with events like Northern Spark, the space would come to life.

Although Northern Spark wouldn't be in our area the next year, we decided to bring the night market back. In 2018, we hosted two market events to complement the Cedar's Global Roots Festival and Palmer's Palmfest, both happening across the street. We started the events early in the afternoon at the request of vendors, but it was nighttime when things started hoppin'. Folks heading to the bars or out for a smoke would pop over and check over artist goods or grab some late-night snacks from Keefer Court's booth. While it wasn't an outrageous moneymaker for everyone involved, there was clearly potential, especially with the crossover traffic. And Keefer Court sold out of its new curry recipe the very first night!

In the late hours of the evening, local musician Jarrelle Barton found his way to the market. Guests sat together in the glow of the lights, listening to the ethereal sounds of his guzheng. Another magical night of music on the West Bank and a moment stamped forever in my memory.

The following year, we decided to try the night market on summer Saturdays, building on the momentum of years prior. It did not go as seamlessly as we hoped.

Coua Lee, creating sand art live at the night market

Fundraising efforts to run the event all summer through fell short, but, learning from our past mistakes, we planned a modest kickoff with gradual growth planned over the coming weeks. We had a pretty small team for implementation, so it was all hands on deck. As we arrived, little by little our excitement kept getting stomped. The power was cut to the lot (apparently the source we used the previous year had been illegally installed). The fence around the perimeter was broken. And the lot was in dire need of some deep cleaning.

After those issues, permit lags, and what seemed like the world's longest and most indecisive thunderstorm, we finally had the first West Bank Night Market of the year. A few vendors backed out because the looming storm cut into their prep time, but staff thought it would be good to give it a go with the folks that were ready for a soft launch.

We gathered as a group to pull things from our storage shed, loading tents and chairs and tables and lights and cleaning supplies little by little into the Dania Hall lot. Our night market would be mostly tabled by entrepreneurs from the neighborhood, excited to test their new products and goods out and share their wares.

Though we had cleaned up the lot earlier that week during one of our neighborhood cleanups, it seemed there were some new additions.

"Uh, what's that big black thing?" I asked.

Toward the front of the lot, visible from even across the street, was a big black lump of . . . we weren't sure. We did yet another round of cleaning, but whatever this was, it was wet, heavy, and impossible to move—least of all into a trash bag. Turned-up concrete mixed with trash? Your guess is as good as ours. We got to work cleaning the rest of the lot again and began putting up tents and lights.

What had formerly been the Nomad and was now Part Wolf, the neighboring bar, was gracious enough to sponsor us with power. This resolved the first of 2019's night market woes. Even though the sun hadn't set yet, the lights looked adorable strung along the tents and over the fencing. Little by little, the vendors arrived; several shop vendors from the Riverside Mall and a few local nonprofits set up tables and goods. We were small, but we were ready!

With everything settled, we did a quick check-in as a group to make plans for the upcoming week. As we chatted, several additional residents and business owners, including a few artists, made plans to join us for some of the upcoming nights. Even though it felt like we were moving in slow motion to get this rolling, it felt good to be in motion nonetheless.

Hungry from the setup and wanting to get some grub before the event kicked off, my coworker Emily and I went to go get some food from Keefer Court. Emily Peck, who I'd met via the Southern Theater, was working with the WBBA part-time. She brought her event and production experience to our little burgeoning market, and her calm and steady presence was welcome. We waited for our lo mein while a group of women chatted excitedly in the restaurant. Walking back to the event area with our food, we saw a few of the vendors taking their stuff down and heading out.

Wait, what?

"They were bored, so they decided to pack up," Weli, one of the other organizers, explained. I must have looked confused. "They'll be back next week," he said. So, that was that.

With the quick outflux of vendors, our little crew began to take down tents and pack things up. As we packed, a few guests arrived.

"What time does the market start?" one man asked, mistaking our teardown for setup. I explained the situation as optimistically as I could, thanking them so much for making the trip and inviting them back the next week. Unfortunately, they were in town for the weekend from Madison and were just stopping by before the show at the bar. Ooof!

But, as they say, don't let the perfect be the enemy of the good.

I felt like we had bunted the ball, the first night of the market a soft hit toward a larger goal in mind. We left with additional vendors signed up for upcoming weeks, a greater sense for the timing of setup and teardown, more volunteers, and friends from the community excited to get the word out for a market geared toward zip code 55454. Our team felt more connected and in sync, including and especially new staff. And on a purely aesthetic note, the Dania lot was now way cleaner thanks to the cleanup we had done prior to setup.

The night market never quite reached the weekly consistency we hoped it would. We simply didn't have the resources to staff it to the capacity we'd need to really support and boost the vendors. The good part was, we were able get the logistics in place for future markets and other activities in the lot. And because we had budget checks in place, we never went into debt to give the program a shot.

Lessons learned: Night markets are best held and at their most magical at night, even if antsy vendors want an early start. And even good programs that serve a clear need can flounder if they are underresourced.

I'll Leave Regrets for Dead and Sing Along

› ERIK FUNK

Erik Funk is a vocalist and guitarist for Dillinger Four and was one of the owners of the Triple Rock. He's a dad, a fellow music nerd, a business owner, and a husband. And with the success of the Triple Rock, he turned the tables on what was normal, what was punk, and what was feasible for musicians making a living in the industry.

> **The future of the West Bank is small, local businesses that serve the people that live there.**

› On his connection to the West Bank . . .

"I used to hang out with the guys from Studio of the Stars. Before the old Bedlam—back with the Extreme Noise [Records] crew. That was '96 or '97; we would see and play tons of shows. That was the first time I spent any time around the West Bank. I think at that time, Cedarfest was what it was known for. There weren't as many big festivals all the time."

Erik Funk

"Now you can't spit without hitting a festival or two each weekend," I put in. "Well, in normal times."

"Yeah." Erik laughs. "When we were going to open, we were looking for density. Before Blondie's, Five Corners bar was almost the one. We took a long look and eventually decided we didn't want that space. Then, a month or two later, Blondie's went on the market."

› On food . . .

"At that time, I was a vegetarian—we all were—and Triple Rock was only a bar. We'd go across the street for falafel at Med Deli. We would eat there and Hard Times. It wasn't as much of a 'scene,' and people weren't so restaurant-oriented then. Nowadays everyone makes themselves out to be a little bit of a foodie."

› On changes in the neighborhood . . .

"Up until more recently, it was a hippie-ish neighborhood. A transient day-drinking scene. The business of live music changed nationally, even internationally. In the short time we were a venue, the landscape changed—it did for most venues of like size on the West Bank. Twenty years later, it became lots of booking agents and far less DIY. Then there was the consolidation among promoters like First Ave. They were able to gobble up and obtain a major market share.

"There are pros and cons to that, of course, but it made it tough for others to compete. And then there was a proliferation of music venues for a while. In 2003, when we opened up, a lot of other spaces thought they should be a venue. It was more than I thought the Twin Cities could support.

"The West Bank had a lot of live music. Because the cast of characters on the West Bank changed so much for those twenty years, I think we're the only ones that consistently operated in one spot. Everything changed hands at least once or twice—the 400 Bar, the Nomad changed hands three times or so.

"Palmer's was the only one that had an original connection to that Original West Bank Music World. There was a swamper [somebody who cleans up after a bar or restaurant closing] named Danny—he gave us our little bit of West Bank cred. We were 'Danny approved.' We came in and at the time didn't necessarily feel like we were joining a neighborhood with a long musical tradition because we were more of the DIY punk scene invading this area."

› On the nightlife . . .

"Back then, there were more theaters than there are now. That wasn't as much my scene, so I didn't interact with them as much. We were trying to be a venue from the start. We had to find a place where we knew we could do it in the future. Honestly, at the time, we were like, 'A little slice of South Minneapolis here on the West Bank'—we didn't come in and try to be a part of the West Bank."

"That's so interesting you say that," I interject. "For so many of us, you were an absolute cornerstone."

Erik laughs. "I guess. I think part of that is just the longevity. Over the span of time, you're gonna be a lot of people's first show ever, first bar ever. If you stick around long enough, you're going to be that place for a lot of people. I feel like we were kind of successful in spite of being on the West Bank."

Gasp—heresy!

"Really, though, just as the years went by, especially in the later years— definitely in the last five years—it was a struggle," he continues. "We originally had a patio outdoors, and it was popular. When we decided to build the venue, we decided to just get rid of the patio. We did not see the smoking ban coming!" He laughs again. Minnesota banned indoor smoking in 2007. "Now places wouldn't think to open without one. Even a year before it happened, it seemed like 'Never! Never in the Midwest!' So . . . that hurt our nonshow businesses, not having that patio. When it's nice out, people want to be outside."

"What would be ideal? That it would stay smaller, local businesses that serve the people that actually live there. It's a dense neighborhood. It's a good, functioning, reasonably safe, pedestrian-oriented neighborhood. That's the best case.

"One of the biggest ways we were useful to the West Bank community was as a pair of eyes on the street. We had someone posted on that corner every night for twenty years. The people that did that job did a huge service to that whole neighborhood. They developed relationships, they saw things before they got out of hand.

"But the future of it as a center for smaller live music venues?" Erik pauses as he ponders. "Triple Rock's space, that's one less now; 400 Bar was one less. I think that trend will continue. But I think, I hope, that the Cedar will survive all. That Palmer's will survive all."

Erik hasn't seen somebody on a tall bike in at least a few years.

The Last Dance

C hange has a heartbeat pattern to it. Nothing is the same from moment to moment when we look at how the blood flows. With each beat, it moves through the body, pumping ever forward. Sometimes there's an episode of irregularity, but the blood keeps moving.

Sometimes we fall in love and our heart skips a beat, but the blood keeps flowing. Sometimes our heart races in fear, and extra adrenaline propels us fast and furious to the Next Big Thing. And sometimes, our heart breaks. And even though it's not a literal break, it can certainly feel like it, and our body moves a little more slowly, a little more sadly.

MN music moms at the Triple-Rock

It was a whisper first before it became real, as is often the case with West Bank rumors.

"I hear the Triple Rock is closing," my colleague Yasameen said to me one day.

"What?!" I responded, agog. "I knew things were tight, but I haven't heard anything about them literally closing. I hope it's just a rumor."

But within a month or two, that whisper proved to be true. Our beloved Triple Rock Social Club, cornerstone venue of the West Bank, home of punk and endless late-night revelry, was to close in the fall of 2017.

It seemed like everything was happening all at once on all sides of life, in a flurry of activity and planning. I was feeling grotesquely pregnant and uncomfortable by that point in my sickly and less-than-blissful second pregnancy.

We went to as many shows as we could and ate there as often as possible. We hosted a kid-friendly morning brunch for Moms in Minnesota Music (much to the chagrin of more hungover guests, I assume).

The Triple Rock's last day would be November 22, 2017. Small Business Saturday would be November 25. My due date fell in between. Unlike the West Bank Music Festival, Small Business Saturday didn't require my presence day of, but the final prep and supply distribution was on me.

We worked with friends up and down the light rail corridor to stuff bags with coupons and Green Line T-shirts for shoppers and diners.

The folks at the Triple Rock were determined to go out with a bang, not a whimper. They planned a series of shows leading up to the closure, with a final night featuring Dillinger Four. Tickets sold out in seconds. A generous friend offered me tickets to join them, but I felt pressed to decline. "The concert's right around my due date!" I said. Madeline had been two weeks late, but I was feeling so uncomfortable, and I had a suspicion this baby would be right on time.

In Minnesota, there's a certain buzz that happens before a snowstorm. The weather reports begin coming in, and we all make our varying predictions. "I don't think we're going to get as much snow as they say," some declare. "It's going to be a big one—make sure to get home early," others say. Inevitably, at least one person will chime in about the Halloween blizzard of 1991.[14] (It's a state law that if winter weather is discussed at a certain length, Gen Xers and millennials must chime in about their 1991 Halloween experience and whether or not their moms made them wear jackets over their Halloween costumes.)

Similarly, the night before an event, there's a buzzing sense of urgency for organizers. It's not panic, but it persists with the same dull roar. As a kid, before a big day I would get that butterflies feeling, up at night thinking about the next day. Not nervous, but too excited to possibly sleep. Nick stayed home with Madeline while I wrapped up West Bank activities, a steady rhythm of urgency pulsing through my body. As the sun set that evening, I drove around dropping off Small Business Saturday supplies, feeling way too pregnant to waddle around with the rolling cart and boxes upon boxes.

As the night wore on, the gentle throbbing escalated into a full roar. I rode waves of contractions overnight, moving from the couch to the rolling ball and back again. I headed over to the bathroom for a warm shower when the pain and discomfort grew to be too much. I didn't wake Nick up, feeling like we had a long day ahead of us and at least one of us should be sleeping.

---

14. A blizzard dropped a record amount of snow on the Midwest on October 31, 1991, and Minnesotans haven't stopped talking about it since.

The following morning, as per our plan, Nick took Madeline to school, where she would later be picked up by a family friend for a fun overnight sleepover. I labored at home a little longer before we headed to the hospital.

And just like that, the slow heartbeat of change continued, and our world shifted again. While our friends said heartfelt goodbyes to the Triple Rock in a night of music and communion, we had our own painful transition of welcoming our second child into the world. While it was a beautiful event, we could feel in our bones the further loss of freedom that comes with the added responsibility. Our lives might have a little less live music in them, at least for a time. In honor of the venue's namesake and its place in our hearts forever, we named our baby Triple. (I'm kidding. We named her Zarina, after my godmother.)

Helping Too Much?

After moving our office to the Southern Theater, I became personally involved with that organization and active in the Seven Corners part of the district. The Southern was on the tail of its own turbulent transition, and executive director Damon Runnals had some exciting plans to turn things around. His ARTshare program was an all-access subscription model crafted for theater artists. A program aiming to help local companies collaborate and grow their audiences together, it was a salve for small and midsize theater companies in need of opportunities, support, and a professional venue for presenting their work.

I started off small, helping with some capacity-building grants as part of the West Bank Business Association's Small Business Services. The Southern then brought me on to do some short-term strategic planning sessions with the board. It seemed a perfect fit for how we intended WBBA services to grow—out of relationships and needs with the West

Bank business community. As the Southern's financial situation grew increasingly tight on the back of some long-term debt, its position became more precarious. Supporting full-time staff became a less realistic option, growth another story altogether. Damon wound up accepting a new position elsewhere, and the Southern was in need of transitional assistance. Knowing the staff and their plan already, I agreed to help on a contract basis for a month or two to get them back into position for a new hire.

With the WBBA in a stable position, I didn't see taking on a big project as a problem—yet. Unfortunately, boards don't necessarily move as quickly as staff does. One month turned into two, two into three, and . . . I got stuck. A desire to help the Southern, a feeling of responsibility toward its staff, and my own stubborn refusal to leave a project feeling incomplete led me to stay on longer than I should have.

The ARTshare program continued on, but despite being a great concept, it was underresourced due to limited cash flow and skeptical funders. Artists helped keep the fledgling idea afloat, working with staff to try to refine contracts, payouts, scheduling, and staffing. The revenue from ARTshare membership was split between the venue and artists participating in the program, with monthly payouts made to each company based on overall membership. It worked not unlike many cooperative models, in which both the burden and the benefit are shared among members. Unfortunately, the building, now over one hundred years old, had additional structural and capacity needs. While there is a lot of funding in Minnesota for art production, there is less available for infrastructure. Boosts from the Minnesota State Arts Board were nice, but they did little to help fortify the walls, which were literally crumbling around us.

At this time, the Southern had a small team of five helping with operations. There hadn't been enough resources to bring on anybody full-time since Damon's departure, but the crew was committed to the mission and vision of the beautiful theater we loved. We had hope in the promise of the ARTshare program and did our best to bolster the concept and access to the arts. We expanded student discounts, added more local incentives, created discount programs for members, and more. We worked together to execute a well-curated season, the only one in the Southern's long history of programming to be entirely open submission. The curation was led by a team of artists representing a variety of genres: performer, writer, filmmaker, and curator Sha Cage; theater maker, director, and educator Jon Ferguson; musician, performer, and spoken-word artist Joe Horton; and dancer and choreographer Kaleena Miller.

Officing out of the Southern was as interesting as it was creepy. As staff and artists transitioned in and out, we all did what we could to help the little theater feel loved and cared for. Volunteer crews painted and tidied the odd little greenroom to make it a more welcoming space for the actors that used it. The greenroom kitchen, a rectangular area adjacent to the changing areas, was particularly odd. We affectionately called it the "bitchen," not because of its '90s flair but because in the middle of the room, right next to the kitchen sink, there was . . . a toilet. Bathroom + kitchen = bitchen!

The basement was another story. A dusty area used mainly for storing paint, lightbulbs, and other supplies, it ran the width of the building—but not the length. Picture walking down steep, crumbling stairs. You flick on the lights and prop open the door, securing it with a rope because god forbid it close behind you and trap you in. Just ahead of you is another light switch, which you flick quickly, making a silent prayer that you don't touch a spider. You descend the remaining stairs into a long, skinny room full of old, unused paint that's surely dry or moldy. To the right is a storage area where the West Bank Business Association stores festival gear—tents, coolers, chairs, and tables. To the left is a storage area full of Southern Theater archives. Event supplies, old paperwork, old theater blueprints. Now, those blueprints—remember that the basement runs the width of the building, but not the length? The blueprints for the Southern show the original basement ran the full length of the building. If you look carefully in the basement, you will find a small square entry point to the rest of the basement, long since sealed by concrete and painted over. What remains in the hidden area of the Southern's basement? The world may never know.

We did what we could to help encourage the Southern to connect its programming to the local community. At the time I joined, less than 0.5 percent of the theater's audiences were coming from within the neighborhood. Less than 0.5 percent! We wanted to help the Southern build better relationships on the West Bank and work more closely with the amazing cadre of artists who lived there. In a short time, our efforts began moving the needle in the right direction, if only modestly.

We also made strides in accessibility. I hoped to do what I could to bring the building up to code and move them further in that direction. We put together an Americans with Disabilities Act (ADA) plan for the organization, complete with quotes and capital expense information for a full building renovation. I started chipping away at those goals, starting with putting in an accessible door in the front. To make it happen, we used Façade Improvement Grant funding from the city of Minneapolis and a grant from VSA Minnesota, a now disbanded organization that worked to create a community where people with disabilities could learn through, participate in, and access the arts. More work yet is needed and long overdue, but at the time it felt like a big win.

After two fruitless rounds of hiring, at what seemed like the last possible moment, the board found an interim executive director with whom it could take a leap of faith. While I was glad to have helped the Southern through a rough transition, I was equally relieved to let go of the weight. As I stepped away from my transitional duties just before Zarina was born, the new hire, Janette Davis, stepped in.

The Southern Theater continued to truck along after my departure. Though the organization continues to have a complicated role and reputation within the Twin Cities creative community, the building, its historic home, and the ethereal acoustics the venue provides remain a special place for artists. The arches will stand strong as long as artists continue to breathe creative life into the building. After all, from ghosts to artists, it's the people that make a place.

Transition II

I found myself revisiting the first year of Maddy's birth often during Zarina's first year. I was able to take a bit more time off with Zarina and was spared having to hop back into a big event so soon after labor. Having eight weeks of leave, even unpaid, seemed like a comparative luxury. I didn't make it any easier on myself, though. Nick and I had planned a move at the same time, and we spent a good chunk of my leave packing and loading boxes.

Though this was mostly workable, it was at the cost of other things I had planned for my leave—not the least of which being physical therapy and rest. I had hoped to do a better job of helping myself heal this time, but in yet another way it seems I am not alone among moms, it was hard to prioritize myself ahead of my family.

Both girls came with me to work for a majority of their first years. Putting aside the financial constraints we had to consider, was it worth the extra effort to keep my daughters with me longer? To nurse longer and see more of their firsts, even if it meant late nights of grant writing, after-hours meetings, and bumping my sleep deprivation up several notches? That's the guessing game we play in a society that doesn't provide us with federally sponsored leave yet requires two working parents. I hope we get to a better equation someday. And, like many parents, I hope our kids won't have as many things on their shoulders as we've had if they decide to have kids of their own.

One winter Sunday morning the year following our move, Zarina woke up at 5:30 a.m.—a little too early for my preference. I sat with her on the couch, wrapped a blanket around us both, and nursed. As I looked out the window frosted with winter kisses, I thought to myself how only one year earlier, Z had been sleeping on my chest in a baby carrier while I packed boxes. Cuddling together in the blanket on a cold winter morning felt like a much healthier option.

Moving but a memory at that point, I tried to lean in to the coziness of winter and the stillness that allows us to slow down the pace of things. I tried to savor the feeling of being needed by my little ones a little bit longer and not rush the pace of a quiet morning. At least, until it was time to go back to work on Monday.

Daily activities: a recap of the #OfficeBaby era

> Wake up
> Nurse
> Prep the diaper bag (and curse your evening self, who opted to leave it for the morning)
> Head to the office
> Park behind Bullwinkle's
> Stack yourself like a pack mule with work bag, baby bag, and baby
> Cross Seven Corners warily
> You have arrived!
> Set the baby up with toys and snacks
> Check mail
> Diaper time!
> Return calls
> Time for baby's morning nap
> #OfficeBaby!
> While the baby sleeps, pop out the laptop
> Grants, marketing, emails—type-type-type!
> Baby wakes up!
> Time for outreach
> Time for baby-friendly meetings
> Lunch together (awww)
> Nurse
> Diaper time!
> Baby is sleepy—afternoon nap! (but not for you, sucker)
> During nap time: grants, thought work, design
> Nap time is over—baby's up!
> Time for one more meeting
> Pack up all the gear (including those diapers) and head for home
> Cook dinner
> Everybody eats!
> Nurse

- Bathtime
- Bedtime for baby (but not for you, sucker)
- While the baby sleeps, pop out the laptop
- Wrap up the stuff you couldn't finish during the day
- Grants, marketing, emails—type-type-type! (sigh)
- Start feeling sleepy
- Remember you wanted to pack the diaper bag before the morning
- Decide against it and head to bed
- Bedtime for mom—huzzah!
- Repeat

💬 West Bank Friendships

› BEN MARCY

 riginally from Springfield, Illinois, Ben Marcy is an adjunct professor at the University of Minnesota and a student in the Organizational Leadership, Policy and Development doctoral program. A regular within the old Bedlam Theatre crew, Ben was also a ten-year resident of the West Bank. I sit down with him on a quiet afternoon to talk West Bank.

> **"The spirit of the immigrant community in the neighborhood ... is powerful and important."**

› On his connection to the West Bank...

"I started my connection to the West Bank via summer classes around 2003. I would go to the North Country Co-op for lunch during the summer when I was taking classes at the U." North Country Co-op was a great co-op on Riverside Avenue that unfortunately closed in the aughts. "I then came back to the U for Humphrey School of Public Affairs in 2006. I was interested in how people participate in policy making beyond political campaigns. I got involved with Cedar-Humphrey Action for Neighborhood Collaborative Engagement, helping students engage with the surrounding neighborhood.

Ben Marcy

"We had all these international connections, but we weren't connecting to the neighborhoods right outside our walls. The neighborhood is unique, eclectic, dense—as well as being a central location of the development with the light rail line. Especially with what the city was planning, it was important for us to be engaged as policy makers for what the neighborhood would look like in ten, twenty years. We wanted to develop a course and platform.

"After graduating, I stayed in the neighborhood and was working on the West Bank Community Coalition board of directors. We tried to build capacity with the Neighborhood Revitalization Program and tried to heal some of the histories over the past few decades and the histories of factions.

"I lived on Seven Corners until moving closer to Cedar and Riverside. I lived in the neighborhood for over a decade, until just recently."

› On food . . .

Ben laughs. "Mayday Books—does that count?"

Mayday is an independent bookstore on the West Bank that specializes in progressive books and magazines. Ben used to go there often.

› On changes in the neighborhood . . .

"The biggest change for me is different from some of the biggest changes for others," Ben says. "I think for me it was the loss of Bedlam. I think there are some spaces that are more meaningful for other folks and maybe for the whole of the neighborhood. But being connected to Bedlam and where it was at the time when it was pushed out of the neighborhood . . ."

He pauses. "It's hard to think about that—it's a trauma to think about that, to people that were working there. It felt like a place that could be theirs when there were other places that didn't feel that way. Dance parties that felt safe in ways dance parties in downtown Minneapolis didn't feel safe, because of their identities. It was really great to see Bedlam productions in the early 2000s. You had young up-and-coming artists, people who were just starting and finding traction in what they were doing.

"It was a weird time because we were in the midst of a recession. It was difficult for people, but it also felt alive. The reason Bedlam was there in 1501 South Sixth Street—there was no market for condos, which is what the developer wanted to do. So, to their credit, they let Bedlam use that space for at least a little while. It was a magic three or four years doing things that nobody else was doing.

"You know, Bedlam created a model for what a nonprofit theater could be. Others have tried to adopt this and look at this model, how it can be a revenue generator, how you can open a space to more people that are outside of your production company and not always be heavy-handed about what's supposed to be in there. There was a shared mission and values. So that was to me, that's personally the biggest loss."

I agree. "I think for a lot of people, it was the community space, it was the church."

"Yeah. I think John Bueche's friend, a pastor, remarked something to that extent: 'This is akin to a church. This has things a church can learn from.'"

› On what remains the same . . .

"The spirit of the immigrant community in the neighborhood. I think that's something that is powerful and important. There's also a strong sense of skepticism and even combativeness within the neighborhood towards authority. That can be troublesome at times if you want to build something but it can also be really important when the city comes in telling you what they are going to do. The community responds 'No, this is what we're going to do to improve the neighborhood' and people organize.

"One of my roommates described it well. He felt at home within the neighborhood and said, 'This is a neighborhood—this is what neighborhoods should feel like. That this is one of the few neighborhoods within Minneapolis where you see a diversity of people in the neighborhood.'"

› On the neighborhood culture . . .

"The arts and culture . . . the losses of the spaces. Not just Bedlam, but the loss of the Triple Rock, the 400 Bar, and other venues. I think those things are pretty important. As far as what the West Bank was known for, it was known for being this vibrant, hearty music scene. When you've lost those institutions—that's something that's suffered, in my opinion. . . . There's still the Cedar, the Red Sea, Acadia. I don't know what they're doing and how that's all playing out, but that kind of experience as being a place for arts and culture. And then you have Mixed Blood, Theatre in the Round, Southern. I guess I'm worried about how many of these mid-size art spaces will be lost and what that means for up-and-coming artists.

"And some of these spaces are really important cultural institutions. The nice thing about Bedlam was you'd have kids come in who were just walking by and had no background in theater. Then they started acting and loving the experience. I think there's such a drive, or has been such a drive, around direct services. It's more about survival than about living. Places like Bedlam were vehicles for living and creating forms of culture. In the early 2000s it was Bedlam working with the East African community to share their experiences, and showing youth how to present them with DIY theatre techniques—it was something fascinating, new, and real."

› On his "West Bank story" . . .

"There's a lot! For some people, it's a story. For some of us, it's just our lives. Being at Hard Times at 3:00 a.m. and watching a coyote walk down Cedar-Riverside. There's other things that were memorable—like in 2012, the Battletrain from the MayDay Parade was outside of Mixed Blood. It had like twelve torches lit and it went rolling slowly down Cedar Ave, just with the traffic. If you weren't from the neighborhood and just driving through, it might have been horrifying."[15]

› On what he imagines for the future . . .

"Well . . . there's imagination in terms of what I would want and imagination in terms of what might happen. I want there to be an establishment of institutions in the vein of Triple Rock. But I don't know if that's necessarily what the community wants now. It's hard to gather and understand what the community wants right now, in this moment.

"I think the fact that there's a loss of that nightlife—and I think that phrase 'nightlife' gets thrown around as people being drunk and irresponsible when I think there was good things that came out—eyes on the street, a sense of protection and people having places to go to and feel connected to. And you have situations where you have young people that need places to go, night-life can be an important aspect of a neighborhood.

"To me, there has to be more space for people at night. I think especially when it's still the case that there's this immigrant story happening, you

---

15. The Southside Battletrain, while not an official part of the city's annual MayDay Parade, is a highly anticipated fixture.

have the space where young people live. The young people are under the constant vigilance of their elders, and the elders have expectations of America, but the kids may be living with different experience.

"Their living space might not be what they are experiencing outside. They have places that they need to go that are structured. The nice thing about Bedlam was it allowed them to figure out what their story is. And that story, it's not all connected to what their parents are experiencing. And I think that's generally what happens with young people, but this may be more extreme for people who are the children of immigrants or who are immigrants themselves."

When Ben was living on the West Bank, he saw people on tall bikes daily.

Transitional Planning

No one lives forever—and even though I loved my work, I knew I wouldn't be in my position forever, either. Transitional (or "legacy") planning can be a scary concept, but it doesn't have to be. Change is inevitable, and it's critical for nonprofits and their teams to plan for it. I knew this included both emergencies and planned departures, and I started preparing for a major transition before my first maternity leave, just in case, and updated the tools periodically after. I crafted organization manuals and left information and lists on how to access accounts and passwords.

But what does transitional planning entail? It wasn't just a matter of making sure files were backed up, but how I organized and planned for the next phase of my position—and the organization. Not only would this leave the organization prepared in the event of an emergency, but it gave a clarity to my current work.

I set to work with the board and staff on creating organizational documents that would help during a major transition, whether slow or sudden.

"Pretend I die tomorrow," I told my board. "What info do you want to have?" We made sure that we updated our bank signatures each year and that insurance account information was current and findable. Working on the process together helped me identify and fill gaps in my documentation.

Now, when I work with other organizations to help with this process, I encourage every leader to identify a trusted colleague they can talk to about transitional planning, preferably prior to the need. I also counsel folks to think through their priorities: What is one big, pressing thing you'd like to make sure is taken care of? Setting a goal around when they'd like to have the process completed is a helpful step for both staff and board. Thinking about how often documents could be realistically updated is key, as is carving out the time to keep them updated.

The cost of turnover is high, the effects of poor execution are dramatic, and there are big positives to planning for transition. In early 2019, we planned another transition—this time a move to Mixed Blood Theatre. Our stay at the Southern Theater had been a good fit for a time, but we wanted to settle in a little closer to the heart of the West Bank. When Mixed Blood invited us in, we ran to the Firehouse and its open arms.

Still Sweeping

Each spring, the WBBA continued its neighborhood cleanings. Our small team organized volunteers, worked with the city to pick up trash, and encouraged staff to join us. The cleanups always had a feel-good, "we did something visible today" quality to them, and I love the community members we'd connect with. But something about them didn't sit quite right.

It can be frustrating when it seems like you're doing the same things over and over. I started to investigate the systems I could put in place to help. Things like getting businesses to adopt trash cans and ash receptacles were one way, and many businesses on the avenue did just that. Over time, it got better; more and more community members participated in these cleanups. Eventually, the association connected with the U of M's College of Liberal Arts to get tons of volunteers from there as well—at one point it used to just be Augsburg that was heavily engaged with the cleanups. I tried to set up some effective systems to leave things better than when I had started.

There was another factor that rubbed me the wrong way. Why was a small, modestly resourced nonprofit doing the lion's share of neighborhood cleanups, particularly on properties that didn't belong to the community? The biggest targets of the graffiti and litter were not the active businesses. So, I began digging. I started with finding out the property owners for given spaces, encouraging them to maintain their properties and adopt trash cans as needed. I started being more persistent about asking the city to maintain sidewalks and city-owned lots. Businesses helped, frustrated with the bureaucracy that would send citations to them for minor graffiti infractions, all while city- and county-owned parcels sat idle next door, accumulating graffiti, trash, and debris.

We learned a lot. We learned that one private property owner had to take another to court over the maintenance of their space. We learned the city and county would point fingers at each other over maintenance, leaving our neighborhood holding the broom. We worked to instill a notion of care among businesses and property owners, not just for the area around their business but for the whole neighborhood as well.

As staff transitioned in and out of the city and the businesses in the neighborhood, cleaning activity would ebb and flow. Where we found the most consistent support was in the institutional partners, particularly Augsburg University, which supported and encouraged a sense of care and mutual support between the institution and neighborhood. What is a good district if not a collection of good neighbors?

Advocating for Women

› MISKI ABDULLE

Miski Abdulle is one of the leaders at Brian Coyle Center. She engages members of the immigrant communities through adult education, family literacy, employment counseling, and women's advocacy, working at the intersection of social services and public health—often intergenerationally, including the particular needs of community elders. She is a licensed social worker and a certified Global Career Development Facilitator.

> " The diversity is very beautiful. We have a buried treasure here. "

Miski Abdulle

As with most of the folks I interviewed for this project, I came to know Miski through our work in the neighborhood. Though we'd see each other at gatherings, we didn't often have the opportunity to work together directly. But she's done amazing work for the women in Cedar-Riverside, and I was certain I wanted her voice to be represented in these pages.

› On her connection to the West Bank...

"My connection is the work itself. I came to the West Bank for work, though I never settled in the Cedar-Riverside area—I live in South Minneapolis, and we were first in Waite House with Pillsbury. There was a lot of Somali need, but they weren't coming there—they were coming here [to Brian Coyle]. I was transferred here in 2006. I've been with Pillsbury since 1997. From 2006 until now, I've been here in Cedar-Riverside.

"Pillsbury—they have theater, childcare, other programs. I am the associate director of the center and Immigrant Women's Advocacy Program. I work in prevention and intervention on domestic violence and assault. We work citywide—we want new immigrant people to know they have resources and support, and people who listen to them."

Our conversation turns briefly to our own immigrant families' histories: my parents and hers. Many times, new immigrants don't yet have networks of friends or family they can turn to for safety—or folks outside their immediate network should the need arise. A confidant like Miski can help, as can having a safe and steady known presence in the community for these types of needs.

› On food...

"Well, I often bring my lunch with me. When I was very new, I used to come back home, then go back to work—I live only two miles from Coyle. But over the years I take food and snacks, so I don't have to go back and forth. I like Davanni's, the Western sandwiches!" She laughs. Davanni's is a local chain that offers pizza, salad, pasta, and hoagies.

"I don't like too much Somali food because I cook the Somali food." She laughs again.

I know just what she means. "It's not as tempting to go out always for your own family food," I agree. "Sometimes I'm picky about curries because I'm craving my own family style."

232

She nods. "Sometimes I go with coworkers, sometimes I go by myself. The other place is the Red Sea—I like their injera. Sometimes, when we have a staff gathering, we go as a group. Or I go by myself, or I go out with friends after a meeting. West Bank is a good spot for hanging out after a long day."

› On changes in the neighborhood...

"People are all grown up," Miski says. "The mothers are getting older, and the children are becoming men and women. There's good and bad things happening with that.

"Another good thing—the trains are available now. People can go to the Mall of America, they work there. There's good and bad with that, also. Sometimes, you know, youth will enter the train with no pay ticket. Or they get in trouble with the police.

"Another trouble is for some women who work at the airport. If they are on a late shift coming back, there can be safety issues. But the more community we have here, I'm sensing the community is getting isolated. There's a lot of division within the community. Like 'This is Somali, this is Oromo'—when we were new, the hosting community was welcoming everyone.

"There's a lot of services, which is good. But sometimes, I hear from people that they just don't know who to trust anymore. They are needy because they are very low income. They are getting older—women especially. Women my age, they don't have the same job opportunities, and the income they have been taking, like SSI, is not enough. So they are just stuck in the apartment."

"Through your work, do you see a shift from generation to generation?" I ask her.

"Sometimes. Sometimes, the mothers I served, and now their daughters, I'm serving them. We don't work with this neighborhood only. Some of the women live in shelters. We do have programs for women in the neighborhood—if women can join, there are sewing classes, computer literacy, specialized classes for women only.

"This program is unique, and we work mostly with families, mostly with women. Usually they are eighteen-plus, but also at Coyle we have a senior program. Sometimes the programs in the neighborhood can be silos—a lot of that because of the politics.

"There's a new wave coming in with the 'Mothers Group.' I think if people sit together and discuss how we want to work together, we can come up with a plan that supports everyone. We often get referrals from other sources and working closely with shelters. We exist and run classes there, but our work is not dependent on them. We can go out and do the work in the community ourselves. If they are from this neighborhood, we can ask them to meet us somewhere else because of privacy and safety."

› On what remains the same . . .

"We are all still working together. More transparency would be helpful. It would be good if people work together so we don't duplicate what we're doing. These are our mothers, these are our women, and if people work together it would be good. Our work will be even more effective."

› On her "West Bank story" . . .

"The diversity is very beautiful. We have a buried treasure here. Especially when we do the Women's Night Out, like with Merrie Benasutti—it's a very, very good story to tell to others. Every year, women come together no matter their culture or their background, living and working and going to school in the neighborhood. Coming together to celebrate womanhood. From 2006, we have done this every year. This is the first year we canceled, because of the COVID. Inshallah, hopefully we will get back!

"There were storytelling sessions we would tell. Very beautiful stories! There's a lot of good things happening in the neighborhood and still going on. The diversity is beautiful. If [people] live in the high-rise, they can come down—there's stores, restaurants, mosques. It's beautiful."

"Diversity is beautiful, but I would imagine that people have to come together and forget about the different hats that they are wearing. Politics and division and this and that. People have to come together as one. We can be different but come together with a common goal around safety, about accepting one another. I would like to see that—increased safety and people to be coming together."

Fires and Unanswered Questions

While New Year's Eve is typically a time for festivity, especially in a bar district, one New Year's Day a different path unfolded. Early in the hours of January 1, 2014, an explosion rocked one of our West Bank apartments, tragically killing three residents and injuring more than a dozen others.

Community members immediately went into triage mode while the firefighters worked in frigid temperatures to control the blaze. Residents lucky enough to escape the explosion were out on the streets in Midwest January temperatures without jackets, gloves, hats, or even shoes, their belongings in flames as the fire raged.

Palmer's Bar, immediately adjacent to the damaged building, opened to residents for warmth and refuge. A triage area was set up at Brian Coyle Center around the corner to temporarily care for and house those displaced by the fire. The water firefighters sprayed to douse the flames froze as it fell. The ethereal beauty, frozen in time, was in stark contrast to the darkness of the tragedy itself.

For all of its complexity and diversity, the West Bank is a closely knit community. In times of tragedy, this plays out in heavy ways. The community rallied together to support the residents, helping raise funds to replace clothes and goods and relocate residents. The Cedar Cultural Center opened its doors for a fundraiser concert, and everybody pitched in.

The West Bank may be the only neighborhood in the United States where a mosque shares a wall with a bar. While residents are not shy or quiet about their differences, they generally accept one another's perspectives. And even though a conversation over coffee may turn into a lively debate or even an argument, one thing is clear: when a West Banker is in need, everybody rallies.

In 2019, nearly six years later, I woke up Thanksgiving morning to find that another fire had ravaged the neighborhood. While it had been extinguished in just under a half hour, five people died, with others injured and displaced from their homes. The fire occurred in one of the high-rise buildings that house many of the community elders. Smoke poured through the building and damaged almost everything on the fourteenth floor. Everybody on that level was left to find new housing, as it was left largely uninhabitable.

Again, the community raced to respond. Leaders from faith groups, health organizations, and other nonprofits rallied to raise funds for the victims. Massive donations of resources, clothing, and food poured in. Leaders came home early from holiday weekends with family, canceling trips to be present and helpful to a community in need.

While it was always healing in its own way for the community to come together, there was a part of this process that was deeply frustrating. Why did a building that housed so many people, many of them older and with limited mobility, not have an adequate sprinkler system to help slow the spread? Who could advocate for our elders?

Representative Mohamud Noor was quick to respond to this latest tragedy. In February 2020, he introduced a bill in the Minnesota House of Representatives to update safety code requirements for existing high-rises. With so many residents in older buildings in the district and throughout Minnesota, it was a critical piece of legislature to move forward. While it has not yet been approved, a vote is anticipated soon.

Hard Times

› ANNA LOHSE

Anna Lohse is a worker-owner of the Hard Times Cafe cooperative. A fixture of the neighborhood, she also served on the WBBA board during some of my first years with the organization. And while a cooperative is about shared power more than it is about individual leadership, Anna's wit and insight bring a lot not just to the restaurant but to the neighborhood, too.

One of the things I appreciate about Anna is her direct and straightforward communication. There's this thing in Minnesota that can happen where people talk around one another rather than to one another—I've been told it's a Scandinavian leftover, part of the "Minnesota Nice" package that we're not very affectionately known for. If you're not careful, you can fall into that pattern of communication, but it's fortunately a little less common on the West Bank. I appreciate Anna's ability to cut to the chase, particularly in a neighborhood where gossip can reign supreme. If you want gossip, go to the Palmer's patio in the afternoon. If you want the news, stop by Hard Times. Anytime I'd stop in when Anna or Brian, another worker-owner, was there, it would

> **" The neighborhood watch during the uprising . . . was one of the most beautiful displays of community I have ever seen in my life. . . . That sense of community is really strong. "**

Anna Lohse

Hard Times Cafe

always turn into a catch-up session. It was a grounding way to start the day (no coffee pun intended). We'd discuss the latest city policy, construction update, or ridiculous political nonsense—of which there seems to be no shortage.

As much as Hard Times is one of the best places for amazing food, it's also a rooted neighborhood temperature gauge, so I knew this book would not be complete without a Hard Times voice in the mix. Lucky for me, Anna was willing to spend a night catching up.

The evening is brisk, with the feel of fall starting to set in. We huddle in blankets on our respective screens to talk politics, religion, and the West Bank.

› On her connection to the West Bank...

"When I was a student at the U of M, I became a regular at the Hard Times. I did a lot of homework there, I studied there, I hung out there. I lived in Prospect Park and on the East Bank. The summer of 2010, I decided to quit school, and I was planning that fall to move to a geodesic dome house in northern Minnesota—but at the very last minute, it fell through. The very day it fell through, I went to Hard Times and they were hiring. I applied on a whim and got hired.

"It's so funny because when they hired me, they thought I wouldn't work out. They hired me and this girl Erica at around the same time, and then we both stayed for a really long time." She laughs. "Now it's been ten years!"

"Lucky them! At what point did you become an owner?" I ask.

"After a year, you can become a worker-owner. I started going to WBBA meetings with Rozina, another worker-owner who was on the WBBA's mailing list. I think even before I was an owner, I would go to meetings, just to be involved. And so, what happens with board stuff happened to me." She laughs again. "You know: when you show the least bit of interest, and everybody's like, 'OMG, you should join the board!'"

› On food . . .

"When I first started working at the Hard Times, I definitely ate at the Wienery a lot. We also ate a lot at the Triple Rock. Lots of Hard Times folks would go there before the staff meeting, and . . . maybe be a little bit tipsy. This is no longer the culture, but it was at the time.

"I always loved Keefer Court and the Red Sea, too. But yeah, the food scene has shifted somewhat. A couple of us eat at Dilla's a lot now. Everyone still eats at the Wienery. But it is a different scene. I mean, not entirely—but losing the Triple Rock felt like losing a lot.

"You know, when I got hired at Hard Times, there was more of a connection between Seward Café and Hard Times."

"It's definitely a different vibe now. Why do you think that is?" I ask.

Anna pauses before responding. "I think it's like . . . our collective is just very different now than their collective. Theirs went through a really huge shift right around when they decided to serve beer. You know, it's like there's this institutional memory that comes with the ownership, and I think the feel of their collective is different now.

"It can be good and bad. When there's a lot of old members, new ideas can get shot down all the time. The institution can be stubborn in that way. But it has kept us doing what works for twenty-eight years—when ideas do move forward, they are well tested and vetted. I also think for a while there was more crossover between us in customers, workers, and workers living at the same houses, things like that. But there seems to be less crossover now."

› On changes in the neighborhood...

"I guess I'll start by saying my opinion is very centered in my experience, which is a very particular experience. It's not of somebody who lives on the West Bank. It's ... I guess I'd kind of say it's the white experience of the West Bank.

"We've lost a ton of venues and a ton of nightlife and a ton of community. I worked overnights for almost two years, and they used to be so busy. We had Medusa, Nomad, Palmer's, Triple Rock, Bedlam ... we had a lot of the punk venues, and a lot of those venues have left. We still have Palmer's and Nomad (now Part Wolf), but it's just not the thriving music scene it once was. So maybe not so much the white experience, necessarily, as the punk experience of the West Bank. You know, we used to always say West Bank was the downtown of the Southside—and it's not that anymore.

"When I got hired, all my customers were my friends outside work, too. I saw them at shows, they lived at the punk houses that I lived at, I ran into them in the community. And now, fewer people are making the trek to the West Bank. I think it's really sad. I miss feeling more connected to the punk community. I feel like so many people left the West Bank after Medusa left, and Bedlam.

"I'm also sad for those types of West Bank spaces I didn't get to experience. These other DIY spaces that I had never been to, that I had never seen. The West Bank Social Club, places like that. It's all the DIY spaces that we let go. And we still have Palmer's and the Nomad, but those are not quite the same.

"I do think the other thing is that the punk community aged. The older punks don't have the energy to maintain a space like that without pay. We're not willing to work and run a space for free anymore, or we simply can't afford to. A lot of spaces have closed down, and nothing has really taken their place. I wonder why that's not happening as much anymore. Maybe we came from a DIY generation?"

We laugh in analog at the thought, though we agree it's a depressing one.

"I mean, I don't know," I answer. "I hope not! Not to bright-side a pandemic, but there's going to be an exodus from commercial spaces over the next year. And I wonder if with cheaper rents and greater availability that comes with that, if more artists are going to be doing things in those spaces they couldn't afford previously."

"Yeah!" Anna says. "And I agree, I do think it's financial, too. I know what the rent is now. Maybe you're right. Maybe after COVID, there will be more commercial spaces. Everything was getting too expensive. I don't know what it would be like to try to run a space like that now, with the current police situation. Is it possible to run an under-the-radar type of space like that anymore? We used to get away with it, even punk show houses. The cops were hardly ever called on stuff like that."

› On what remains the same . . .

Without skipping a beat, Anna says, "There's definitely still a strong sense of community. I feel like it's hard to imagine another neighborhood where you walk around, and you walk two blocks to the left and you know 90 percent of the business owners, you walk two blocks right and you know people on the street. Sometimes it feels like I'm on Sesame Street." She laughs. "Like, 'Oh hey!' 'Oh hi!' I feel very safe on the West Bank. I've always felt safe.

"I feel like the neighborhood watch during the uprising [following the death of George Floyd] sort of sealed for me how strong the community is. Seeing the response of the community—how it was led by the youth in the neighborhood, particularly. How close it was to the riots that were happening. We're directly between south and downtown, where most of the riots were. And our neighborhood was left nearly completely unscathed. It was because of active participation from hundreds of community members, each fulfilling different roles. People up high looking down low, letting folks know 'Hey, there's this guy walking around the corner. Looks like he doesn't live here—does anybody want to talk to him?' That night, and that team, it was one of the most beautiful displays of community I have ever seen in my life. It made me proud to be on the West Bank and participate in some way. That sense of community is really strong still.

"The stubbornness has not changed at all, either, which I really, really appreciate. That unwillingness to bend to the whims of the city. I appreciate this deep desire to preserve the community. The West Bank does not care about bureaucracy—that has not changed at all. And the West Bank regulars are still the same, though there are some fewer. I see the same people daily that I saw ten years ago. So, to have that continuity is comforting."

› On the neighborhood culture . . .

"Well, I'm older. It feels like the community is older. It felt like when I first arrived on the West Bank, it was more of a party scene. We were all having a good time, not in a disrespectful way, but bar hopping and things like that between all the bars on the West Bank. It felt like the culture was alive and young and vibrant.

"I don't want it to sound negative, but it does feel like the culture is different now. It's . . . more serious. It's definitely older. I look at the regulars at Palmer's, for instance. When I was there, there were people that were twenty-one. I go there now, and I still feel like I'm the youngest person there, and I'm thirty-one."

I agree. "Anna, now we are *elder* activists."

She laughs. "Yeah, and we lost a lot of the venue spaces. So, the only people who stayed on the West Bank is the hard-core committed crowd. There's less of an alive, vibrant nightlife. It's a lot quieter."

"True. I wonder if some of that is cultural, too," I ponder. "I spoke with Abdu, and he was talking about how for him, the West Bank has a very active nightlife for the Somali community in ways that he doesn't even find in Africa."

"That's true," Anna says. "Yeah, Dilla's is hopping at night! There are crowds of twenty, thirty people there in the evenings."

› On her "West Bank story" . . .

"I mean, definitely the riots and the neighborhood watch, to me, was completely unique to the West Bank. These young kids that were, like, seventeen years old patrolling the neighborhood to keep watch. A young girl in a hijab riding around on a bike checking in on us. It was great. It was a multigenerational effort. The moms were bringing tea. Everybody was helping.

"There's also this one overnight story that always sticks with me," she adds, laughing. "So, I used to work overnight shifts. And occasionally, I'd have to kick people out. Some people think a girl is not going to be good at that, but I was actually always super good at it. I would raise my voice, and all of the regulars would stand up and put their eyes on somebody, and they would leave.

"But there was one where I could not get this guy out. I was talking to him to get out for like ten minutes and he just wouldn't leave. Then he started getting a little testy, getting in my face, like he was going to do something. And at that moment Marshall walked in, one of our regulars, and he's, like— huge. He's this big, intimidating guy. He walks in, sees what's happening, rips his shirt off, bear hugs this dude, and just walks him out of the café. Then he came back in, I gave him a muffin, and he sat down and played two games of chess. You know, it was like it was nothing.

"This is what it's like here. This is what we do for each other. And it felt like one of these moments where I was watching a movie of a thing happening in my life. That moment always stuck with me."

› On what she imagines for the future...

"That one's hard." Anna takes a thoughtful pause. "Every time we lose a West Banker, I get more scared we're not going to be able to preserve it. That we're not going to be as stubborn. Right now, we have folks that feel this ethical obligation to the place, to care for it. I worry about things like the development project . . . will it come and change the neighborhood entirely? Or if they ever find a way to properly connect the West Bank to downtown, will downtown encroach into the West Bank?

"I have no idea, so it's honestly hard to say. Looking at it ten years ago, I wouldn't have thought things would be this way, either. But especially after George Floyd's murder, and with all the protests, and everything that's happening with COVID, so many things could happen. The West Bank could be revitalized. Or buildings could become empty and cheap, and people could do creative things. Or it could meld into [the rest of] Minneapolis. Whatever happens, I hope Hard Times remains for a long time.

"The thing I like most about the West Bank—it's not a cultural monolith in any way. I don't understand how it works, but it totally does work. The way that people are part of a community together but don't feel the need to convert each other to anything. It's the craziest thing to me. There's intense respect from all sides. If it became more of a monolith, that might not be there. That quality feels so special to me. I hope that the neighborhood retains all the different African cultures. It's not just Somali—there are so many other cultures to the West Bank, and most people don't realize that about it. Being there is one of the coolest things; you get to know all the tiny little pockets of culture. And they kind of bicker with one another occasionally, but everyone lives in harmony. The riots were a perfect example of that. On the group text we had going, stuff would pop up very rarely and people would say, 'No, no, not on the text!'" She laughs. "But no matter what, it didn't stop anybody from helping each other."

The last time Anna saw a tall bike was the same day I talked to her—and that's not counting the two in her front yard.

Accessibility

While an older neighborhood oozes character, older buildings are not without their downsides. They have the charm of an earlier era, but also the narrow doors and archaic plumbing.

Moving from California to Minneapolis came with several learning adjustments, and perhaps some anxiety. The first time I used a basement bathroom, it felt beyond strange. See, in Southern California, basements for houses aren't a thing—but earthquakes are. I remember one time I went to Camdi, a little restaurant in the Dinkytown commercial area neighboring the University of Minnesota. I had to step through the kitchen to get to the bathroom, winding my way down narrow stairs and following a long hallway to a tidy but small basement lavatory. I wondered where I would go in an earthquake. What would I hide under? Would the building collapse in on me? *Would they be able to find my body in the rubble?* This fearful anticipation seems far away now, but it was a part of my everyday thought processes. Earthquakes are never far from the back of your mind when you grow up perpetually waiting for the long overdue "Big One" to finally hit.

Earthquakes may not be a concern in Minnesota, but there are other issues with buildings built to earlier standards. The highlights are the tin ceilings, beautiful woodwork, and sturdy brick exteriors. The downside is that the spaces were designed before ADA was law.

The Americans with Disabilities Act, which became law in 1990, "prohibits discrimination against individuals with disabilities in all areas of public life, including jobs, schools, transportation, and all public and private places that are open to the general public."[16] Not enough of our buildings and businesses met these requirements, and the idea that a building's age exempts it from having to comply is a prevalent myth.

Gil Penalosa is known internationally for his work on the "8 80" concept—the idea that if a city was built well for both an eight-year-old and an eighty-year-old, it would be good for everyone. Slower traffic on streets to ensure safer crossings. Benches for sitting, eating, and resting. With my experience walking around with a baby in a sling, I wanted to include folks a little older and a little younger than that age spread, too. The strides we made were uphill, for sure.

Widening the sidewalks in our district was one clear improvement, but we wanted to make more. Businesses, particularly nonprofits, wanted to do more to get their buildings up to date. The cost for renovation, however, was often out of their price range, and few had the capital resources to cover it. Occasionally, grants would pop up for nonprofits that allowed for capital improvements, but those were all too rare. We made tiny progress with door and bathroom improvements here and there. Local lawmakers and government officials seemed hesitant to fund these types of upgrades through bonding or infrastructure grants, and foundations seemed hesitant to cover any capital or building upgrades, focusing on programmatic elements.

Gil Penalosa says, "We must evaluate cities by how we treat their most vulnerable citizens; the children, the older adults, the poor and those with disabilities." West Bank guests and residents are of all ages and abilities. A district that serves everybody that uses it—what a radical concept.

---

16. ADATA.org contains information, guidance, and training on the Americans with Disabilities Act.

The Hunt for More

The year 2019 felt like a beast. (Little did I know what 2020 had in store!) I tried hard to focus in on the things I value. I tried to invest time and energy in family, work, art, writing, and planting seeds for opportunities. I was successful in some ways, less so in others.

"You gotta put yourself out there more!" I heard from colleagues and other well-intenders.

That saying gives me agita. Yes, putting myself out there can lead to opportunities, but it can also lead to a unique type of fatigue. A roller coaster of joy and rejection that's particularly draining when you have a deep emotional connection to your art and your work and the things you are submitting.

That year, I participated in a project stemming from the LitHub article "Why You Should Aim for 100 Rejections a Year." The premise: unless your work is absolute crap, and I mean terrible, aiming for one hundred rejections entails several things:

1) You're putting yourself out there, period.

2) You're learning from the process.

3) Among those rejections, hopefully you're also getting at least a few acceptances.

Part of the reason I decided to put myself out there more was because even though I was happy, I was feeling a strong inclination for more. A drive to learn more, do more, challenge myself more. The West Bank certainly had challenges, but that's not what I meant.

I had so much to be grateful for. I was working with amazing people, doing work that was helpful. I wondered—if I loved my work so much, why was I looking for more?

As the girls grew older and increasingly independent, I set off into an introspective and thoughtful time when I reconnected with me and what it meant to be me in this new, mom-ful iteration.

While rejection was harsh, the acceptances I did receive were good fits. I presented in my first art show in years, a group show that was part of the conference of MidWest Mixed—a group making space for conversations and learning for multiracial people in the Midwest. Their topics have always felt on point and timely, and sharing creative space was a connection I intensely needed. I was also able to write several pieces for Pollen, a nonprofit networking organization I had grown to love dearly.

Another one of the acceptances I received in 2019 was to the James P. Shannon Leadership Institute, which hosts yearlong, bimonthly cohorts for "community-serving leaders to clarify core values and define the purpose of their work." I was excited to embark on a centering effort, especially at what felt like an increasingly momentous time.

It's okay to want to grow and challenge yourself. And the path to that growth is not always linear or up or down—sometimes it's within.

Community-Led Development, Community-Led Hope

The community-led work on behalf of West Bank residents is critical to the overall well-being of the district, and the organizers are beacons of light. While the seeds of community-led activities had been planted long before, additional efforts began to take root in 2018 and 2019—among them Abdirahman Mukhtar's group Daryeel Youth.

The kids in Cedar-Riverside always impressed me with their wit and humor. Some kids, however, need extra care. Abdirahman helped provide this with Daryeel's Friday nights on the Cedar Cultural's plaza. He also began another initiative, #ForHooyo (*hooyo* meaning "mother" in Somali), an effort to curb violence among the youth. In addition, a group of Somali mothers formed to help with outreach and drug prevention and recovery for kids in the neighborhood affected by the opioid epidemic.

I appreciated the times the West Bank Business Association was able to offer programming that served the needs of both businesses and residents. There were the cleanups, of course, but that wasn't all. In the spring of 2019, a partnership with Springboard for the Arts allowed us to connect youth with businesses for mentorship and training and create another round of pop-up creations and events. That fall, I painted a new mural for Keefer Court to honor the Kwan family and their history in the neighborhood.

One afternoon in late 2019, a restaurant owner contacted me about an idea she was working on.

"I'm headed downtown to drop off some things," I told her, "but I'll stop by your place on my way back."

I took the light rail downtown to the Minnesota Makers store, which had opened earlier that year. The shop, much like the Manchester visitors center I had appreciated, hosted a bunch of Minneapolis guides and maps—including the shiny West Bank Area Directory and walking tours we had developed. The shop had run out of the first batch, and today I was delivering a replenishment. I felt a swell of pride as I dropped off the maps, remembering my visit to Manchester and the hope it seeded in me at the time. Adjacent to our maps and directories, the store featured a big selection of Minneapolis- and Minnesota-themed artwork and hand-crafted goods: locally made chocolates, wood carvings, screen prints, wild rice recipes, and more. I knew I wouldn't be going back to California for the holidays that year, so I picked out some things for my family, putting together a little Minnesota care package with ease.

I hopped on the light rail back to the West Bank and headed over to Sagal Restaurant to talk to Fartun. Sagal, located right on Cedar Avenue, is a diner featuring Somali food, including great sambusa—one of my personal favorites. We always joked about having a sambusa contest on the West Bank among the restaurants but never got around to it. The rivalry among the finalists, I'm sure, would be hotly contested—everyone prides themselves on their sambusa.

Fartun wanted to talk about creating a facility for youth in the neighborhood, a medical clinic that could serve as an annex to other healthcare resources in the neighborhood. It would be focused on treatment and recovery, provided in a culturally specific way that could better meet the needs of the community. I shared with her the idea I'd had for the city lot in years prior for a building space and community resource, along with the WBBA's draft plans. I helped brainstorm how the clinic could be combined with other uses so it would meet the zoning and suggestions for Cedar Avenue and complement the corridor.

I thought to myself that WBBA might not be in a position to lead a big project, given our board temperature. But whether it was partnering or even just information sharing, I wanted to do what I could to support one.

When Is It Time to Go?

When is the right time to leave a job?
How do you know when it's time to move on?
And what do you do if it's a job you love?

Everybody has different views on this. In spite of its challenges, I enjoyed my job at the WBBA and valued the work I was doing tremendously. The closer I grew to the people I worked with and my partners, the more I felt huge pangs of guilt even thinking about leaving. I read countless blogs and articles on the topic and did at least a year's worth of self-evaluation, including bugging my friends and colleagues about the topic. After a while, however, I felt as though the hypothetical possibilities had me bursting at the seems.

Growing any further was unlikely, especially for a risk-averse board that was content to stay the size it was. Beyond this, there were signals that my time to go was coming.

There are a variety of legitimate reasons for someone to leave a position. Some signs that you are nearing the end of a role and it's time to move on may be:

> You're not growing in the ways you'd like to be growing.
> Your vision for the organization—or your role—is not aligned with leadership or those with the power to set that vision.

- Your needs aren't being met. Sometimes this can be temporary, as can happen with a small and growing organization, but a lot of people get roped into what becomes a long-term bad situation.
- It's toxic. Can it be fixed? If so, do you have any control over this?
- Your work is done. Some roles are temporary, and even some organizations are temporary. Sometimes the end is clear.
- You've outgrown the organization—or the organization has outgrown you.
- The mission is no longer in alignment with your values. I've had friends wind up leaving organizations that clung to outdated concepts of marriage and gender, for example, or who failed to respond to timely and urgent needs.
- You are not valued. For whoever needs to hear this right now: you deserve recognition in your role, no matter the size, shape, or scale of your workplace! I remember watching an interview with the CEO of a company that provided on-site childcare, car services, artists in residence, and more. His employees had lots of loyalty to the company, and vice versa. He saw his employees as the most important assets, and every day his most important assets walked out the door. It was his job, he thought, to make sure they were excited to come back.
- You no longer care about the work, or take care with your work. The nonprofit sector has huge issues with employee burnout; too many organizations drain people like batteries and replace them with fresh sets as they leave the sector in droves. Are you burnt out? Don't blame yourself—but don't sit in that space for too long.
- You want to learn more, and you need a job change, degree, or learning opportunity to do that.
- Your friends and colleagues are tired of your whining.

For me and the work on the West Bank, our visions were aligned. I just wanted more of it! More growth. More learning. More policy work. I felt guilty even thinking about exploration, as my values aligned so well with my work. But unlike marriage, a job is not "till death do us part." (And even in marriage, there's always divorce, trial separation, or an open relationship!) In spite of my guilt and loyalty to the role, I still found

251

myself wanting more. And with my efforts to nurture our programs, grow the association, and expand the work we were doing, I felt like I was trying to collect water in a colander. The work remained, but my energy just kept slipping through the holes.

What's one more sign it's time to move on? When another door opens.

The Friendliest Face on the West Bank

› BIHI!

I first met Abdirizak Bihi at Brian Coyle, and we connected over our overlapping work in the West Bank community. Bihi is a Somali American social activist and a natural community organizer, a charismatic social butterfly in the Cedar-Riverside community. He is the director of the Somali Education and Social Advocacy Center and works to educate Somali leaders and community members; he is also a former board member of the Cedar Cultural Center and one of the founders of its Midnimo program.

> " I think the history of activism has always been here on the West Bank.... The culture of West Bank is the feistiness, the passion for everything. "

If you're in the neighborhood, you'll likely see charismatic and sharp-dressed Bihi, who's always up for a chat as he's walking from place to place. If you're in the area for an event, you may just find yourself featured on his livestream—he's always using social media to support fun activities and other West Bank goings-on.

I don't remember when I first caught myself doing it, but somewhere along our relationship I started calling Bihi "Uncle" instead of his name. One of the things Sri Lankans and Somalis have in common is respect for those older than us, and a way we show that respect and affection is through language. The terms *auntie* and *uncle* are used even for non-blood relatives as a term of endearment or respect (and occasionally out of exasperation). While Bihi isn't too much older than me—I'm somewhere between him and his daughters—it started popping up naturally.

Given the care he takes of the neighborhood, it fit.

› On his connection to the West Bank ...

"I moved from Somalia to DC in 1996 and moved to Minnesota in 2000. I first came to work as interpreter at the Hennepin County Medical Center. Housing was a big deal at that time, and I moved here to help people access housing. I helped 1,300 people find housing! While I was there, we helped make a multicultural office in Hennepin County—in that office, there were probably over ninety languages spoken. There were so many needs: needs for housing, translation, interpretation, advocacy, helping set up halal stores, helping get space for mosques."

Having helped so many people with housing, it's no wonder he knows everybody! Bihi seems to have an endless network of friends on the West Bank.

› On food ...

"The restaurant called Sagal used to be an Ethiopian restaurant. It was managed by a woman who immigrated here from Ethiopia. The whole family used to work in the restaurant. Everybody used to come—it used to be full all the time.

Bihi and friends at a neighborhood cleanup

"It was the place for refugees and immigrants to meet. We used to bring information about jobs, calling cards to call back home. We used to bring a lot of information—and you could go to the café and at any time you'd hear different languages and see people: Somali, Oromo, Ethiopian, Eritrean.

"Also, Enuye used to hire from here and give space to folks that needed it. She has a great story, too. She used to make injera at home in M building and everybody would pick up and buy from her."

I met Enuye while doing outreach in the neighborhood, and remembered her kindness.

› On changes in the neighborhood...

"There were a lot of old neighbors that are not here anymore. The old hippies, they were very welcoming—especially for people with challenges and barriers. I think it would have been difficult for immigrants to live in any other neighborhood. You know, I would see an elder being helped across the street or being shown how to use the light. It was a very welcoming and inviting place for new people.

"So, the immigrant community, this neighborhood was the starting point for a lot of Oromo and Somalis. Almost everyone in the state has started their life here. If you go to Willmar or St. Cloud or St. Peter or Moorhead or Duluth—when I go to any of these places, I run into people that identify with Cedar-Riverside. They say to me, 'I used to live in F building!' Or 'I remember Chase House!'

"But before, you know, the neighborhood was actually more diverse. A lot of those hippie elders have moved out or passed away, and new faces and new cultures have come in. I documented at one point there were ninety-one languages in the neighborhood!

"I established Somali Link Radio that comes out every Tuesday, 6:00 to 7:00 p.m.—the only English-speaking Somali radio in the country. But now, anyone under twenty-five, most likely their first language is English. That's a fast transition for an immigrant community!

"The other thing: the street businesses have changed. There used to be some Hmong businesses. There's a few Southeast Asian and [other] Asian businesses left, but it's fewer. I also noticed that there were a lot of bars before, and many of those places have changed from nightclub into a mosque or another kind of business or community center. So there's a lot of that change—the businesses are looking like the community that lives there. And that makes sense. In the 1800s, the men who were running restaurants were the Norwegian immigrants; now you see the same change is taking place [for the East African immigrants]. Lately, I've been seeing more accommodations for cyclists. The Samatar Crossing is a gateway to the city. People-wise, culture-wise, that part of our neighborhood is evolving. . . .

"Within the community, there's lots of change taking place generationally. The other thing is students. When the school is open, you'll see thousands of kids. You also see all these young people from the community going and walking, mostly girls, to the U of M and Augsburg. Education is so important. This community went through a lot of challenges. I think the history of activism has always been here on the West Bank."

› On advocating for the West Bank Somali community . . .

"One morning, I saw a huge long line at Cedar Cultural Center. I kept saying to myself, 'There is something good in here.' And there were people from Duluth, Eau Claire, from Burnsville. And they drove all the way to see something good. I sent an email to Robert Simonds, the director at the time, and asked, 'Why don't you include us?' And he said, 'Can you come and see us? ... We've been trying to connect with the East African community in the neighborhood for so long.' That's when I joined the board. We worked together with Adrienne Dorn and Mary Laurel [True] to come up with Midnimo.

"We started local and then grew. We would look up a band we loved and ask, 'What happened to the band?' Oh—they fled Somalia. So then, the West Bank Social Club and Augsburg College supported the effort, and they started backup bands for the artists we were putting together. And then, instead of us looking for artists from around the world, artists were calling, asking to be invited. . . .

"One day, I was visiting relatives and I saw a flyer somewhere else in the neighborhood that said, in English, 'Come to this meeting! We are deciding whether or not to have a light rail station here.' There were homeowners that were concerned about what light rail might bring. And we, the Somali residents, were not invited to that meeting.

"So I reached out to [Hennepin County commissioner] Peter McLaughlin about this. I told him, 'I thought we left dictatorship in Somalia! I thought we came to a democracy! We were never informed!'" Bihi laughs. "And I reached out to Sharon Sayles Belton, the mayor at the time, too. I said, 'This is unacceptable—nobody ever asked us. Don't we have rights?' Then they decided to have a flyer in Somali, and we got the word out and we changed that decision!" He beams with pride.

"Then, years later, the conversation about the Green Line started. We advocated for the station to stay on the other side, on the street side. We also advocated for a skyway from the F building. We came to a solution

256

somewhere in the middle. But we did so much outreach for that effort. I would door knock to get elders to come to the meetings. Everybody hates to go to meetings, but I would push them to come. A few years later, we would have a conversation with elders, and they said, 'It is so great! Now I can go to St. Paul, and my daughter can go to the university, and it's so easy.'"

› On what remains the same...

"The culture of West Bank is the feistiness, the passion for everything. That is still the same. When we are voting, it's not easy, but people are passionate. It's a West Bank thing! . . .

"Another thing I can tell you is that the hospitality of people—for example, when we had a fire in 2014, people sprang without thinking to help others, together. The people who jumped out of the buildings, their things were taken into Palmer's to be kept safe for them.

"And the most recent fire, we raised $100,000. We gave away food and furniture, and the Cedar Cultural Center and People's Center and Dar Al-Hijrah Mosque helped. Those things never changed—we are there for each other."

› On the nightlife...

"There were a lot of bars—there was so much at night. For a while, people didn't want to go out because after September 11, some people would come to enjoy bars, and they would change into angst and yell at people. There was some fear around that. You know, it takes only one incident to create big fear. There was an elder that was punched—that was the beginning.

"But there were outpourings of support, too. I remember people would come from all over the community, bring flowers to the mosques. And then, for a while, some of the new immigrants coming to the neighborhood didn't drink, didn't smoke, didn't go to clubs.

"After September 11th, things cleared out for a while. But then, in a few years, the music scene was booming again. People were coming to 400 Bar, people would come and enjoy the Zombie Pub Crawl—that was a big thing that we lost. It was so much fun, but strange for the people that were unfamiliar. I remember the elder ladies used to say, 'Tonight is the devil's night.'"

I laugh. "That's how my dad used to describe Halloween."

Bihi laughs his own contagious laugh. "I remember Cedarfest, Somali Week. But a lot has changed in terms of nightlife.

"One of the things that surprised me is—we accepted that a person from Burnsville might have [negative] perceptions of the neighborhood. But when I engaged people, I was surprised how many people, even Somali Americans, said things like 'It's not safe at night.' So, I started to become a valet to help with car parking. I would walk them around, as a tour guide.

"The West Bank is the melting pot of the Midwest. In West Bank, you can eat Chinese food, Vietnamese food, Somali food, all in the same block. Same with churches. We have three mosques and a church. It's very interesting—people are surprised how much stuff is available in such a small area. Services are available, too, from Brian Coyle and the Cedar Riverside Opportunity Center. There are a lot of resources."

› On his "West Bank story" . . .

"Oh my god." Bihi laughs. "It's so many!

"One story that I usually share: When I first moved to Cedar-Riverside in C building, almost twenty years ago, I was working from home. One day, a neighbor of mine called the police—because the cable company told them it was $9.99 service, but they were billing her $70. I came off the elevator and ended up interpreting to help. The police were surprised why she called 911. They were speechless for a while, but she didn't know who else to call! So we helped her.

"Fifteen years later, her daughter happened to be in my office when we had an issue we could not fix. Even somebody who had an IT background wasn't able to fix it. She asked if she could try. She fixed it! That's the thing: by staying in one place, you get to see people grow. Not everybody makes it, and you see some of them on the streets. But an overwhelming majority of young people do well . . . and eventually they are helping us and doing things for us."

› On what he imagines for the future . . .

"One of the things I strongly believe is that downtown will grow. Sooner or later, twenty or thirty years, downtown will either come to us or we have to go to downtown. The space, the idea for the lid over the freeway—I think people think that's not going to happen.

"I believe you can cover that small area of the freeway and make a park, to stop downtown coming to you. I think we should think about that space as a park or soccer stadium or something communal rather than having downtown and businesses move this way. This will endanger our affordable housing and increase our housing costs.

"I see the new population on the West Bank is the future. The millennials in the community come with their own ideas. I also think a lot of buildings are in danger for development. My kids said they would love for us to move into a house . . . but we don't want to live anywhere outside of West Bank.

"I see a future where business will be the real deal. This population is growing. Purchasing power is growing. More businesses will be coming here. I hope that when that happens, people will have a stake in the neighborhood."

Always out and about walking in the community, Bihi says he sees a few tall bikes every day.

Yanked through an Open Door

I got an email, a text, and then another email. One by one, friends were pinging me about a new position that had opened up at Twin Cities LISC. My colleague Kathy had moved to another position, and after about a year of vacancy and program evaluation, the Creative Placemaking role had opened up again.

I put my best foot forward in my résumé and cover letter. I got my references together and tried not to get my hopes up too high. I let a few key people at the WBBA know I would be applying, including KJ Starr. I sent everything in with excited professionalism, and then . . . I heard nothing.

Things continued on the West Bank at their typical fast pace. We moved into a new year of technical assistance, new clients, and projects to prep for spring openings. After a particularly tough executive committee meeting that ran over by nearly an hour, I plopped back into my chair, exhausted.

"You okay?" KJ asked. "That was pretty brutal."

"Yeah, I'm fine," I said. "Just gonna send a few things before heading home." The sky was dark, the Midwest winter still holding a tenacious grip on our temperatures and our daylight hours. I clicked refresh on my inbox and gasped.

"Oh no, what now?" KJ asked.

"They want me to come in for an interview," I responded.

"Oh my god!" she practically screamed. "You're gonna get that job. You're gonna get that job and you're gonna leave me, and then I'm going to be screwed."

"You wouldn't be screwed," I said with a laugh. "We wouldn't let that happen. And you're too awesome for that anyway. And besides, this is going to be incredibly competitive. I feel lucky to have gotten an interview."

"Still. That's uncanny timing."

"I know." I was still in disbelief.

We scheduled my interview for two weeks out. Shortly after that foreboding executive committee meeting, I came down with the world's most brutal head cold. Feeling wrecked and stacking up Kleenex like it was my new hobby, I pleaded with my body to heal. Stuffy nosed and watery eyed, I practiced mock questions with a willing friend and prepped my interview outfit. The weekend before the interview, my head began to drain and defog. Miraculous timing!

I hoped my impressions, sans Kleenex, were enough to lock in a second interview. I hoped all the way into the following month, when I still hadn't heard back. As the weeks crept by my hope started to fade—until I got a call from one of my references.

"Keep your phone by you!" she said excitedly. "I think they might be offering you a job!"

"What?!" I shouted back into the phone. "I thought they were doing second interviews! I never heard back, so I'd pretty much given up. I didn't think the interview went that badly."

"Nope!" she assured me. "Sounds like it went pretty dang well."

And then things went from slow to fast: I had a call that night that included a verbal offer, and there was a formal job offer in my inbox by the following morning. I met first with a subset of my WBBA executive committee, who were surprised but supportive. We talked through next steps, and I started making phone calls and visits to the remainder of the board. I gave ample notice and assured the board I would do everything I could to help through the transition.

"Besides," I said, trying to keep the conversation light, "you helped me prep all those emergency planning documents anyway. We're already in pretty good shape for even unexpected transitions!"

The idea of leaving was bittersweet. I thought back to those days of debt and furlough and how far we had come. With reserves in the bank, active grant contracts to hold us through the year, and a series of applications already submitted, it felt good to have the organization in a healthy and stable position.

If I was going to take this leap, what better time than now?

A West Bank Essential

› ELTON TRUSCLAIR

Elton is a West Bank *essential*. He's one of my night-owl friends—I first met him after a late-night event on the West Bank. I had seen him biking around many times before, his uniquely decorated bike as much a fixture of the neighborhood as his friendly face. Over the years, I got to know more about him. We'd find time to connect in between his travels to and from New Orleans, and summer nights on the West Bank would often be capped with long conversations.

> " It's about us. It ain't about just you. "

Jamie and Elton, 2019

I meet with Elton one afternoon at KJ's house, as they live near each other. The three of us sit together outdoors, masked and grateful for the in-person company. As we begin our conversation, a young man rides by on a bike.

"Hey, nephew!" Elton calls out and waves. The young man stops and says hi before biking on again.

KJ notes, "That's a Hard Times baby, that one. He's a West Banker, born and bred."

"Yup, yup." Elton nods. I love that about Minneapolis, how well the families in this neighborhood in particular know one another. "KJ, do you know how old I am?" Before she can guess, Elton says resoundingly, "I'm *sixty-three*. I've been in Minnesota thirty-one years. I've been on the West Bank for twenty-eight years."

› On his connection to the West Bank . . .

"Well, I worked at the old Loring Cafe, and man, the place was artsy-fartsy bohemian. We could wear our drawers to work as long as we put on an apron." Elton laughs. "An Ethiopian dude brought me over, and he showed me around. He said, 'Man, I gotta take you over to the West Bank.' This is when I first came over here, in the '90s. Man, the West Bank was so different than it is now. A lot of Ethiopians, Hmong folks, a lot of bike kids, a lot of Black kids, and a bunch of Cuban kids. A shitload of Latin Kings!" He laughs again, a deep laugh.

As we chat, a chicken runs past me on its way to the other end of the yard. Having recently become a mother to two new chickens and a refurbished coop myself, I'm overjoyed to see them. KJ laughs. "Yeah, Abdu and I met here, and the first time he saw the chickens, he flipped out," she says. "He said, 'I had fifty chickens in Somalia.' It touched his heart."

"That's awesome," I say.

Elton joins in: "Yeah, we had chickens. Growing up, we had to feed the chickens and slop the hogs. Kids do that now, they'd have to take a shower before they go to school! You know what, when the hogs were having babies? We had to *be there*. They made us stay there to make sure the hogs didn't eat the babies. The hogs would eat their babies!"

"Yeah! Pigs would eat a farmer!" says KJ. "They're terrible. I stay away from them."

"They're just prone to eat," Elton says. "You gotta watch them, keep them fed. But yeah, my grandmother used to raise chickens. She had little baby chicks—we called baby chickens biddies. My grandmother used to bring them in, because the snakes—I'm from the bayou. I was born on the bayou, in a cabin. We'd bring them in the house, the snakes were so bad. Everything out there is out to get you!"

› On changes in the neighborhood...

"You know, it wasn't about one group of people like it is now," says Elton. "It was everybody. Like when they had Cedarfest, I always went. Everybody had their shops out. It was great.

"And then we had that place—Global Village. That was our spot! We got all our unique and rad stuff from there. I loved that place...

"Back to the Cedarfest, it went all the way down to the Cabooze. The whole street—that was the greatest. The last time I seen it like that was the Zombie Pub Crawl. When that ended, that was the end of an era. It was so many people. It was the biggest crowd I ever seen on the West Bank. It just was like—people were acting like zombies all over people's fences."

KJ chimes in: "You know, I was driving on Washington Avenue with my kids just before one. And I thought, 'Oh shit. It's a little late to be out.' And the zombies came out and, like, started 'attacking' the car. My kids were terrified—I had to explain to them it was just people. My kids had to be with us during one of them at the Wienery because we were open, and they slept on a shelf behind the counter."

"After that, it hadn't been anything that big since," says Elton. "That was the end of an era. Because the neighborhood was more accepting of crowds back in the day."

› On food...

"On the West Bank, I'd go to Hard Times. Hard Times Cafe. Once I hit that place, that was our spot. If I had a problem with any white kids with that racism, I would sic Airaq on them. We did the Hard Times every day and every night. The bars used to close at 1:00. Then we'd go to Hard Times, cleaning, drinking, partying. But we had to work—if we weren't working, we couldn't stay."

Elton pauses and adds emphatically, "Everybody hung out at the Hard Times. They just wanted to hang out with us, to look at us.

"The Hard Times was a freak show after 1:00. The style fashion show, who can dress the weirdest—the differentest, you hear me? That's how these buttons started. This is my fifth blue-jean vest. I started this jacket in '92 and just grew. Everybody knew each other in the neighborhood."

I agree. "Minneapolis is a small community."

"It is, it is. And even when I didn't live in the neighborhood, I'd still come in because I had a car. I had a '66 Ford Fairlane. I lived in Richfield at one point and moved out there the same night of that mega storm. That big snowstorm."

"Wait, was that the Halloween one everyone talks about?" I ask.

"Yep. Yep."

"Oh my god. Everybody has a Halloween storm story!"

Elton laughs.

› On changes in the neighborhood . . .

"Seems like as the Somalis came the Ethiopians left," Elton says. "They weren't matchmaking. . . . And I remember the first Somalis that came there. There weren't many. Then, it was like they kept saying, 'This is the spot, this is the spot.' That's when it changed. And a lot of other changes. When the Black boys from Chicago was bringing they ass down here with them guns.

"Everyone was hanging out at the Viking Bar. And then, Keith bought Palmer's, and he invited the young punks to feel welcome. He catered to the poor white kids. We always had a lot of Black kids, know what I'm saying? The Black kids were over at Viking. Viking was pretty packed—well, it was packed until the dude killed the bartender."

KJ chimes in once more: "Oh, and the Viking is haunted, by the way."

Elton nods. "Oh, yeah."

› On what remains the same ...

"Well ... it's hard to say because of COVID lately. Because the Hard Times, Palmer's, Cedar Cultural—as long as you've got those places. Those are key spots."

› On his "West Bank story" ...

"You know, we had nights where the police wouldn't mess with us. And if somebody else tried to start something, we'd railroad them out. After the bars closed, we'd hang out there. Nobody said turn the music down. We'd be out there partying in front of Palmer's and the Nomad. Nobody ever fucked with us. The Somalis were new then and couldn't complain. They used to not complain. Some of them were mad 'cause they couldn't understand us."

"Why was that?" I ask. "Was there a language barrier?"

"Yeah. This was a long time ago."

"But that's gotten better though, right?"

"Yeah, because they're older. And the kids now. We didn't like them hollering and running around. They were saying n***** this and that. I told them they don't know nothing about that word. They're just using it to try to get in, to fit in."

› On what he imagines for the future ...

"I see it just like it is, right now. It seems like it's just this little 'home on the prairie.'" Elton laughs. "A *big* home on the prairie. You know, the newer folks coming in, they accumulated a lot, and they're spreading out. They're buying houses in rich neighborhoods, like no Black guy'd ever do.

"I think the West Bank is gonna stay pretty much just like it is. I don't see it changing. If they do make a change, I hope it's for the better."

"What would better look like?" I ask.

"Cleaning up they stuff!" Elton says. KJ nods.

All three of us have been involved in various efforts to help address litter and other issues in the neighborhood, from cleanups to graffiti removal. When we installed the decorated utility boxes, it was Elton who helped us prep everything and get the boxes ready to go. During this very conversation, KJ is working on job descriptions for new safety and cleaning ambassadors for the neighborhood.

"What else would you like to see change on the West Bank?" I ask.

"The Native Americans," he says. "I'd like to see more people helping them, try to help those guys. You know, too many people are too selfish. I don't care if you rich or poor. You get a person thinking it's about just them, that's bullshit. It's about us. It ain't about just you."

› On the importance of family and helping others . . .

Our discussion turns to family—the gift of living close to family and having cousins and aunties and uncles nearby.

"Cousins help you grow up," Elton says, and I agree.

I ask how his family is doing, given the recent double storm to hit the gulf area.

"My family is from Beaumont, Texas, all the way to New Orleans. And my brother lost his home. I told him, 'If you need me to come down for two weeks, I'll come down.' But my mother will be like, 'Don't let that boy come down here. It's not a good time.'" He smiles. "Mom's always looking out for me. I love home. It's a ghost town, though." Elton puts on a funny voice: "It's a ghost town, my dear!"

Jamie and Elton, 2020

I smile, recalling our conversations about the West Bank's haunted history.

When I ask Elton the last time he saw somebody on a tall bike, he chuckles before responding: "Per's my mechanic."

Closing Time

When I started my role at the West Bank Business Association, one of my first gatherings outside official activities was the vigil for a small boy in the neighborhood who had passed away. I didn't know him, and I didn't know his father, but his death was a tragedy, and the neighborhood was shook. In a heartbreaking accident, he had lost his life as the result of a found gun. I didn't know the right thing to say or do at the time, and I said so to my new friend Pastor Jane following the vigil.

"Sometimes," she told me knowingly, "sometimes the right thing to do is just show up."

At the beginning of 2020, I was on my way out, but there was a lot still to do before I left. I wanted to be fully present during the time that remained, and I did my best to wrap up loose ends and leave the organization in a steady state with files organized, money in the coffers, and grant proposals out the door. And then COVID hit.

Our technical assistance transitioned quickly into emergency planning—fast-tracking websites, adding online ordering capability, and helping with social media. Approximately a third of U of M students, many of them international, were still in the dorms. Many, according to my interns at the time, "couldn't cook a meal if their lives depended on it." We shared information about to-go options and student discounts, boosting already tight relationships between the campus kids and the restaurants. We helped businesses with Paycheck Protection Program applications, and KJ waded through thousands of pages of government guidance, translating the legalese into everyday language our businesses could understand. Abdu then translated that into Somali to help get the word (and the resources) out to those who needed it most.

Restaurants immediately switched from prepping food for customers to prepping food for elders, sending meals to Riverside Plaza via youth volunteers. Some took advantage of the downtime the pandemic necessitated to update recycling and composting infrastructure. Others added walk-up windows for safer carryout orders. Some created temporary outdoor seating options for dining customers. And most businesses placed their emphasis on local customers, fortifying relationships with patrons who lived nearby. Residents and regulars made it a point to get out and support businesses. Once again, community members rallied for one another.

A few weeks before my official last day, I made plans to go back into the office to gather my remaining things. A photographer wanted to meet with me to follow up on a story for the *Minnesota Daily* announcing my departure from the West Bank and into my new position.

It was the Monday morning after a weekend snowstorm. When I parked in the lot next to the theater, it was clear nobody had been there all weekend; the ramp to the entryway was covered in about six inches of snow, with no visible footprints (an unusual sight for the typically bustling West Bank). The front door stuck against all that snow on the outside, such that I had to open it with a pull, pull, pull.

After gathering my last things and loading up my car with slow, snowy steps, I met the photographer outside. We walked, socially distanced, down the block to the intersection of Cedar and Riverside. We took a few photos by the Keefer Court mural and chatted, noticing how quiet things were in the district. We talked about our families and the response to the pandemic.

Music is something that bonds my husband and me, perhaps more than anything else. We often recall key albums fondly or with disdain, having sworn off some artists entirely due to impalpably negative associations with villains of our past. Science says that smell brings back the most acute memories, but we disagree. Smell may be most intense and visceral memory trigger for some, but for us, it's music.

Not surprisingly, guiding the West Bank Music History tour and walking through our visual and audio playlist always left me feeling emotional. We end that tour, momentously, with "Closing Time" by Semisonic. "Closing time, one last call for alcohol so finish your whiskey or beer. Closing time, you don't have to go home but you can't stay here."

As we walked up Riverside Avenue to take the last photos, a light snow began to fall. The photographer asked questions about the organization as I pointed out the work we had done over the years: the utility boxes, the signs and banners, the extra trash cans, the murals. From the Cedar-Riverside intersection you can see so much of it. I pointed out the folks we had worked with—the business owners, their kids, the generations that surrounded us. I thought of my tenure on the West Bank officially drawing to a close, a new adventure on the horizon.

"Closing time, every new beginning comes from some other beginning's end."

To be continued . . .

ON WHAT THEY IMAGINE
FOR THE FUTURE . . .

**"I think my dream and my hope is that more Minnesotan/
Twin Cities folks who have influence realize that a big
part of what the West Bank is could be lost if we don't
do something and save what we have now."
—Mary Laurel True**

The West Bank we know now wouldn't be what it is were it not for the people and protests[17] that have made it so. Neighborhoods naturally evolve to meet the changing needs of their communities. I worry, however, that this neighborhood is at risk on multiple sides—university encroachment, downtown sprawl, and exploitation from the owning class. The power a neighborhood holds can be whittled away by commercial and institutional interests.

Many books and studies have already been written about gentrification, and I don't aim to duplicate those efforts. But the West Bank story is still being written. Unlike many of the surrounding neighborhoods, it remains largely local and fiercely independent. Without intervention, much about what makes the West Bank special, including its remaining cultural and creative assets, will be lost. In a neighborhood where the percentage

---

17. Widespread neighborhood protests put the brakes on raze-and-rebuild development projects in the '60s and '70s, preserving historic buildings in the neighborhood as well as single-family homes.

of residents who rent is scores higher than the national average, where markets and institutions encroach from all sides, where household wealth is limited, what options are available for preservation?

"I'm afraid of gentrification. Because of the lack of affordable housing and how the city is changing." —Abdi Mukhtar

One of my last technical assistance meetings for the West Bank Business Association was with a West Bank shop owner to draft up an update to his business plan. He's been in operation for two decades, but he's really not making much money. His rent continues to increase, but his income dwindles. He had a plan in place to purchase his building at one point, but the owner changed his mind. So, he continues renting, though he'd prefer that money go toward investment in his own building. If he owned the space, he said, he could make improvements. Stories like his are not uncommon.

Creative placemaking can be a powerful tool. It can be used as a marketing gimmick, but it can also be used as a tool to help fight displacement. At the business association, we aimed for the latter while understanding the market influenced our ability to do so successfully. Time will tell whether our programs and efforts will be impactful in the long term. With time, we will also be able to understand why some things worked and why others did not.

The trajectory of Bedlam Theatre carries with it both warnings and lessons. Paralleling the theater's moment-by-moment programming, most of its time on the West Bank involved a series of month-to-month leases. When it moved to its second location, just off the light rail line, its staff knew losing the space to future development at that location was a strong probability. "We thought, 'We'll hang out here until you do that,'" says John Bueche, a cofounder of Bedlam who also served as its executive artistic director. "But as the recession set in, the move became more permanent, and people—especially community members—became attached to the space."

"How can we intervene in ways that help mitigate displacement and alienation?" —Mark Valdez

Affordable rental opportunities and stabilized commercial rent prices help. But when most owners aren't local, accumulated wealth leaves the district. Creating ownership opportunities for residents and commercial renters within the district slows change down even further while creating additional opportunities for wealth building. There are a variety of creative ways to accomplish this, including cooperative ownership models and legacy property transfers. But ownership is also a mechanism fraught with complications, a colonial approach to preservation on what's already stolen land. It's also not a failsafe, as owners can always cash out and move on. Nonprofit enclaves and cooperative models are options for long-term solutions that can last generations. In any iteration, property owners and commercial developers have to be a part of this solution.

"I feel one of the biggest threats to the West Bank is the geography of the buildings." —Pat Starr

Other factors can help with neighborhood preservation on the West Bank.

Local governments can create investment funds and programs supporting local ownership. The city of Minneapolis's new "opportunity to purchase" program is one such pathway; while it has a lot of promise in residential situations, it could be expanded to include commercial properties as well.

Those with power in terms of property ownership and government jurisdiction could stop battling one another and focus instead on caring for what they've been entrusted to care for—together. At one point during our cleanups, we discovered Cedar Avenue was being neglected by the city on 311 calls. Folks would redirect tickets to Hennepin County, where they were subsequently ignored or passed back. When we dug for more info after reports went unaddressed, we found the contracts the city had with the county to maintain the avenue. In another instance,

Fine Associates, a local developer, took Sherman Associates to court for the maintenance of Edna's Park—and won. But getting them to maintain it, even with a court order, is a cumbersome and repetitive task.

Who maintains a public space, and who keeps those responsible accountable?

Residents can and should be empowered to guide neighborhood decisions, and developers should let resident feedback guide them. Tools like the Equitable Development Principles & Scorecard, from Twin Cities organization the Alliance, help—as does having a good, vetted community engagement process for any new development or redevelopment opportunity. There's a long history of developers subverting grassroots projects on the West Bank for their own purposes while dragging foundations along for the ride. Who benefits?

Another way to slow the gentrification: universities and institutions could back off their plans to continue expansion, growing up and in rather than expanding ever outward. They could make sure buildings, including residence halls and dormitories, connect with the neighborhood rather than exist as silos.

And those who love the West Bank for all that it is can step up, too, by patronizing, supporting, and advocating for the businesses and people we love.

EPILOGUE

Much of writing this book involved mining my brain for memories—touch, taste, smell, sound. How I long to be in a crowded music venue, annoyed by the too-tall interloper who stealthily moves in front of me, blocking my previously unobstructed view of the band with their sweat-soaked T-shirt. The stale smell of the beer on the floor of the venue as fans meander out after a show, the crunch of the plastic from cups left abandoned. The crisp winter air hitting my face as I exit the venue, cut sharply with the dusty nicotine fog of relieved smokers lighting up on their way back to their cars.

I long to be with my family in California, digging my toes into the sand. Washing dishes with my nieces while we blast the best terrible pop music. Laughing over cards and tea after dinner. Rolling my eyes at my dad for blocking the path to the kitchen again, yet finding comfort in his steady presence.

It's tremendously, achingly hard to feel so far away from the people and places we love.

Like any good pause—from vacations to maternity leaves—there are opportunities amid the challenges. The pandemic is an opportunity to check in with ourselves, to reexamine our values and our priorities. To separate the wheat from the chaff in our lives and recalibrate. To center.

What kind of world do we want to step back into?

What do we miss, and what are we most excited to return to?

What should we leave behind?

When I was younger, I spent much of a high school summer immersed in online gaming. I role-played with friends online, playing poetry tag in the time between. With chatrooms and AOL Instant Messenger, the simple imaginary world was immersive and wholly addicting. I knew it was a problem when I stepped out the back door into a backyard barbecue my parents were hosting and just being outside felt weird. The touch of the wind on my forehead. The smell of the grill. The loudness of birds and traffic. I tapered off my gaming after that unsettling experience.

As things gradually reopen and the world whirs back up to tempo, let us never forget our collective muted pause and how this affects us and all of our senses. Whenever you step into spaces, new or familiar, fully immerse yourself in your surroundings. Step into your favorite local restaurant and remember that the door sticks a little as you open it, or it shuts too quickly and you feel like you slammed it. Remember that one stool that's a little crooked, so you always avoid it. Remember the bathroom that always smells a little like piss, or like too-fruity air freshener. Remember that the ketchup there tastes a little different, with a grainy texture and sweet saltiness you adore, because they make their own from scratch.

Enter spaces with care and kindness. Appreciate the fact that when you are a regular at a venue, it's less because you're so cool and more because there's a human on the other end of the counter that makes you feel welcome.

As we step back into a new normal, we can do so with an appreciation of community and connection—actual connection. We can recognize the simple gift that is our presence with one another.

And may we never take the delicate stitch of togetherness for granted again.

Where to Find Interviewees

> Miski Abdulle: linkedin.com/in/miski-abdulle-64809845
> Scott Artley: linkedin.com/in/sartley
> Kate Barr: twitter.com/KateSBarr
> Merrie Benasutti: linkedin.com/in/merrie-benasutti-66a51812
> Abdirizak Bihi: linkedin.com/in/abdirizak-bihi-1362a924
> Allen Christian: houseofballs.com/
> Angie Courchaine: facebook.com/pinwheelartsandmovementstudio
> Erik Funk: linkedin.com/in/erik-funk-1a93a179/
> Cam Gordon: linkedin.com/in/cam-gordon-84651b10
> David Hamilton: linkedin.com/in/david-hamilton-33196723
> Claudia Holt: linkedin.com/in/claudia-holt-a315393/
> Michelle Kwan: linkedin.com/in/michellekwansells
> Anna Lohse: linkedin.com/in/anna-lohse-9b324a113
> Abdurrahman Mahmud: linkedin.com/in/abdurrahman-mahmud
> Ben Marcy: linkedin.com/in/benjamin-marcy-aa00bbba
> Rana May: ranamay.com
> Abdi Mukhtar: tusmotimes.com/author/abdirahman
> Dan Prozinski: linkedin.com/in/dan-prozinski-01bab480
> Russom Solomon: linkedin.com/in/russom-solomon-20ba1143
> Andrea Swensson: andreaswensson.com
> Mary Laurel True: augsburg.edu/sabo/2019/02/14/
  staff-feature-mary-laurel-true
> Mark Valdez: linkedin.com/in/mark-valdez-4a73125
> Jennifer Weber: linkedin.com/in/jennifer-weber-3aa3a459
> Tony Zaccardi: twitter.com/tonyzaccardi

Cedar Cultural Center	thecedar.org
Daryeel Youth	facebook.com/DaryeelYouthMN
Hard Times Cafe	facebook.com/hardtimescafe
House of Balls	houseofballs.com
Keefer Court	keefercourt.com
Palmer's Bar	palmersbar.net
Pillsbury United Communities	pillsburyunited.org

Pinwheel Arts and Movement Studio	facebook.com/pinwheelartsandmovementstudio
Propel Nonprofits	propelnonprofits.org
The Wienery	wienery.com
West Bank Business Association	thewestbank.org

How to Support Their Work

At the end of our sessions, I asked interviewees how to best support them during this time. I encourage readers to please support these incredible artists and West Bank venues—during COVID times and beyond.

David Hamilton, Cedar Cultural Center

"Follow the Cedar along on this journey. Make donations, watch the livestreams and the programming."

Abdi Mukhtar, Daryeel Youth

"I'm really trying to see how I can continue what I've been doing with Daryeel. Some of the young people want to get into rehab."

"Trinity has been helping with First Friday efforts. I'm not a 501(c)(3) yet, but donations help. My goal is recruiting one or two of the young adults to do the Friday work. A lot of the youth always tell me 'if I get a job I can change my life around.' So if I can give them stipends, but also, a requirement can be getting into treatment or getting the help they need."

Mark Valdez, Exiled in America Project

"With Exiled in America, I think some things people can do to help is share the workshops, videos, and of course contributions. It's an expensive project. Introductions are helpful, too, to folks that are working in housing that we should be talking to."

Scott Artley

"Honestly," Scott says, "I don't need anything right now. I feel like I have survivor's guilt right now for even having a job. Support artists right now!"

"Hear, hear!" I agree emphatically.

"As I get older, I realize the important inflection points are the political ones. If you find artists are important, if you want to make sure there's a space for D.I.Y. punk shows. Complain to politicians. Come up with solutions! Work outside of the system. Have your illegal venue. Be okay with the consequences of that.

"If I were to ask for anything, it would be more political courage. It takes an individual level to exert an influence on that."

Allen Christian, House of Balls

When I ask how we can help support him right now, Allen tells me to let you know that the House of Balls is still *safely open* by appointment and drop-in if he's around. You can ask about the work, and guests are always welcome to leave a donation, too.

"Don't be afraid to come on over!" he says, ever the host.

Andrea Swensson, the Current

"You can listen to *The Local Show*—that's always nice!" Andrea smiles. She hosts this weekly program on the Current, which highlights Minnesota artists past and present. "And support local artists. Always."

Miski Abdulle, Pillsbury United Communities

"We need more resources, and we need to engage not only the women but also children and young adults. We want to make sure that mothers are getting help with youth that are fallen and need support.

"For immigrant women, we would like to have more resources, educational resources for people to come together and help us and help families to survive. Because people now are losing jobs, and even if they are a small business owner, they are not getting help."

Anna Lohse, Hard Times

"There are just so many unknowns right now. People can pay attention to our social media, to get updates. Pay attention to the communication we're trying to have. . . . It's hard. I want to say 'Come to Hard Times and buy food'—but also, we should all not leave our houses right now!'" She laughs. "I mean, honestly, we're only open right now because we must be."

I sympathize. "This is the situation businesses are in. There's just very little choice right now."

She nods and continues. "Of course, I can say 'Buy some Gordie bucks!' or 'Buy a T-shirt!'—but realistically that's not what's gonna keep us in business. . . . There are just so many unknowns. Another round of PPP loans would be helpful. But if it slows down too much and we can't make rent, we'll do a GoFundMe fundraiser or something like that." She sighs. "It's so hard, though. We take great pride in being a business, and we believe a business should make money. And we believe if you're not making money, you're not running your businesses properly. We've been strict and principled in that and having to make money the right way. And it feels crappy to think about things like GoFundMes just to stay open.

"So, we're open, we want to make enough money to at the very least pay our bills and pay our labor. But . . . okay." She pauses. "Here's what I'll say: Once this is all over, come every day . . . and then, give us all your money!" Anna laughs again. "Come and be a regular!"

Abdirizak Bihi

"We keep talking about equity and racial justice. We talk about people of color and immigrants. We should also support the equity in housing, economics, education.

"I think we need more after-school programs for kids. Spaces for young people to get mentoring. This young generation, it's a challenging time for them. The kids are living in two different worlds, their world and their parents' world. That's painful. To be a kid, but positively. People like Coach Weber shouldn't be struggling to pay for basketball. I think there's a generational gap, and one of the biggest challenges is space where young people can go."

Michelle Kwan, Keefer Court

"Continue to come and enjoy our food! That's what's going to keep our doors open. At least we're breaking even—we can pay our staff, our vendors, our product keeps going out and we're not wasting food.

"That's what happened with COVID. I was looking at my parents and [thinking], 'Wow, this really could be the end of Keefer Court.' But my mom and I were able to do a lot. We had one baker, one chef. We didn't have as much in terms of wages—but those first two weeks were so hard. Then things turned around. I think the extra funds with the stimulus, people felt like they could come out, and it helped.

"Another thing people can do: tell your friends about us! Word of mouth is our best marketing tool. It has always been."

"And anything else you want the reader to know?" I ask.

"Come to the West Bank! Just come hang out, sit at Palmer's. There are days where I'll go to Palmer's after work by myself and the community just engulfs you. You find all these connections. You make forever friends at Palmer's. It's a family.

"And there's so much to *do* on the West Bank!" she continues, increasingly excited. "I encourage people to come to the neighborhood for food, events, entertainment, and the people. Cedar Cultural Center has amazing shows. Their Global Roots concert is great, and you can enjoy a lot of it for free! Blackout Improv is at Mixed Blood. You can get to know the community but also experience so much more. There's so much culture and history happening. Come experience the West Bank from the inside, not from the outside."

ACKNOWLEDGMENTS
AND APPRECIATION

With gratitude for everyone on the West Bank that welcomed me with open arms, helped guide my work and learning, and challenged me to always do better.

My most sincere thanks to everyone who took the time to interview for this book. Our exploration helped guide this love letter and affirm my urgency and the need for this project—and the importance of lifting up West Bank voices, especially right now.

To my colleagues over the years at WBBA: Abdu, KJ, Scott, Lucas, Zahra, Kari, Raven, Angie, David, Jordana, and Eben. I'm grateful for each iteration of our tiny team, and for each one of you.

To Lisa, Juliana, Jill, and Jennifer—thank you for welcoming me to the West Bank and my role. There is no finer group of ladies I'd rather get kicked out of a comedy club with.

Many thanks to my early readers: Sarah, Rachel (*goddess of books!*), Ava, Mark, Ash, and KJ for your insight, constructive criticism, and support. Each iteration helped refine this text, every note was like a chisel to a sculpture to help it take shape. It would have been a rough cut of stone without you.

For my sister, Susie. Thanks for making sure music was a part of life even when it was Forbidden, for taking me to my first concert, and for instilling music in me as a part of how I define myself. I hope we can dance on the West Bank together sometime soon.

To Corina, Kevin, and Ryan, for breathing visual life into this vision and making your magic happen with creative flourish.

To Andrea, my kindred-spirit writing comrade. Thank you for the late-night mom solidarity, the mirror checks against imposter syndrome, and the solidarity during a tough year. Brownies 4evr.

To Madeleine, thank you for being such an incredible voice partner, from syntax to style. To Dara, for saving me from the depths of despair and dancing with me to the finish line.

To Adrienne, for helping usher me into this role and onboard me with grace.

To Nick, Maddy, and Zarina, who put up with having a brooding writer in the household who gets stuck on the words running through her head more often than she'd care to admit.

And to all the West Bankers, past and present, who hold it down.

FOR FURTHER EXPLORATION

Books

Cyn Collins, *West Bank Boogie: Forty Years of Music, Mayhem and Memories* (Triangle Park Creative)

Ahmed I. Yusuf, *Somalis in Minnesota* (People of Minnesota series) (Minnesota Historical Society Press)

Blogs and Articles

Conflict Minnesota, "Rent Strikes on the West Bank," conflictmn. blackblogs.org/rent-strikes-on-the-west-bank

Creative Exchange: Connecting Community in Cedar-Riverside, https://springboardexchange.org/connecting-community-in-cedar-riverside/

The Current, "The 400 Bar May Be Gone, but Its Stories Live On," blog. thecurrent.org/2013/01/the-400-bar-oral-history

The Current, "West Bank Music Festival Highlights the Diversity and History of the Cedar-Riverside Area," blog. thecurrent.org/2012/08/west-bank-music-festival-highlights-th e-diversity-and-history-of-the-cedar-riverside-area

The Growler, "Holding Court: For 30 Years, the Family-Run Keefer Court Has Defined Chinese Baking in Minnesota," www.growlermag. com/holding-court-for-30-years-the-family-run-keefer-court-has -defined-chinese-baking-in-minnesota

The Line, "West Bank Arts Foundry: Connecting Artists and Businesses," http://www.thelinemedia.com/innovationnews/ westbankartsfoundry-3192014.aspx

Minnesota Daily, "In Cedar Riverside, Art Initiative Connects
Community with Mentor," www.mndaily.com/article/2019/06/n-cedar
-riverside-art-initiative-connects-community-youth-with-mentors
Minnesota Daily, "West Bank Leader Reflects on Her Work with Business,
Art Community," mndaily.com/191588/news/ctjamie
MinnPost, "The Cedar's David Hamilton: Our Plan Right Now Is
to Be Very Cautious," www.minnpost.com/artscape/2020/04/
the-cedars-david-hamilton-our-plan-right-now-is-to-be-very-cautious/
MPR News, "#ForHooyo: Moms at Heart of New Campaign to Curb
Violence in Twin Cities," www.mprnews.org/story/2019/04/06/
for-hooyo-moms-campaign-curb-violence
MPR News, "Mpls. Agrees to Pay 'Zombie' Protesters $165,000," https://
www.mprnews.org/story/2010/08/23/zombie-lawsuit
Star Tribune, "In Minneapolis, Pizza and Tea Buys a Connection
with Somali Youth Crying for Help," www.startribune.com/
in-minneapolis-pizza-and-tea-buys-a-connection-with-somali-youth
-crying-for-help/503665382
West Bank School of Art, http://westbankschoolofart.blogspot.com
Anduin (Andy) Wilhide, "Cedar-Riverside: From Snoose Boulevard to
Little Somalia," Augsburg Digi-Tours, http://digitours.augsburg.edu/
tours/show/1

Videos

The Co-Op Wars, Radical Roots Films, http://www.radicalrootsfilm.com
Diners, Drive-Ins and Dives, season 4, episode 4, "Burgers and Dogs"
(featuring the Wienery), foodnetwork.com

ABOUT THE AUTHOR

Jamie Schumacher traded the warm beaches of Southern California for the snowy lakeshores of Minnesota. Her goal was to find an affordable place to live where arts, culture, and community could coexist. She found all that and more, but it took a few months for what she found to thaw out completely.

While starting the arts nonprofit Altered Esthetics, she worked closely with community members in Minneapolis to support the burgeoning Northeast Arts District. She headed to the University of Minnesota for a master's degree in innovation in nonprofit management (which she draws on to encourage nonprofit boards to conquer their fear of trying new things). She continues to speak at seminars and workshops, sharing insight about cultural districts, creative leadership, and rough transitions.

While working as the executive director of the West Bank Business Association, Jamie helped secure Cedar-Riverside's role among Minneapolis's city-designated cultural districts. She now works with LISC Twin Cities, building the capacity of the more than two dozen cultural and creative districts of Minneapolis and St. Paul.

Also a visual artist and an accomplished writer, her written work has been featured by Pollen, the *Star Tribune*, and the Minnesota Women's Press. Her book *It's Never Going to Work* was released in 2018 and details the ups and downs of starting an arts nonprofit. (Spoiler: it did work, at least for a little while.)

Jamie currently lives in Bloomington with her partner, Nick, their two daughters, a rescue pup named Rufus, a still unnamed betta fish, and four chickens. While she is available for hire, she would also like to warn you that she dabbles in the dark arts with only limited success. She is available for speaking engagements if you sign a waiver, carry liability insurance, and keep a fully charged fire extinguisher on-site.

www.jamie-schumacher.com
Twitter: @purenoumena

CREDITS AND PERMISSIONS

Kevin Cannon, book cover and map illustration, 2021

Athena Currier, author Illustration, 2018

Corina Sagun, interior Illustrations, 2021

Chester, *Thank God for the West Bank,* 2014

Charles Samuelson in front of Samuelson's Confectionery, Seven Corners, Minneapolis, Minnesota Historical Society http://collections.mnhs.org/cms/largerimage?irn=10340151&catirn=10751601&return=

Rana May, West Bank Landscape, and Planner images by Jamie Schumacher

Jamie and Elton, photo taken by KJ Starr, 2020

Nur B. Adam, author bio photo, 2020